Congratulations! It's Asperger Syndrome

of related interest

Asperger's Syndrome
A Guide for Parents and Professionals
Tony Attwood
ISBN 1 85302 577 1

Pretending to be Normal
Living with Asperger's Syndrome
Liane Holliday Willey
ISBN 1 85302 749 9

Asperger Syndrome and Long-Term Relationships
Ashley Stanford
ISBN 1 84310 734 1

Embracing the Sky
Poems Beyond Disability
Craig Romkema
1 84310 728 7

Hitchhiking through Asperger Syndrome
Lise Pyles
Foreword by Tony Attwood
1 85302 937 8

**Our Journey Through High Functioning Autism
and Asperger Syndrome**
A Roadmap
Edited by Linda Andron
Forewords by Tony Attwood and Liane Holliday Willey
1 85302 947 5

Congratulations!
It's Asperger Syndrome

Jen Birch

Jessica Kingsley Publishers
London and New York

First published in the United Kingdom in 2003
by Jessica Kingsley Publishers Ltd
116 Pentonville Road
London N1 9JB, England
and
29 West 35th Street, 10th fl.
New York, NY 10001-2299, USA

www.jkp.com

Copyright © Jen Birch 2003

Library of Congress Cataloging in Publication Data
Birch, Jen, 1955-
   Congratulations! It's Asperger's syndrome / Jen Birch.
      p. cm.
   Includes bibliographical references.
   ISBN 1-84310-112-2 (alk.paper)
   1. Birch, Jen, 1955-2. Asperger's syndrome--Patients--Biography. I. Title

RC553.A88 B524 2002
616.89'82'0092--dc21
[B]
                                                              2002023982
British Library Cataloguing in Publication Data
A CIP catalogue record for this book is available from the British Library

ISBN 1 84310 112 2

Printed and Bound in Great Britain
by Athenaeum Press, Gateshead, Tyne and Wear

THANKS

To Mum,
who has loved me from the day I was born
(not always an easy task),
and who still loves me.

To Keith Birch Photography,
Auckland, New Zealand,
for cover photograph (www.1or2pictures.com).

To Christina Birkin,
for being my Technical Manager
for all things beyond the actual writing of this book,
and for lots of enthusiasm towards the project.

To John,
for being the first "guinea pig"
on whom my writings were tested,
and for lots of loving encouragement.

To Autism NZ,
for the invitation to be Keynote Speaker
at their National Autism Conference, Auckland, 22–24
March 2002,
and for the opportunity to launch this book.

To all my Friends,
for your love and caring along the way.

Contents

To the Reader 9

Part One

રી

1. Life at Park Fields 13

2. The Cognitive Realm: Understanding My World 26

3. Feathers with Everything! Part I 35

4. Death Comes to Park Fields 38

5. Identity and Boundary Issues 45

6. In the Workforce: Part I 56

7. Feathers with Everything! Part II 64

8. Some Social Situations 67

9. Co-ordination Issues 84

10. Other Special Skills and Interests 93

11. Aunty Hazel: A Story 99

12. The Psychiatric Hospital 114

13. Asking for Help 131

14. In the Workforce: Part II 136

15. Married to a Mole 146

16. The Training Course 150

17. In the Workforce: Part III 157

18. Feathers with Everything! Part III 166

19. Going to University, and Three Important Friends 169

Part Two

∂

20. Revelations 195

21. How I Chose a Cat Instead of a Kookaburra!
(Or: More Cognitive Issues) 211

22. Feathers with Everything! Part IV 216

23. My Life Now 222

24. Some Implications of very Late Diagnosis 237

25. The Stone Age Connection 247

26. Helpful Hints for others with Asperger Syndrome
(and our helpers, and the community in general) 253

GLOSSARY AND NOTES ON THE MAORI LANGUAGE 267

BIBLIOGRAPHY AND SUGGESTED FURTHER READING 269

To the Reader

Everything in this book is true. I have not been able, of course, to include every detail of my life over the last 46 years. This would have made the book too long, too tedious for the reader, and an impossibility to write! Therefore, a lot of events, as well as some people who should have been included, have, unfortunately, been left out. Also, in the latter stage of writing this book, I was admitted to hospital rather suddenly for major surgery for bowel cancer. This took two weeks out of my writing schedule. (At the moment of writing this – February 2002 – I am back at home, recuperating, after a successful removal of the cancer.) Of the people who are mentioned, I have changed the names of most of them to protect their privacy.

The book has been written in two different threads: the roughly chronological thread, and the thematic thread. I felt the need to include a number of thematic chapters, so that some of my important life issues could be identified; otherwise, such issues could easily be diluted to invisibility within the narrative. This structuring method may seem haphazard at first, but I believe it comes together by the end of the book. In any case, the strict chronology of my life is not, to me, the most important guiding principle of my story: the chapter called "Revelations" is the demarcation line between one major time chunk and the other.

John's arrival into my life has acted as a bridge, connecting the first time section to the second.

Thank you for reading my book!

Should you wish to contact me, please write to:
Jen Birch, P.O. Box 17–426, Greenlane, Auckland, New Zealand;
or, e-mail: jenbirch@actrix.gen.nz

Thanks also to my brother, Keith Birch, who provided the cover photograph. Should you wish to find out more about his photography, please visit www.1or2pictures.com.

Part One

Part One

Chapter 1

Life at Park Fields

My grandparents had named their farm "Lone Pine Farm," though all that was left of the pine, by the time I arrived, was a stump. My parents started by buying the other end of the farm, and called it "Park Fields." As Dad was a whiz at welding, he crafted the words "Park Fields" in perfectly formed letters of steel, and attached them to our roadside gate.

My parents built what was originally a car-shed, in the middle of a twelve-acre paddock. There was no driveway at first, so groceries and building materials had to be carried from the road, through the grass, by hand or in a wheelbarrow. One of Dad's many skills was making concrete blocks, and so this shed, and many others, were constructed from these. With a coat of white plaster, the car-shed became our house.

When I – the first-born – came along, I was noticeably yellow in hue. This was jaundice, which is comparatively common in babies. It can also be a sign of other health conditions, however. In those days – 1955 – the blood tests which are nowadays taken at birth were not done. After the jaundice had disappeared, I still had a slightly yellowish – sallow – complexion and tooth colour, which has remained for life. A doctor told me recently that this is attributable to jaundice at birth. I was a very quiet and placid baby, sleeping all day, even when major carpentry projects were being carried out in the next room. On the other hand, a trip into a shop would guarantee a screaming attack, which Mum says seemed to have been brought on by the moving displays, which were the fashionable method of advertising at the time. Mum would have to park my pram or push-chair in such a way that I could see nothing, as whatever I saw set off the screaming.

I never learned to crawl, but managed to propel myself around the linoleum floor on my stomach, using my limbs as flippers. My first attempts to walk were at 22 months. Prior to these first steps, the Plunket Nurse had been concerned, and had mentioned the term "Cerebral Palsy." When I finally achieved this motor skills milestone, all was assumed to be well.

I loved our cosy little house, kept warm by the Aga coke-burning stove. Mum often made pikelets or pancakes on the hot plate on top of the stove. We kept our towels, and our clothes to be worn the next day, on the rail by the Aga, which ensured that they were always toasty-warm. Every day Mum had to empty out the cinders which were left over from the coke, and frequently there was also a "clinker": a hard piece of rock which would not burn.

In keeping with its design as a car-shed, one side of our house had a "Big Door": the whole end of the house, which happened to be we children's bedroom, could be rolled completely open on a set of wheels. On a sunny day, this meant that my brother Keith and I could play inside and outside at the same time. I thought that this was a completely normal and common-sense arrangement; and it would be many years before I realised that no one else had a "big door". At other times, the fact that the big door was on wheels and not, therefore, flush with the ground, meant that a wide range of small creatures could enter our bedroom at will. Again, I found it completely natural that slugs, snails, earthworms, slaters (woodlice) and a variety of spiders were to be found on the floor, and it made sense to look before stepping.

Mum took me to the local play centre, but I was unable to interact with the other children. All I wanted to do was to stay in the book corner for the whole morning. One of the highlights for the other children was finger painting, but I would not touch the stuff, as I have an abhorrence of sticky substances on my skin. (For the same reason, Mum had to leave an unbuttered corner on my toast every morning, otherwise I would not eat it, because I did not want to get butter on my fingers.) One day, the play centre organised a cartoon film viewing for the children; I was three years old. Again, the moving, animated figures (of Tom and Jerry) terrified me, and I screamed so much that I had to be taken out. The other children loved it.

Grasses, flowers, and all types of creepy-crawlies were a constant source of fascination for me. I could, and sometimes did, spend hours hidden in the tall grass or amongst the shrubs and trees, watching whatever lived and moved. I learned some of the names of grasses and weeds from Dad, and the names of many garden flowers and shrubs from Mum, Aunty Freda, and Grandma, who were all keen gardeners. Most of the weeds were just as attractive to me as the garden flowers: just a few examples are the blue linseed, shepherd's purse, ribwort plantain, and the rushes and sedges. One morning, as a youngster, I gathered a bunch of rushes with flower heads as a gift for my teacher: she seemed less enthusiastic than I was about them, and some of the other children chuckled.

I grew up as a gardener. Every summer I would gather the hard, purple Scarlet Runner bean seeds which were leftovers hanging on the bean fence. The bean fence was one of the items which bore Dad's style: constructed from long, thick logs, it was sturdy enough to grow pumpkins on. I collected empty tins and punched holes in the bottoms with a hammer and nail. These I filled with dirt and one bean seed each. The beans came up and grew wonderfully, until the first frost arrived. Invariably, they would be scorched until all were dead. (I never realised until leaving the district as an adult that frosts were heavier at Karaka than in most other parts of Greater Auckland.) On frosty mornings, the cow troughs and puddles would be covered with a layer of ice. Every year, we had to have the same lamentations from me over the dead bean plants.

The rest of my gardening efforts were more successful, however. I would carefully dig a row in the ground, and sow carrots, turnips, radishes, peas, sweetcorn… and, one year, a whole gardenful of kohl-rabi. Mum thought my seed-sowing methods quite amusing, as I would meticulously place one turnip seed per inch, instead of just tipping them in. Even though, as a youngster, I did not like eating turnips, I liked planting them, as the seeds were so appealing to me. When one turnip plant ran up to seed, I spent hours, (days!) methodically harvesting every tiny seed from every pod, and carefully storing them in a container. I saw these as a useful commodity which I would be able to sell to nearby farmers; this enterprise never came to pass, however, as Mum usually managed to stop me from carrying out my childhood business ventures.

Aunty Freda, Grandma and Grandad lived at the other end of the farm, and I was a frequent visitor. Aunty Freda was (and is) an excellent cook, so there were always cakes, biscuits, and lollies, as well as book-reading, and every variety of being spoilt. Aunty Freda also had numerous goldfish ponds, and it was one of my treats to feed out the wheat germ from the tin. The fishes' little mouths would come up to the surface and open wide, while I watched the food being sucked inside. There were gold ones, black ones, white ones, and multi-coloured ones. Aunty Freda had some varieties which, as an adult, I have never seen again. When it was time to clean out one of the ponds, all the fish would have to be caught and held temporarily in buckets. Aunty Freda had a soft muslin net for this purpose, and, although the catching had to be done very gently, she would allow me to wield the net for some of the time.

Aunty Freda was also a whiz at making pipe-cleaner men. Working so fast that I could not follow her movements, in a few seconds she could transform a couple of pipe-cleaners into a little figurine. I loved the fact that they had movable limbs, so I could play with them for hours – making them climb trees and traverse the African jungle.

Grandma had had poultry before I knew her. Grandma's old hen-house still stood, ramshackle and abandoned, two paddocks away from the house. There was a metal tub for a water trough, with a white, very dead, hen still floating in it. I would stare at this unfortunate fowl with dread fascination. But by the time I knew my Grandma, she was a semi-invalid and housebound. She owned two large golden syrup tins full of old pennies – some a hundred years old, as I found out when I examined the lot. Once, she bought a boxful – a gross, it said on the side – of marshmallow Eskimos, some of which we chewed our way through on every visit.

What Grandma and I did mostly was to play "Farm." She had bought me a lot of toy farm animals over the years, and they stayed at her house so that I could play with them there. Using tooth picks for fences, I made paddocks for cows, calves, bulls, sheep, horses, pigs, poultry – along with a race and a cow-shed. The cows would then have to walk to the cow-shed to be milked, so I would "walk" them along the race (the farm track). Once in the cow-shed, they would be put in their milking stalls and have the (imaginary) milking machines put on. Grandma would be sitting in her big, red chair for all of this, (as she could not get up and down), with me playing at her feet. At the moment of turning on the milking machines, Grandma was in charge: she supplied the appropriate sound effects, "Choof, choof, choof, choof," as each cow was milked. Then, as in real life, the finished cow would walk out of the hatch-way at the end of the stall, and the next cow would have her turn. Many are the hours we must have spent at this!

Another memory I have of Grandma is her interest in making scrapbooks. She had a number of these, already completed; many of her pictures came from flower catalogues and farming magazines. I caught on to this hobby, making my own scrap-books on and off throughout my life. Grandma made her own flour-and-water paste, mixing it energetically in a small jar. The sound of that rapid stirring was the first time I remember having an ecstasy attack in response to auditory stimuli; I still feel like a purring cat when the sounds are right. In keeping with her national heritage, my Grandma placed a lot of importance on a particular vegetable. Some of her scrap-books were specialised ones, full of nothing else but pictures and their captions – clipped from the Journals of Agriculture – of potatoes.

Then there was digging for kauri gum. Apparently, in years gone by, gum diggers had excavated a part of our farm, and Dad showed us where. Armed with a trowel and a sharp stick, I scraped and delved along the banks of a tiny stream at the bottom end of the farm – "The Flat," we called it, and we children were not supposed to go there without permission. The stream was in existence only in the wetter seasons, and seemed to be the tail-end of a larger one on the farm next to ours. Most of the kauri gum had, by the time I became a digger, crumbled and dissolved, manifesting as an orange, gritty patch in the soil. Oh, the thrill, on occasionally extracting a good, hard nugget of gum! I saved these up in boxes… as well as my carefully harvested crops of acorns and horse-chestnuts. I was a collector, a hoarder – a trait which would become something of a problem in years to come.

Mum remembers that I could never be hurried. When getting ready for school, for instance, I had to go through all of the steps, no matter what, at the same pace. I was not able to change the routine, nor leave out any parts of it, even if we were in a hurry. Mum learned, she says, simply to allow enough time beforehand. On reaching the school gate, there was then the matter of getting me through it. During my first months there, I would not walk through into the school grounds without someone from the school (whom I trusted) taking my hand and bringing me in. An older pupil, Linda – being a kind, caring and trustworthy person – took on this role, until I no longer needed this form of support. (Thank you, Linda! I never did thank you properly for this.)

Mum covered my school exercise books with spare wallpaper. The type that she had on hand was embossed, and she would top that off with a picture from a used Christmas card on the front cover. I felt that I had the loveliest school books in the class.

At home, I was not much of a household helper, preferring to be outside, usually in my own private world, or hidden in a corner with a book. One of my few household skills that I recall was "pricking the sausages." As a young child, Mum had told me that the sausages had to be pricked with a fork before cooking, otherwise they would burst and look messy. My resultant savagery towards the sausages meant that one would have to look hard to find an unmutilated piece. My other speciality was the bean-slicing. As we had an enormous bean fence and Mum owned a green, two-holed bean slicer, I could have hours of fun poking the beans in and watching the slices come out the other end. I also learned how to make the porridge whilst Mum and Dad were at the early morning milking, so that it would be ready when they arrived home famished.

At hay-making and silage-making time, the farmers of our immediate neighbourhood helped one another. Morning and afternoon teas were a meal in themselves when feeding a gang of hungry men, so Mum was kept very busy preparing five meals a day, as well as milking cows twice a day, doing all the usual chores, and caring for my brother and me. Typical morning teas would include scones, pikelets and lamingtons – all home-made, of course. Sometimes I was the little helper who carried the basket of food and the billy of tea to the workmen. One way of stirring the tea prior to drinking it was for someone to swing the billy over his head, again and again; the trick was to keep the lid on and the contents in.

There were two hay-barns on the farm: one was known as "Grandad's hay-barn," and this was the original one; at the other end of the farm, at Park Fields, was "Dad's hay-barn." Hay-barns were just one more enthralling part of my secret childhood life. One could find a hiding-place between hay bales; and tunnels; and a look-out from the top hay bale, peeping out through the strip of ventilation netting just beneath the roof. Sometimes Dad's hens would lay eggs here, which would be looked for and found.

A secret place

Joined to Dad's hay-barn was his truck shed, constructed from his home-made concrete blocks. A few feet from the truck shed was an empty piece of land; it looked like Dad had had this in mind for some building or other, but never got started. This forlorn-looking patch had a character all its own, and I would go there for certain types of adventures. It was the only piece of ground near our house which became flooded after heavy rain, so I would paddle around it in my gumboots for hours, poking around with a long stick, to "test the water depth." Like, I suspect, most children, I loved messing around in puddles. (Unlike most children, however, my Mum would remark that I was the only child she ever knew who could make mud pies without getting muddy.) There were even unique plants to be found in this desolate spot: tauhinu and salsify grew nowhere else on our farm, which added to the mysterious quality of the place. These two plants also looked right for the part: stark in appearance, they seemed to belong to a harsh, lonely environment. Deepening my sense of other-worldliness still further was the secret alliance between the salsify and me. Dad told me a number of times that he wanted to eradicate all salsify from the farm. (Why he was so concerned about salsify is a question in itself, as there were only ever one or two salsify plants growing at any one time, whilst other types of weeds were an ongoing challenge!) Though usually a compliant child, I saw no harm in one or two salsify plants, with their striking purple flowers. I loved them for their unusual appearance, and for adding atmosphere to one of my secret locations. Therefore, in spite of Dad's reminders to report any sightings, I never did. Yet here is another strand to the strangeness of his request: had he walked the few steps to the same spot that I did, he could have seen the "forbidden" plants for himself. Oh well, aren't people funny!

Dad's truck

Dad had an old Studebaker truck which he and I loved driving around in. The driver's seat was a wooden nail box, and the indicator was a yellow tin hand on a pole, which could be lowered out of the window at the appropriate moment. There were sizeable holes in the floorboards, so that I could watch the grass or the road swish past underneath. One of its purposes was to go to the quarry, where we would collect loads of gravel and sand for making concrete. The other main reason for its existence was hay-making. To save time, Dad had the hay-bale-loading gear permanently attached to the front and top of the truck. Thinking back, I don't think anybody else's truck ever looked like this.

Mum usually – if not always – had trouble trying to get me to eat my vegetables. At lunch time, sometimes peas were part of the meal. Although I love peas and every other vegetable *now*, as a child I hated them. If I knew that Dad and I were going out in the truck after lunch, I could store the peas in the side of my mouth, and, finally, when the road started swishing along, I could spit the peas out through the holes in the floorboards.

One day, at school, we were all out in the playground when an unmistakable vehicle drove up to the petrol station opposite. "Look at *that!*" somebody yelled.

"That's my Dad!" I piped up, bursting with pride.

Paspalum and cow plops

Paspalum, a common grass of New Zealand pastures, is useful for resisting drought longer than other varieties. When left uncut, it grows tall flower stalks which ooze a thick, brownish, very sticky substance.

As primary school children, my brother and I would walk down the drive to the farm gate, from where the school bus would pick us up. The drive consisted of two wheel tracks covered with stones, passing through the front paddock, with a strip of grass between the wheel tracks. When the cows had recently grazed the front paddock, there were plenty of fresh "cow plops," entailing the careful watching of one's footsteps which was normal life for us. When the cows had not been in the front paddock for a while, there were the old, dried-out cow plops, and the dreaded paspalum: its long flower heads reached right over each of the stone tracks. There was no avoiding the sticky flower heads which wrapped themselves around my bare legs, and no avoiding the glue which stuck tenaciously to my skin and to the hairs on my legs. I could collect quite a lot of this gunk by the time I reached the front gate. One could not simply wipe it off with a tissue or with water: it needed serious washing with soap. Possibly, I disliked it even more than others did, due to my aversion to sticky substances on my skin. Oh well, at least it was not poisonous or otherwise harmful to humans! During my childhood, however, I once heard that someone's pet goat suffered from ergot poisoning from those paspalum seed heads.

I often enjoyed rolling through the grass, (as long as it was not paspalum in flower). I chose a safe place where the cows had not been for a long time, and felt the pleasure of the fresh grass, its natural smell, and the motion of rolling over and over. One day, I did not realise that a cow had, indeed, been let into an area where usually there were none. Getting back on my feet after a rolling session, I discovered that my white cardigan was now mostly dark green – I was liberally manured with fresh cow dung. I ran crying to my mother for a clean-up – something I did not usually volunteer for!

Walking up and down the race (the central farm road for tractors and cattle) could be an occupational hazard. By the time I began this activity, most of it was concreted, but one last stretch of it was not. Twice every day, the herd of cows would walk up the race to the cow-shed for milking – with someone walking behind, to remind them to keep moving. On the way, they dropped a lot of cow plops, which, over time, amounted to ankle-deep cow dung for us to walk through – in our tall gumboots. (Not for us the ankle-height gumboots – they were for townies!) Right from the age of one's earliest steps outside, the gumboots were a normal part of one's attire. I had to learn to fold my trouser legs in such a way that they would slip into the gumboots, thereby protected from dirt. My earliest memories include the routine of carefully tipping my gumboots upside down, and tapping them sharply before putting them on – to ensure the removal of the spiders, bees and wasps which would find their way in. As for the un-concreted stretch of race, it was a deep morass: when I was ten years old, the cow muck (cow plops en masse) threatened to spill over the top of my tall gumboots. My brother and I accompanied Mum to the cow-shed for the afternoon milking. I could, if careful, drag my footsteps through this deepest patch without a spill-over into my gumboots; my younger brother, however, had more trouble. His method of walking somehow caused the cow muck to work its way, in spite of his gumboots, right up his trouser-legs to his crotch: he would then be soaked in it from the waist down. Every day, Mum had to store spare clothes at the cow-shed for him to change into.

My bike

Dad bought me a pre-loved bicycle for four pounds; it was painted light blue. As with all new things in my life, I was not too keen at the thought of what this would entail. I was small for my age, and the bike was too big for me. It had a hand brake (which could not exactly be relied upon, especially on a downhill slope), and a free wheel.

We had a circular stone driveway, in the middle of which stood our orchard. At other points of the driveway were our house, Dad's workshop, the truck shed, and the implement shed; the last-named building housed such farming equipment as the silerator, wagon, and cultivator. The driveway served as the ideal place on which to learn to ride the bike. With either Mum or Dad holding on, I would pedal round and round the circle. This meant that Mum or Dad had to run, in order to keep hold of the bike. As I was not exactly a "natural" at keeping my balance, in the process my parents must have run hundreds of circuits each. After I finally began my circuits, rather wonkily, on my own, it would take only one particular stone out of place to tip the balance. That same stone would then act as a menace every time I approached it, causing me to run into it and tip over. Seeing this, Dad jogged up to me and asked me to point out which stone was the culprit; he then removed it, so that I had one less obstacle to contend with.

I did learn to ride the bike, though I could easily part company from it. When I began High School, the other neighbourhood kids and I rode our bikes up to the corner where the school bus picked us up, from there to drive us through many of the side roads of Karaka, on the way to Papakura. When we first lived there, the roads were gravel, not sealed. Along one side of the road was my family's tree plantation: macrocarpas, eucalyptus and wattles. When the wattles were in flower, I loved sniffing in the sweet, almost sickly, scent as I rode. Then it was time for the hard slog up the hill; I could have got off my bike and walked, but I did not want to look like a weakling in front of the other kids.

The neighbours opposite us used the public road to get their cows from one part of the farm to the other – on foot. When the cows were on the road, so were piles of cow dung, but we were all used to cow dung. Worse was the difficulty of actually getting in between the cows and through to the other side – for me, anyway. This process necessitated the unspoken communication of negotiating road space with others – creatures who had all day and who considered that they had right of way. On one occasion, I misjudged and rode my bike into the back leg of a cow. She did not appear to notice, altering neither her gait nor her demeanour in the slightest. I, however, fell heavily on to the ground, bruising one hip black and blue, and badly grazing an elbow. I was shaken, hurt, bleeding, and humiliated, for my neighbourhood companions were laughing at me for my ineptitude. Trying not to cry, I managed to catch the bus and get to school, where my friend Joelene suggested I get medical attention. Joelene kindly took charge of the situation and ushered me to the sick bay, where a teacher bandaged my wound.

Dad's method of keeping mosquito larvae out of the cow troughs (and thereby reducing our number of mosquito bites) was to keep fish in the troughs. Most of these were brown cold-water fish, invisible once they were in the murky water, unless they ever ventured to the top. Apart from their diet of mosquito larvae and whatever else was in the troughs, they needed no feeding. A few of the fish were gold or other colours. One of my intense interests was to peer into the cow troughs to see what was living there. I learned who the inhabitants were of every trough on the farm: not only fish, but large diving beetles, water boatmen, backswimmers, red swimming spiders; and, finally, to my delight, planaria (black flatworms) became part of the fauna of one particular trough. I sometimes had jars of water beetles in my bedroom – which was how I discovered that water beetles can fly, because they escaped by night.

I dimly recall the time when Dad's workshop was built; again, the con-crete-block-making machine was put to good use, and a very spacious building was the result. (Apparently, as a toddler, I had amused myself by climbing into Dad's cement barrels; this caused Mum a lot of trouble in trying to get the cement out of my clothes.) Dad's workshop was beautifully arranged, with red silhouettes of his tools on the wall, showing where to hang each one after use. At one end, he built three hatchways which connected with the three storage piles outside: one each for sand, stones, and scoria – his concreting materials. Another area of the shed was devoted to his welding equipment: arc and oxygen tank varieties. Along the back wall were lengths of steel and pipes, as Dad was highly skilled and inventive in metalwork. A pipe bender was part of this equipment, and I was the person called upon to operate it. Once in the pipe bender, even the toughest steel pipe would become quietly compliant and miraculously assume the required shape. What a sense of power this gave me! As a small child, operating the pipe bender made me feel like Hercules.

I quickly found additional uses for the lengths of steel and pipes. One particular length of steel had raised edges, so that tilting one end created the perfect runway for marbles. More lengths and pipes were added at either end, linked in places by a wide rubber pipe; there were plenty of available materials in Dad's workshop. The finished marble alley ran the length of the workshop. Now I would spend days, weeks, putting my marbles in one end and listening to the sounds they made as they went through. Sometimes I would pour a number of marbles in the starting hole all at once, so as to see which one would come out the other end first and "win the race." Usually, though, each marble was put in singly, and the next one put in at the exact moment that the last one came out the end. This was because I loved the sounds, which varied as the marble reached the different pieces of pipe, and the best way to prolong the experience was to use only one marble at a time. There was a strict rule about putting the next one in at precisely the right moment, so that there was no cessation in the sound effects – until I had used up my tin of marbles. As I had been collecting marbles from an early age, I had a sizeable tin full. When the tin was finally empty, I would collect the marbles from the catchment area and start all over again. The repetitious rhythm of the sounds in the pipes, and of my movements in putting the marbles in, was deeply enjoyable, satisfying and hypnotic; it was something I did not want to stop. Decades later, just weeks before my forty-sixth birthday, I would discover a similar rhythmic sound and movement which would have a similar effect.

When other children asked me what I did on the weekend, I would find that my interests were far from the norm. Girls of my age would play with dolls, and at being mothers; dolls bored me, except when I was being "School Teacher," and they were my "pupils." To aid me in giving my lessons, I wrote lots of little "school journals" on scraps of paper, stapling them together as booklets. Water-beetling, tadpoling, gum-digging, marble alleys, and poultry raising would last throughout my teen years – and, the last-named, for a lifetime – so that I would no longer divulge what I did on weekends. My secret life became ever more secret, as I increasingly realised that I was not like other people.

Chapter 2

The Cognitive Realm: Understanding My World

As a young child, I started each day by rubbing my eyes vigorously with my fists, so as to produce the pretty, moving lights which I thought were fairies. Mum tried to discourage me from this, lest I damage my eyes. I fancy that I remember the heady excitement of being able to make myself "invisible" by closing my eyes – and the disappointment when Mum finally convinced me that she could, indeed, see me!

I lived by the rules; rarely disobedient, I liked and needed the security that rules provided. My parents were not, for the most part, strict, so I was not hemmed in by many rules in any case. When I was old enough to wander the farm without being in any danger, the paddocks, orchards and plantations were mine to delight in. I had to tell a parent where I was going, but then I was usually free to go.

I found that each sphere of knowledge had its own set of facts, or rules. Certainly, as soon as I became five and could read, I could discover many more facts than was possible through my own observations. Of course, there were thousands more species of animals in books than in my real life, so I read about every species I could, from ants to spiny anteaters. Everything in the world was run by rules, it seemed: reproduction, genetics, arithmetic, cooking, motor mechanics, snakes-and-ladders. To find out the facts, the rules, was to achieve mastery over life. Alas, the older I became, the more the uneasy feeling grew, that the rules for living amongst people were elusive and liquid. This was the only set of rules that could not be nailed down and kept down.

Thinking on the spot was difficult for me – hence, I can see now, my dependence on knowing the rules. Knowing what to do beforehand was, and still is, very important for me. I have been told, and, in fact, been reprimanded and ridiculed at times, for not being able to act spontaneously. My lack in this area is, I now know, at least partly due to my mental processing speed being too slow for fast-moving situations. As an adult, I assisted with an Access Radio programme for five years. I wrote scripts for myself and for my co-presenters, so that, live on air, I would know exactly what to say and when to say it: everything was timed to the second. This meant that I could function in this milieu – except when anything changed. A co-presenter in one programme expected me to adlib, by asking me questions which were not in the script. This completely threw me: I could not even think of an answer, let alone say it. My mind was on one track, and that was the script. I knew that I was live on air, and that a gap in broadcasting was being created, because I was being expected to answer unscheduled questions, and I could not! I was also a little annoyed, because my co-presenter had "broken my rule" for how to broadcast a programme. This slower processing speed also means that I have trouble making fast decisions.

On the other hand, if given sufficient data and time with which to think matters through, I can reason things out as well as, and often better than, other people. As a young child in primary school – I think I was five or six years old at the time – I worked out a satisfying way in which I could do my adding for arithmetic. From that moment on, I have added in units of three. This method allowed me greater accuracy and speed than did my previous efforts, and caused my father and headmaster to ask how I was doing it. I have kept my secret until now, however.

At around the same time, I was pondering the phenomenon of English definite articles: the words "a" and "the." The difference was that one used "a" when one has only just encountered the thing, and "the" when one has encountered it more than once, I concluded. It's hardly rocket science – but it seemed to be another indicator that my interests and my internal world were different from those of my peers.

When the rules of the world changed with little or no warning, I would be taken by surprise, and would be unable to cope with the new situation.

For instance, at the annual Sunday School picnic there was the lolly scramble. Every day for my whole life I had lived by the rule of "Don't snatch; be polite; wait aside to see if the other person wants it first." Every time I saw a lolly fall, I waited politely aside to see if anybody else wanted it; by the time I thought it was time to try to get it, it was too late. Then, at the end, I found myself in the position of looking foolish, because everyone else had handfuls of lollies and I had none! The vicar would then hand me a few lollies which he had kindly saved for the occasion. I was left with the feeling, however, that I was somehow incompetent, and that the situation was confusing.

Another such change to the rules occurred in the secretarial course I took while in my teens. A teacher had set up an exercise whereby we would conduct mock phone calls, asking for an interview, as practice for when we finished the course. We were put in pairs, with one girl to make the call, and the other to answer the phone at the work premises. The teacher instructed the "workplace receptionist" to offer an interview, and to negotiate the day and time. My role was to be the job-seeker. In real life, until my thirties, I was largely phone-phobic, but, for this exercise, at least I had already been told what to expect and what to say. I made the pretend phone call, all psyched up with what I had to say. My partner at the other end, however, had decided to play a joke, and answered, "The job has gone!" Now, my prepared script of day and time was unusable. I just sat there, numbly muttering "the job has gone!" not knowing what to do next. My classmates and the teacher laughed at the joke, and, when I realised that it *was* a joke, I did too. There was no malice in it; it was just a classmate having a bit of fun by suddenly changing the rules, which I was unable to do.

Another example of this occurred in a workplace. One day, I had run out of work, so, being conscientious, I kept asking the supervisor if he had anything for me to do. Eventually he got sick of this, and asked me to stop following him around with this question. "Please sit down," he said, "and wait until I find something for you to do." I did as I was told. Staring into space seemed foolish when I could be reading whilst I waited, so I picked up a book... still awaiting instructions. Some time later, the sales rep came in and demanded "What are you doing sitting there!!!" I felt very hurt and upset, because I had been obeying the rule, yet now the rule seemed to have changed with no warning.

Thinking quickly under pressure adds more stress to any situation. I still have trouble checking my change in shops after a purchase, partly due to the slow processing speed, and partly because people are waiting for me to leave: the shop assistant is usually perplexed as to why I am taking so long, and any customers behind me are being inconvenienced! The shop assistant, seeing me work my way through my coins, sometimes asks "Is everything all right?" I have had to tell my local shops "Don't worry about me; I am training myself to check my change." In the process, I usually get a "hot flush" of embarrassment. It is appropriate, for me, that the word "Cognitive" – knowing, perceiving, understanding – can be shortened to "Cogs", because we can think of the brain as using cogs to link up our thought processes. In fact, when I am trying to think under pressure and it's not working, I feel the sensation of those cogs turning frantically in my brain – but failing to mesh.

Thinking quickly under pressure and in a situation of conflict is just about the worst scenario for me. This adds a heap of negative emotions to the mixture. As I greatly dislike conflict in the first place, such a situation is usually impossible for me. The other person(s) have the advantage in that they can think more quickly, and as it is usually they who have chosen to have the confrontation, this means that they have already thought ahead as to what they will say and do, whereas I am taken completely off guard. I might as well hold my breath in such a situation. I need to go away and mentally go over what happened (mentally process it), and it may take a week, or much longer, for me to understand what it was all about. However, one usually needs to make one's response, if any, before too much time passes, so it usually helps me if I write down my response, and then still wait a day or two, in case my understanding, and emotions, change regarding the situation. Dealing with conflict is such a big subject that I cannot do justice to it in this chapter, but I have touched on some of the reasons why it is problematic.

In my early childhood there was no television in our home. Looking back, I am sure that this was a blessing. Not only did I get "hooked on books" instead of on TV, but I was saved from seeing scary programmes until I was older. Visual images which were too frightening for me have been a problem, right through to the present day. My nearby grandparents bought a TV when I was young, but I saw mainly children's programmes there. Speaking now of my teen and adult years, if something terrifying appeared on the TV screen, I would have to run from the room, with my hands over my ears. It was much too frightening a prospect to switch the TV off, as that meant going right up to the appliance and touching it – which meant getting much too close to its evil contents. That is, I feared that whatever scary thing was on the screen might be able to reach out and grab me. I still avoid watching programmes or movies which are too scary or horrific for me, as the visual memories – flashbacks, I suppose one would call them – can last for years. Therefore, why give myself extra trouble and anxiety by cluttering up my brain with disturbing images? I am less tormented, now that I am 46 years old, by such disturbing screen images – mainly, I suspect, because I do not watch many TV programmes or movies, and I am choosy about what I do watch. For this reason, I consult a TV guide booklet as to which programmes are on, so that I will not accidentally switch on a horror movie, for instance!

Still on the topic of TV and film, I also had another, related, problem, until practically the present. I could not, emotionally, separate "fiction" from "non-fiction" on the screen. It was bad enough seeing real-life suffering through the media: this can upset me very much, and I can take only so much of this. When the visual offering was "just a story," though, I could not switch off my "real-life" reactions to it, and often still cannot. As a younger person (especially), even being told "It's just a story!" made no difference to me at all. This means that I react with horror to what I see, whilst others around me are calmly enjoying themselves, and even laughing. In fact, others' laughter at what I perceive as disturbing events makes it all the worse, as I feel as though I am in a chamber of horrors, surrounded by torturers who delight in others' pain (the others who are on the screen). I find so-called "comedies" to be often distressing for this reason: people or animals get hurt, and the people around me are laughing at this. Therefore, I have learnt to avoid "comedies" for the most part, and I daresay that I am considered to have no sense of humour.

New things have also been a lifelong challenge. As a preschooler, I was told that my grandparents were about to give me a special present. I was taken into a room at my grandparents' house, where a shiny, new tricycle greeted me. I immediately burst into tears! This was not the response my family expected, or wanted. This new piece of technology, which also meant the whole new concept of cycling, felt frightening to me. I wanted to remain with my familiar playthings and surroundings. Similarly, my grandmother once gave me a large, beautiful cloth doll. My Mum tells me that my immediate response was to grab him by the arm, swing him round and round my head, then fling him as far as I could into the distance! Again, this reaction was not of the "socially acceptable" variety. My parents retrieved the rejected doll, who, over the course of time, became familiar to me, with the result that I loved him very much for the rest of my childhood.

New things are still regarded with caution, if not suspicion, in my world. My Mum recently acquired a new hand-held phone with her Fly-Buy points, and gave it to me, insisting that I would find it wonderful. Oh dear, I did not like it in my space at all, let alone the thought of using it. Whilst my ordinary, fixed-place phone was still on hand, I could not bring myself to use the new one. Mum kept asking me whether I had used the new phone! Finally, the only way I could force myself to try the new phone was to unplug the old one, and take it back to the Post Office. After that piece of surgery, I discovered that I quite liked the new one after all!

It is usually the same with new clothes – I avoid the whole issue until someone forces me into a clothes shop. Well, why do I need new ones, when the old clothes I got 25 years ago are still perfectly good! In fact, people sometimes breathe the word "retro" around me in hushed tones; I didn't know what that meant, at first. The purpose of clothing is for protection from cold and sunburn. Old clothes are trusty, familiar and soft; new ones look and feel strange and uncomfortable. Why would one, then, want to have the new ones? It's a weirdness which *other* people have, but they try to force their peculiar notions on to me. And "fashion" – and "labels!" – it's like other people are escapees from Planet Bizarre.

Now I will tell you how I experience tasks of more than one step: I get all of the necessary tools and materials assembled before I attempt to start. Otherwise, I might get part-way through the task, find I lack a necessary item, and then become very frustrated; or, I might forget what I am doing part-way through and get distracted, then feel annoyed or frustrated later on when I discover that I have left the task half done. The assemblage of items also acts as a reminder to continue with the task, and as a reminder of which step of the task I have reached.

When moving from one room to another, as part of a task, or to find something, I usually forget what I went to the new room for. I then have to physically retrace my steps to the starting point and begin again. I need to take with me a visual cue as to what I want in the other room (e.g. a pencil, if what I am looking for is a stationery item), or I need to keep talking to myself on the way about what I want to do there. Otherwise, as soon as I get out of sight of my original visual cue, I get distracted by some new stimulus and then change to dealing with *that*, instead of what I went for. Then, some time later, when back in the original setting and again seeing my original visual cue, I feel annoyed and frustrated that I did not complete the task I intended to do, so I then start out all over again; but, the same sequence of events can keep on happening. (This is even worse in the two-storeyed unit where I am currently living! – as by the time I get to the top of the stairs, I've forgotten what I went there for, and have to go back down again… and vice versa.)

I have noticed during my lifetime that certain actions are labelled as "Common Sense," and I do not always agree with this assessment. Sometimes I have been referred to as lacking common sense. In that case, I thought, (beginning in my childhood), I must have "Uncommon Sense," which is just as good as, or better than, "Common Sense" – it's just a different way of going about things. There is, however, a stigma about doing things differently from the "norm."

One problem (which may or may not belong in this chapter) has been that of self-damaging acts. As a child, I started by picking at the outer, fleshy part of one ear. After causing bleeding and a scab, I could not leave it alone, but kept picking at it so that it could not heal. My Mum put some ointment on it, which probably helped, because I have never liked the feel of ointment or any other sticky substances on my fingers! In later years, any small blemish on my face would be picked at uncontrollably, until I made a mess of my appearance. Then, I would feel disgusted with the way I looked, and a self-destructive cycle would be in place. So concerned was I with one particular blemish that has tempted me into scratching at it for a lifetime, that I recently had it surgically removed. When the time came for the surgery, I then had a terror attack (which is another story for another time). I achieved the desired result, however, in that I removed a major source of self-destructive behaviour. An unwanted side-effect is that I now have an extra line on my face, which is the surgical scar. I still have to watch, though, for the first signs of pulling out eyelashes: once I've pulled one out, the urge becomes stronger and stronger to keep going until they are all out, which I have done many times. These behaviours seem to be responses to stress, and sometimes excitement. And when major frustration or upset occurred, I would sometimes (until recently) bash my legs with my fists until I was covered with bruises; next day, I would feel pain on walking. This would give me some kind of release, but I am glad that I seem to have (touch wood) overcome that particular behaviour. The fact that my last few years have seen major improvements in my life, e.g. having the understanding of friends and family, has helped very much in this respect.

Once, in my thirties, I went to the airport. Watching the crowd, it soon came to my attention that some individuals' top halves were walking in opposite directions to their bottom halves. This both riveted my interest and began to make me feel uneasy. When I pointed out this phenomenon to my companions, they responded with "Oh no, I hope she doesn't have one of her turns now." Later on, I came to the conclusion that some sort of reflective surface was acting like a mirror, causing the optical illusion.

Walking down the main street of Otahuhu last year, I was jolted to see *half* a man standing on the footpath and waving his arms, that is, his top half. Previously, this had the potential to be quite a fright. This time, however, I told myself that there had to be some rational explanation. On closer inspection, the man proved to be down a manhole, with only his top half sticking out. I was proud of my new powers of analysis.

As will be a recurring theme in this book, things happening around me at high speed are often a source of stress for me. Sudden noises such as cars backfiring, brakes squealing, dogs suddenly barking, balloons bursting, and fire-crackers banging can produce a fright – although I am now familiar with some urban noises, such as fire engines rushing down the road, sirens blaring (as long as I am not too close to them). As I grew up, I began to notice that other people did not usually react as strongly as I did to these phenomena. I would spend all of Guy Fawkes Night, for instance, with my hands clasped tightly over my ears; prompting the query (and this was when I was in my twenties), "Is she retarded?" Even a soft sound can cause me to jump, if it is unexpected. Also, things moving quickly into my visual field can have the same effect – especially when on the road, as this is the place where everything is moving at top speed. Driving, and being driven, are among my top stressors – especially as I am aware that there is more than a fright at stake here, but a mistake could lead to a trip to hospital or the morgue. My mental processing, decision-making and reaction times seem to me to be too slow for the much faster road conditions that now exist. Accordingly, I have given up driving for the more relaxed travel methods of bus, train and my own legs. When someone else takes me in their car, I can be a bad passenger, letting out gasps and yelps of fear. (Of course, some persons' driving is more anxiety-provoking than others'!) Another traffic situation which can be very scary for me is the parking building. Recently, my partner John drove (with me in the passenger seat) into a parking building – which I found too much like playing Dodgems, with cars suddenly coming at us from all directions. After I let out a series of involuntary yelps, John said "Try to save your sound effects for when there really is an emergency!" To which I replied, "But every time I really *do* think it's an emergency!" In other words, I am reacting with "Red Alert" every time something moves around me – and it is not something I choose to do. It is very stressful, and tiring, to live in a world which is producing the "Red Alert" reaction in oneself every few moments. Ultimately, it is probably unhealthy. That is why I have, very recently, chosen to remove one major stressor – driving – from my life, and I modify my life to make it more relaxing for myself wherever I can.

Chapter 3

Feathers with Everything! Part I

The first poultry that I had contact with were Dad's laying hens. The laying hybrid of the day was the White Leghorn–Black Orpington cross, and we had six of these. They were white except for small black patches, randomly placed. By the time I was old enough to notice what went on, it seemed that they were never replaced when they became old. After ceasing to lay, they should have been used for the dinner table (according to farm efficiency practice), but they just lived on and on. Years later, I was told that Dad was unable to kill them, hence their longevity.

When I became old enough to have pets, I acquired some barnyard bantam hens and roosters from my uncle and Aunty in Te Puke. These came in hues of red, brown and yellow, and thus brightened up the fowl-yard scene. They never managed to rear their chicks, however, because of the rats and weasels which were abundant on the farm, until the day that Mum built me some chick-rearing pens. Now that I could successfully rear chicks, I could breed this hen to that rooster, and see what sort of offspring resulted. The poultry population skyrocketed.

Using bantam hens as surrogate mothers, Dad hatched wild ducklings (mallards) from eggs he found on the farm. This event afforded amusement for the family and visitors, as the proud mother hen paraded her "chicks" around the lawn and orchard. Finally came the day when rain created a large puddle in the driveway: the ducklings, now past their babyhood stage, discovered the joys of rushing in at one end of the puddle and aquaplaning out the other. The bantam mother tried, with increasingly worried clucks, to call her offspring out of the nasty water; but eventually she marched off in disgust, never to bother with them again.

From my relatives in the Bay of Plenty, I acquired a batch of muscovy duck eggs. As the bantam hens often went "clucky," i.e. broody, there was a bantie available to hatch the duck eggs. Knowing little at the time about muscovy ducks, however, I had not realised that they are half-way between a true duck and a goose in some ways, for example, the incubation period for the eggs. Instead of the four weeks required to produce "true" duck-lings, muscovy eggs take five weeks. This caused a miscalculation in our plans, as I was due to spend my school holiday in Te Puke with my rela-tives, yet the eggs had not hatched, and we did not know when they would. Thus, Mum ended up with the responsibility of being midwife to the muscovy babies whilst I was away. This was no easy feat as, this time, the bantam hen seemed to know that she was being tricked, and was throwing the ducklings out of the nest as they hatched. Poor Mum was regularly journeying down to the hen-house, some distance from our house, to check on, and rescue, the newborns!

When a holiday in Te Puke was coming up, I would write a long list of instructions for Mum about how to take care of my poultry. Mum recalls that I was a tyrant where this subject was concerned! The muscovy duckling incident, however, had been unintended, as they had hatched on a different date from what we expected.

The four muscovy ducklings grew up into four beautiful white ducks: three females and a drake. As adults, they roamed at will, soon discovering the farm water troughs. This was seventh heaven for the ducks, but the result was troughs full of feathers and duck-poo. This was our cows' drinking water, and the cows had to come first: the disobedient ducks had to find a new home.

During a holiday with my aunt and uncle in Te Puke, a neighbour had some guinea-fowls she did not want (we would later find out why!) We had a very smelly journey back to Karaka, with a pair of them in the back of the Anglia. Guinea-fowls are very strange creatures to say the least, and had to be acquired as a pair; not that anybody but a total expert can tell the sexes apart. They had big, fat bodies, with long, scrawny necks and tiny heads. On top of the head was a curved horn like a rhinoceros. The plumage of this variety was blue with an overlay of white dots; and super-scuttling little feet poked out from the underside of this ball of feathers. My nick-name for them was "Citroën-birds," because their legs were concealed by their plumage, causing their little feet to look like the half-hidden wheels of a Citroën. They let out frequent, very strange and very loud cries, and these could go on for hours. Their mating rituals involved the male performing somersaults in front of the female. I have recently read more on the courtship behaviour of guinea-fowls: they need a lot of space in which to run very fast and to do any other gymnastics they feel are necessary, for example, the somersaults, otherwise they will not breed. Trying to catch them during the day was impossible, as they could run straight up walls, so fast that one could not even see their feet move. All this was entertaining, except for the fact that the pair of guineas became territorial over the hen-house and then would not let the hens enter. They attacked the hens mercilessly, yet, in return, we never saw so much as an egg from the guinea-fowls, let alone any chicks. At this, a decision had to be made: the hens would, of course, stay, but the guinea-fowls had to go to a new home.

Chapter 4

Death Comes to Park Fields

My grandparents' garden had a little wooden gate separating it from the "cow-shed paddock." A chain and a nail at usual fence height served to fasten it, but, since this was too high for me as a child, another chain was attached lower down, so that I could have the satisfaction of "opening and closing the gate by myself," whilst an adult attended to the topmost chain.

On the left side of this gate was an old punga house, by now somewhat tumbledown. Constructed from large scoria stones and punga fern trunks, it had served as a frost-free shelter for tender plants such as begonias. Snowdrops, cinerarias and fuchsias were also favourites to be found throughout my grandparents' garden.

Early one evening, when I was ten, there was a phone call to my grandparents' house. I forget which one of the adults answered it, and then instructed me to take a message to Mum at the cow-shed. The message was for Mum to ring the hospital when she had finished milking. I unfastened the chains on the little garden gate; by now I was big enough to reach the top one. A feeling of dread filled me as I wondered, "How long are they going to keep up this pretence?" I duly delivered the message, offering to write it on the blackboard installed for messages, but Mum said that that wouldn't be necessary. Mum had to finish the milking first.

Days went by, and I wondered if I dared to hope that all was well after all. But just as I had dared to hope again, one morning Mum called my brother and I to her. Grasping the back of one of our kitchen chairs, and looking down, Mum said something about Dad having "gone to sleep." I, too, clutched the back of the chair that was before me, with the terrible knowledge of what these words meant: it had been applied to dead animals enough times. My grief was immediate, and Mum and I were crying; but my younger brother, only six years old, did not comprehend what the words meant, yet began crying because we were, because he could tell that something terrible had happened. Some additional explanation must have been given to him. My despair was total: I knew from this moment that three-quarters of my soul had been wrenched away, never to return; and that now I was unprotected and unsafe in a frightening, dangerous world. I knew that only with my Dad alive could I possibly remain protected; that my Mum could not, despite her love for me, fulfil this role, and, therefore, I was henceforth totally vulnerable.

This devastating new state of affairs haunted me every waking moment. For the first two days I cried a lot, and after that the tears got stuck somewhere inside. Every second of every day the knowledge "Dad is dead" repeated itself to my aching heart, with the physical accompaniment of a blow to my diaphragm. "Dad is dead," thud; "Dad is dead," thud… The thought of never seeing him again was unbearable; I could not escape the pain and terror of this massive life change. With my soul ripped apart and mostly gone, I knew that I could not survive any more. Not in life as we know it.

A neighbouring family gave me a copy of Robert Browning's poems – too sophisticated for me to read at the time, but the thought was appreciated – and gave my brother Dr Seuss's *One Fish, Two Fish, Red Fish, Blue Fish*. (Thank you, kind people.)

After three days at home, my brother and I returned to school. There it was "life as normal," as if nothing had happened. Therefore – and as it was the sixties, in rural New Zealand – we were forced to join the conspiracy of silence: the assumption that if something is not mentioned, it does not exist. In those days there were no such things as school counsellors, or any sort of counsellors that I could have got access to – nor had I heard of the concept of counselling; and I would not until adulthood. No school teacher, or any other adult, ever took me aside to ask how I was getting on without my Dad. My childhood days were lived decades before such things as self-help books, popular psychology, support groups, computers or e-mail were heard of – in my part of the world, anyway. Nowadays there are helpful support groups that one can belong to, in person or via the computer networks. Lacking the knowledge of where to turn for help, however, was (and for some people, still is) a huge part of the problem.

Back at Sunday School next time, my Sunday School teacher asked me – in front of the class – how my father in hospital was. Everything in my ears and eyes suddenly became blurry, buzzy and distorted as my mouth apparently uttered the words, "He died last week." The Sunday School teacher then hugged me, though this afforded me no comfort.

Over the months and years – eventually to become decades – there was no recognition that I might have been suffering, and no opportunity to be helped. Family members, both immediate and extended, got on with their lives, and, if they were grieving, then they, too, kept silent about it. I picked up the strong message that death – of people, at any rate – was something unmentionable. (Here's a quick glance to the present: recently, on television, I saw an advertisement about rural drivers and alcohol; the announcer said that rural New Zealanders are strongly into denial when it comes to alcohol-related road deaths. Hmmm, I thought – how about strongly into denial over any form of death? I wonder whether this state of affairs has changed at all in the last forty years.)

During my school years I had the pain sharpened each time another child asked me what I was going to buy my father for Father's Day, when my father's birthday was, what did he do about such-and-such… One day I was absently running my fingers through the sand in the metal sand-tray my Dad had made for the school. A younger child came up, and, needing to hear acknowledgement of my father, I told her, "My father made this!" The little girl looked at me scornfully and sneered, "You haven't even *got* a father!" Another spear-thrust through my innards, then.

Another time, I managed to get a couple of primary school classmates to listen to my "interesting information" for a few minutes: that my Dad had been in Japan just after the nuclear bomb blasts, and that this had been the cause of his leukaemia and death. They did not seem to want to stick around to hear any more of this. I am sure that a teacher had been lurking around close enough to hear or notice, yet, again, no one came to find out if I needed to talk about this.

My Grandad and Grandma were very old by then, and, like everyone I knew in those days, did not talk about feelings. During the following two years, Grandma, and then Grandad, died too.

The death of a child's parent can, in itself, cause developmental delays. The occurrence is not something that will ever go away. A hurt knee will (usually) heal, a defeat in rugby will soon be forgotten, or may be rectified next week. The permanent disappearance – desertion – abandonment – of a child by his or her parent leaves an aching void which may never be filled. One's caregiver – in the case of a father, one's protector – is gone for all eternity. This can fill the child with terror, despair and hopelessness. The child is not in a position to find or access help for himself or herself. Other family members have their own loss to deal with, and may not be able to deal with the child's loss as well (even if they realise what the child is feeling). If the child does not speak about the trauma, it does not mean that all is well – it may actually mean the opposite, as all of the horror is bottled up inside. So it was for me.

Part of what a child has to do, in order to become an adult, is to gradually split himself or herself off from the parents. This is also intertwined with the child's, and teenager's, budding sexuality. For instance, a girl child learns, unconsciously, how to be a female through the gradual process of observing her mother and father, and through the father's interactions with the girl child. Part of what a father does is to comment, verbally or non-verbally, or both, on the girl child's progress to womanhood. Every time he smiles at her, or tells her she looks pretty, or discusses her concerns with her, the father is affirming and encouraging the girl's development into womanhood. If he disappears permanently out of the girl's life, she loses the most important person on her journey to adult femininity. If her father dies or deserts the family permanently, the girl child has nothing to "split away" from, when she needs to reach this milestone in her development. Of course, boy children are also affected by the death of a parent, and the death of the mother is equally disastrous. A missing parent creates an impossible developmental task for some children, who cannot split away from that which is not there. Therefore, this is one way in which the death of a child's parent creates a developmental problem. The child may not be able to meet his or her teenage milestones, and may have great difficulty in taking his or her place in the fully adult world. Aside from this is the daily loss of the sharing of common interests, the nurturing, and the guidance that the child now lacks.

Some "experts" think that the child's grief reaction is due to the child fearing his or her own death. Now that the child has seen someone die, they reason, the child is afraid that the same thing could happen to him or her. From my own perspective, this is another piece of nonsense to add to my collection. There is already enough for the bereaved child to grieve about, without anyone needing to add this extraneous item. I was horrified (and all the other feelings I have mentioned) purely because I would never see my father again – it was not my own death I feared; in fact, I would have preferred to die on the spot, rather than be in the position of having a dead father. And now that I have (in January and February 2002) been in danger of my own death, due to contracting bowel cancer, I still feel the same way: the knowledge that I could have died, and the terror I have at times felt in hospital, was as nothing compared to the horror and despair of my Dad dying when I was ten. Where do these "experts" get their assumptions from? Not from those with insider knowledge, it seems.

Every birthday, Christmas, and Father's Day now became a day of sadness, a day of mourning for the person who was not there. For weeks, months, and years afterwards, one somehow expects the missing person to suddenly appear, to be at one's side, but then the stab in the guts reminds you that he (or she) is gone for ever. Nothing could put my life back together again. (Actually, a substitute father – e.g. a stepfather – may well have been able to do this; but, without this, I now had no male role model in my life for the crucial ten years of my childhood and adolescence.) Added to this was the knowledge that the worst thing I could imagine – the death of one of my parents – was not only possible, but *had actually* happened. Therefore, my child's mind reasoned, the worst possible things can and do happen – anything, no matter how terrible, can happen at any time. This fact ripped away any vestige of confidence I had about living in the world. The world – the universe – God – is ready and willing to destroy anybody and anything at any time. I was to live with this feeling for the rest of my life.

Many ramifications follow from such a life-changing event. For instance, my younger brother had decided that he wanted to learn tennis at the local tennis court opposite our primary school. Each weekend he took his tennis racket to the court, and waited for his turn to play. Other children had their fathers with them, however, and the fathers decided who would play and when. My brother would come home each time with the news that he had not been able to get a game. Eventually he gave up. He, like me, had no one to fight for him any more.

The child with a dead parent grieves not for the past, but for the future. It is the child's future which is now changed for ever: the parent will not show up for the child's birthday, or the school sports day, or the "Father and Son" day at school, or the yearned-for fishing trip, or for storytime before going to sleep. Giant, and unwanted, sacrifices have to be made constantly: the child will have no more camping trips (if this is what Dad specialised in), no more electronics projects (because Mum doesn't know how to do them), no more tennis, no more peering under car bonnets, no more trips to the Transport Museum (with the person who could explain what you were looking at), no more rough-house wrestling, no more pats on the shoulder or hugs in the way that Dad used to do it. Each of these missing occasions, which used to be shared with the now-dead parent, has changed into a painful feeling. As the child grows into a teen, without his or her Dad there is no one to guide the teen into the outside world and the working world – or, at least, in my teen days, this was the province of the father rather than the mother, so I missed out in this sphere too. I am telling you all this not just for my own sake, but so that there may be more understanding for those children who come after me, living the same experience.

Lived experience is the true teller of how it is. I have not lived with blindness, a missing leg, or rheumatoid arthritis – for which I am thankful. Nor have I lived inside a Maori life, or that of an African tribesperson, or that of a person of mixed race. All of these lives, and millions more, are unique to the individuals who live them in reality. Therefore, I cannot claim, and do not claim, to know how it feels to be these individuals. Following on from that, I know that I am not in a position to judge these persons and to give them irrelevant advice which would be inappropriate to their lived reality. People can help one another, yes; but helping depends firstly upon *not* assuming that we know what the other person's life is like; the first step is to acknowledge that we do *not* know, but that we can listen, observe, share and (up to a point) learn. The "Insider Knowledge," though, remains the domain of the individual who has lived it. Anything else is theory, and therefore suspect. Too many times I have been judged by those who do not know, in the first place, with what I am living. In other words, "Before forming your opinion, walk a mile in my shoes." Make that ten miles. Make that a lifetime – because for a child to lose its parent is a lifetime sentence.

Chapter 5

Identity and Boundary Issues

From early childhood, I had noticed that I did not fit in with the little girls. Dolls, dressing up, playing mothers and fathers, playing house, interest in make-up and jewellery, pretty clothes, hair-dos, boyfriends – these things seemed to fascinate little girls, but not me. In spite of Mum's considerable skills as a tailor, and her natural wish to dress me up in pretty clothes, I hated even trying on new attire, and would revert as soon as possible to my shirt, long trousers ("longs") and gumboots. (Jeans had not yet been invented, or, at least, were not yet known to my rural family.) When "dressed up," I felt so uncomfortable and unnatural that I would rather stay home in my old clothes than go anywhere; but then, also, there were so many interesting things to do at our farm home, and few outings could match this. The exception to this, which my family undertook once a year, was our trip to Auckland Zoo. Even though this was probably the high-light of my year, one year I announced: "If I can't wear my 'longs', I don't want to go!" Such was (and is) the intensity of my need to feel "comfort-able" in my favourite clothing, rather than dressing up. "Image" based on one's clothing, hairstyle and adornments is a concept which I find puzzling and distasteful. I assess others on their personality and behaviour, not on their clothing labels, and I find it hard to understand why other people cannot do the same! At any rate, I found that this whole area of life was one of difference between myself and others, and particularly between myself and little girls. On the other hand, neither was I interested in the "macho" activities of the day, such as sports and boisterous adventures. I was aware of wondering where I fitted in to the scheme of things. There-fore, one of my identity issues was "Am I a boy or a girl, or something in between?"

Growing into my teenage years – at least, chronologically speaking – I was left behind by my peer group in some ways. In my emotions and interests I was still at my childhood level. Friendships and romances were in full swing amongst the other teens, whereas I had not yet begun to understand how to connect with people. One of the very few people I had ever felt connected to was my father, and he was gone. Though I did not realise this at the time, I did not know how to understand body language, or facial expressions apart from the most blatant ones, or eye messages, or indirect ways of using language. This kept me on the outer in many social situations; and, therefore, being uncomfortable and unskilful in social situations, I avoided most of them if possible. It felt like I was on a separate planet; once I commented to my Mum, "I feel like an alien from outer space." Mum did not know what to do with such a statement. Thus, another of my identity issues was: "Am I an earthling or an alien?"

A further identity issue was, for decades, that which I will call "The Unwanted Possession." This title is borrowed from Wilfrida Ann Mully's article of the same name, which describes this phenomenon in a way to which I can really relate. It is included in the book *Manlike Monsters on Trial: Early Records and Modern Evidence,* edited by Marjorie Halpin and Michael M. Ames (1987).

The dark was always a challenge for me. From an early age, I had nightmares every night, vividly recalling them in the morning. Every night, for many years, I spent my sleeping time being frantically chased by something or someone: dinosaurs, wild beasts, dangerous criminals, or the police. I spent every night running for my life, terrified. One morning, I told this to my Mum. Mum, seemingly, did not know what to do about this, as she said nothing, and I did not bring up the subject again. As an older child and teenager, I would pull the bedclothes right over my head, at risk of suffocating. I was afraid to open my eyes and see anything inside my room; the worst thing to look at was the doorway, in case anyone – anything – might be coming in.

Even though I was afraid, I frequently took walks in the dark – to see if I could overcome my fear. From one end of the farm to the other was half a mile. Sometimes I didn't switch the torch on, just to see if I could manage without it. There were no street lights; only paddocks and the race (the farm track), so it was considerably darker than being in an urban area. Even so, I could discern where someone had strung a thin wire across the race to guide the cows into some gateway or other; I would duck underneath it. The stars were bright; I knew the Southern Cross and its two Pointers; and the night sounds could include wild ducks quacking, pied stilts yipping, crickets shrilling, and cows chewing their cuds, coughing and belching. I never did lose my fear of the dark this way, but I derived some sort of satisfaction from completing the walk.

Much worse was having to make the long journey from my bedroom to the toilet at least once a night. When I was thirteen, Mum had extension work done on the house, which added a sitting room, hallway, and large sewing room, all of which had to be traversed on the way from my bedroom to the toilet. I seem to have been blessed with a "Woolworth's bladder" (made worse, of course, by anxiety), so hanging on 'til morning was never an option. Mum was, for much of my lifetime, a professional tailor, with one of the tools of the trade, a full-length mirror, fixed to the wall of the sewing room. The worst part of my trip to the toilet was going past this mirror. I was terrified to look at it, yet it drew my gaze like a magnet: I had no power to look away. Horror swept over me, every time, as I expected to see: red glowing eyes, brown shaggy fur, snout and fangs… by the time I had ascertained that this was *not* what I was seeing, I had already had the terror attack.

So it went on into my twenties and thirties. Even after I no longer lived at my mother's house, sometimes I had to sleep with the light on – when living alone, no one would need to ask me why. The nightly sounds of floorboards creaking meant, surely, that an intruder was approaching my room. I would shut the bedroom door, because then, at least, there was no dark gaping entrance-way in which someone or something could be lurking, ready to come in. Since the door would have to be opened first, this would give me an extra second's warning.

I developed a relationship of sorts with this monster, "The Unwanted Possession." Worn out by the fear, I would beg it to come and do its worst and get it over with. Its refusal to do so proved to me that it was more interested, for the moment at least, in intimidation and mental cruelty: in *scaring* me to death. Its name – after I reached my (chronologically speaking) adult years – became known to me as Jenny Pierson. Therefore, if I could kill Jenny Pierson, I – the real me, Aquila – would be set free to realise my potential. I mulled over this possible course of action.

"The Unwanted Possession" entered psychiatric hospital with me. Even though the hospital staff seemed unaware of my life issues, I felt safer from my closest companion with all those other people around me. ("All those other people" were soon to become a major problem in their own right, but that is another matter, for another chapter.) In the evening, without much else to do in the hospital ward, I could even go running outside in the dark and feel a measure of protection. The hospital driveway, which encircled a large green field, became my running track. Every time I passed beneath a particular huge tree, whose branches hung over the track, I lifted up my arms in the sign of victory: I had succeeded again, I had run the circuit in the dark, and the monster had not yet killed me. I had defied fear and death, and felt the thrill of courage rewarded. Therefore, another of my identity issues was: Am I a human at all, or am I some kind of an animal or a monster?...a supernatural being?...

Added to the identity questions were boundary questions, that is: If I am possessed by another entity, where does it leave off and I begin? Does Jen exist at all – apart from providing the convenience of a physical body for something/somebody else? If somebody else wants to do something to me or with me, where does he/she end and I begin? I often felt "taken over" by a more powerful individual – and every other individual had more power than I did. I wanted power, not so that I could dominate others, but just so that I could "hold my own space." I was unable to do this. It was not simply a matter of apathy, or of being too afraid to assert myself; certainly, fear always played a big role in my life, but there was more than fear going on here. It was an inability to own my own source of personal power; if it was there all the time, I could not locate it, could not access it. Also, my brain seemed to be working at a much slower pace than others' brains did. In my specialist subjects, I was mentally quick; but in most other areas, it took me so long to work out what was going on – if I ever *did* work it out – that by the time I worked out what action to take – if I *could* ever work it out – it was often too late, or it was the wrong decision, or the whole situation had altered again by then, and I was therefore still several steps behind. This became part of my boundary issues, due to the confusion it added to any situation. Over time, it caused me to be afraid to do anything at all, because if I chose a course of action, it would be without the full set of necessary data, thus causing a likely misjudgement. This situation fed into my painful feeling of a lack of personal power. If I had a decision to make over a long period of time, for example several weeks, I would be more likely to come up with a satisfactory result; but quick-fire assessments and on-the-spot judgement calls were always problematic for me, and often still are.

Part of my life was spent in an eagle–wolf dichotomy. I fancied being a wolf, with its powerful persona, and its life as a member of the pack. A wolf possessed power, and enjoyed comradeship, which were things I lacked and wanted. I – Aquila – was an eagle, soaring loftily overhead, majestic, connected to the heavens, but – alone and solitary. As Aquila, I was also a spiritual entity who was helping to save the unique wonders of the world. It seemed that I had to be one or the other – wolf or eagle – not a combination. It was a struggle, because parts of my eagle-hood were intensely special to me, and I did not want to lose them in the process of seeking wolf-hood. One of the doctors, in the acute ward of a psychiatric hospital, wrote in my medical record "She believes in this eagle–wolf idea to an almost literal degree."

Growing into adulthood (chronologically speaking), I was still without the "normal" interests other people seemed to have, such as getting married and having babies, or "doing one's big OE" (Overseas Experience.) I kept up my attendance at Bible study groups throughout my teens, and so it was that I found myself at the occasional Christian pot luck dinner. At one of these, a young woman of about my own age asked me, "Do you like cooking?" – I answered in the negative. She continued, "Do you like sewing?" – with the same response from me. To this, the young woman exclaimed, "What *do* you like, then?" – with the implication that there were no other worthwhile interests in the world. I decided that, OK, I would try again with telling my truth, so I said: "Poultry keeping." At this, my conversation partner sort of stared, and asked, "What?" So I clarified the subject: "Chooks, ducks, geese." That seemed to end the conversation. Again, I perceived that I was the "odd one out," the person with interests which no one else shared.

In my teen and young adult days, a popular saying was "Be yourself." There was a problem, however, if you could not work out what your "self" was; and an additional difficulty if your "self" was something which other people found too weird, so that you did not fit in to any circle. These were extra matters that I had to deal with. Later on in life, I was again exhorted to "be yourself," but, paradoxically, this was by persons who did not respect what my "self" was, and who seemingly wanted me to be *their* version of what my "self" should be. So these were empty words uttered by shallow thinkers. When I hear these words, or similar, nowadays, I season them with a few pinches of suspicion. Before I take them seriously, I try to observe (over a period of time, if possible) what kind of a person the speaker is: does he or she really mean those words, or are they just glibly repeating a common saying?

Later still in life, after a particularly disturbing relationship with a man, I found that I was "off men" for the foreseeable future. It just so happened that, around this time, into my workplace came some particularly friendly and kind-hearted women. On hearing of my misadventure, two of the women invited me to their houses, and to meet their other friends, and to stay the night sometimes. Their friendship gave me comfort at a time when I needed it. Through them, I was introduced to more and more interesting and unorthodox (meant in the most positive sense) individuals. Some of them were in romantic relationships with each other. Though I was not in close friendships with many of these people – indeed, I had little idea of how to form close friendships – their company helped me to feel better about life. After six months or so of this, I felt that I had made a happy discovery: the solution to my identity confusions. Now I had the answer, so I thought, as to why I had always felt different! So it was that, one evening at dinner with my Mum and my elderly spinster Aunty, I made the excited announcement: "All my friends are gay, and I think I'm gay too!"

Then began, for me, a "honeymoon period" – that is, the euphoria of a new and exciting life. I rented out my unit in Papakura, in order to move in to a lesbian household in one of the Auckland city suburbs. There were four of us in the house; four humans, that is, and a lot of cats. The cats could open the fridge door and help themselves, as well as having other, less endearing, habits. My room was in the attic, with a ladder for access; I was delighted with the amazing view in all directions.

When I say it was a "lesbian household," let me just make sure that one misconception is cleared away first. On telling my friend Timothy (years later), for instance, he seemed to think that this meant that the household was a sexual free-for-all! No – we were flatmates, not romantic partners. One flatmate had a partner who sometimes stayed over, and the rest of us were single, at least at the start.

A huge part of the excitement was, for me, going to the gay night clubs. As I had not been in *any* night clubs ever before – whether gay or straight – this was bound to be a memorable experience. I was fascinated by the moving lights and smoke machine, and would watch one particular rotating sphere for as long as I could, until someone interrupted my reverie. The music was thrilling as well; some of the songs had a great dance beat, which would make me feel like moving my body – if one could get any space on the crowded dance floor. At least with such a crush of bodies, I did not have to worry as much about my dancing ability; I felt reasonably inconspicuous in the crowd. Whether I had anyone to dance with was not of overriding importance; sometimes I just felt like jumping around on my own.

On night club nights, I was the driver for the household, as I had a car at that stage, and did not drink much (if any) alcohol; whereas the others wanted to drink, and one was already barred from driving due to a drink-driving charge. For other outings, too, I was often the driver. After phone orders were placed with the "tomato lady," I would drive my flatmates to the address to pick up the goods. I would not realise until much later that the "tomato lady" was actually a drug dealer.

One night, one of the flatmates (the one who owned the house) was ranting and raving all night about her girlfriend. "I've finished with her! Anyone can have her now, because I don't want her!" she repeated for hours. It occurred to me that here was an opportunity: perhaps the discarded girlfriend, Jessica, would go out with me! We already knew each other, and had been friendly towards each other so far. The next day I phoned her and Jessica and I arranged an outing. Our friendship grew.

A few weeks later, there was trouble in my flat. The house-owner, Vanessa, was angry that I was going out with Jessica. She now let it be known that it wasn't true that "I've finished with her – I don't want her." Another of the flatmates remarked to me, "People don't always say what they mean, you know! You shouldn't have assumed that she meant it." I felt confused, as well as upset; because if people could mean the opposite of what they said, how could I be expected to know what they really meant?

Relations in the household now took a downward turn; at least, where I was concerned, for I was the one who had misbehaved. Vanessa no longer saw me as her buddy. For me, there was the confusion as to whether Vanessa and Jessica really had got back together. We did not all go out night-clubbing as a joyous little gang any more. Besides, I found out rather quickly that going out until 3 a.m. and getting up for work the next morning did not go together very well. The "honeymoon period" was over.

Three months after joining that household, I was made the offer, by another lesbian household, to come and live with them instead. The people making the offer were of a very sedate lifestyle, compared to where I had been living. They wanted another quiet-living flatmate, and I was glad enough, by then, to return to my usual quiet ways.

At the new house, I was surprised to be contacted by Jessica again. She had broken up with Vanessa and wanted to be back with me again. Euphoria, ecstasy! We had a blissful reunion, and began seeing each other twice a week. Sometimes I stayed overnight at her house, in her bed. As we were both in good jobs at the time, we planned a holiday to Wellington together; I was so nervous about losing the plane tickets that I made Jessica look after them! On reaching our motel in Wellington, the young man at the counter suddenly became flustered, apologising that a mistake seemed to have been made, for our room had only a double bed. He would try to rectify matters, he said. "No, wait," I replied; "that was what we wanted!" Again, the young man was all a-fluster, not knowing what to do.

Our room gave us a wonderful view; then again, any view of Wellington would have been wonderful for me, as I love Wellington. The historic buildings, the forested green belt, the staircases in the streets! Whilst we were there, a gale suddenly sprang up, blowing scaffolding from a building site down the street, and forcing pedestrians (including Jessica and me) to shelter in shop doorways. Oh, the magic of huddling together against the storm; Jessica was excited by the unexpected fury of it. We browsed through book shops, craft shops, art galleries… ate in cafes and restaurants… explored new streets, and just strolled around. This was heaven, if ever there was one.

Back in Auckland, I began writing the occasional story and poem again, which I had done so enthusiastically in my childhood. My new household had a very friendly atmosphere and was a welcome new start. Everything was going well for me, until... I don't think I ever really understood what happened, but it was something to do with Vanessa, from my previous flat, again. Her hold on Jessica was far stronger than mine. Whether they really got back together or whether Jessica was simply doing whatever Vanessa told her, it finished between us. I was devastated.

In my sadness, I became a lonely wanderer of the streets, at times. There was one positive aspect to it: my senses were heightened so that I perceived things – usually natural phenomena – more sharply, which then became transferred to my poems. Mind you, some – or all – of the poems might be absolute rubbish, for all I know. As I often have trouble understanding other people's poems, I am hardly an authority on what constitutes poetry. Anyway, as I filled up more and more pages of my display folder with these writings, I had the idea to publish them. As it is extremely difficult to find a publisher for poetry and stories, I looked around for a desk-top publisher, whom I would pay to print a book for me. I was still in my relatively well-paid job, and – now that I was single again – bought few luxuries, so I could afford to pay for this.

Eighteen months came and went in my second lesbian household, by which time I concluded that it would be better for me to live alone. I was not able to cope with living with other people – whether gay, straight, or anything else – for more than a short-term arrangement. It was excruciatingly difficult for me to leave, however – as it was, at least, the "known" environment, and going anywhere else would be the "unknown" again. In hindsight, I don't know if this was the right decision, but, I did it: I sold my lovely little unit in Papakura, and bought one in Mount Eden, another suburb of Auckland City. My new home was right beside the mountain; a bus stop and a post box, my essentials of life, were on the other side of the road.

Now, though, without my flatmates and without Jessica – and alone for most of the time outside work hours – my mood was more often down than up. I felt desperate for friends and for other people, but I knew that I could not cope with people when I had them. This caused me to feel that there was no solution to the loneliness I felt; and my failure at relationships of various kinds had caused my self-esteem to plummet. I arrived at the space where I did not want to live any more, and I had thoughts of ending my life. To give myself more time to think it through, however, I made a bargain with myself: when I got my book published – thus leaving something of myself in the world – I would be free to leave the world.

I called the book *Popcorn? Milkshake? …?* Most of its contents were "serious," but a few of the poems were deliberate doggerel, intended to be humorous. Although I had had some short-term romance in the gay world, some of the scenarios described in this book were imaginary. Looking back on it, I can now see that there was an element of wish-fulfilment – and of trying to convince somebody – myself – that my gay orientation was the reason for my feeling different. This was no longer convincing to me, however, as I could perceive for myself that, having entered lesbian society, I was still on the outer! In fact, I was even more of an alien in my new milieu, because the "women-only" community prided itself on such things as "women's intuition," "the feminine mystique," "women's knowledge;" and these were things which I never understood in the first place. Therefore, without men around to balance up the equation, I was even more baffled than before as to how to live amongst people.

Some of my poems were pure nature worship: "City by Storm-Set" and "Communion." I do experience a "spiritual" sort of feeling about features of nature, although I dislike applying the word "spiritual" to it, as I feel that it is a very overworked word, its meaning stretched so far as to mean anything. There are not a lot of vocabulary choices for this sphere of life, though. And as far as nature goes, I am the first to admit that I love nature when it is beautiful and kind and nurturing… not when it is savage and death-dealing, as in tornadoes, storms at sea, and malaria. Therefore, I am rather one-sided in my love of nature, (though I suspect most folks are, when it comes to the crunch: most of us would not sing songs of joyful Nature worship whilst a tsunami breaks over our heads.)

So my book was published; but, in spite of continuing to struggle with feelings of worthlessness, I did not end my life. A large part of the reason was that, although I felt like a useless sort of offspring for anyone to have, I thought that my mother would be upset if I committed suicide. As described in my chapter "Some Social Situations," I was to go through some more variations in my sexual orientation… an area of life which has caused me a lot of confusion.

Author's Note: I definitely do *not* wish to imply that identifying as gay or Lesbian is, in most people, due to confusion. As far as I know, all my gay friends and acquaintances stayed that way. I believe that for the vast majority, sexual orientation is something that does not chop and change. In my case, confusion was something I experienced in many spheres of life, and sexual orientation was just one of those spheres.

Chapter 6

In the Workforce: Part I

My first paid job was that of Library Assistant at Papakura Public Library, South Auckland. This was 20 minutes' drive from our rural home at Karaka. The Head Librarian was a small, kindly, white-haired Scotswoman. The library had a manual card-stamping issue system for my first few years there. The youngest, or newest, staff member's task on first coming to work in the morning was to numerically sort the cards of the books which had been issued the day before. This was a predictable, methodical task which suited me nicely. Over my four years there, I did a variety of library duties: issuing books, covering new books, shelving, a stint on Interloan, and even book-buying for the Junior and Young Adult Sections.

All of the library staff had two evenings per week rostered to work, as well as our daytime work hours. Our work was arranged so that our total hours for the week came to only 37.5 hours. We had a dinner break between the daytime and the evening shifts. Because I lived out of town, I stayed in Papakura for the dinner break. My Mum arranged with two acquaintances in Papakura that I would have dinner with them on these two evenings, instead of eating alone somewhere. It was very caring of these people to give me their friendship and all those dinners for four years.

I was in my element around books. As the junior staff member, it also fell to me to take the wicker basket and walk down the street to the stationer's, from where the library's magazine subscriptions were collected. On fine days, this errand was a delight that few other things could match.

Light-hearted moments happened from time to time. While shelving, one day, I found in my hands Sir Winston Churchill's *History of the English-speaking Peoples*, Volume One. Just to see what kind of content such a book would have, I opened the book at random: at the top of the page was the chapter heading, "The Boys." This seemed, to me, to be a little "chummy" for such a classical history book, so I opened at another place: this time, the chapter heading was "The Girls." Now I really was surprised! It took more exploration to finally discover that the book was actually a saucy novel about, yes, boys and girls – but with Sir Winston Churchill's book cover having been wrapped around it!

During my first two years working there – and having reached the age of eighteen – my physical energy ebbed lower and lower. In the mornings, especially, my body felt very tired, unrested. My face had become puffy-looking, too. One morning, on returning to the house after feeding my hens, I commented to Mum, "I am so tired that I can hardly put one foot in front of the other."

"Right, we are going to the doctor!" Mum responded, and made the appointment. In spite of my protests about going, the outcome was worth it: I had an underactive thyroid gland, also called hypothyroidism, which had progressed to the "classical" stage of myxoedema. This explained the very low energy levels and the puffy appearance. More explanation was provided by the dictionary: the word comes from the Greek *myxa*, meaning "mucus," and *Oidema* – "a swelling." An excess of mucus had caused swelling of my tissues. In the longterm, this condition can damage the heart. The good news was that it was easily treatable, with thyroid hormone tablets, (thyroxine), which I was immediately prescribed. The doctor explained the next bit: the treatment would get rid of the excess mucus, which would exit the body via urine, and there would be a lot of it! Sure enough, I was visiting the toilet very frequently over the next few weeks, until the mucus – and puffiness – had dispersed. At the same time, my hair – which I had grown to half-way down my back by this time – was falling out. This is also a symptom of myxoedema. Every time I put the brush to my head, it would come out with a large handful of hair attached. My locks were now looking so depleted that Mum and I agreed that it would be better to get my hair cut short. After this was done, the hair situation stabilised due to my thyroxine treatment – but with an amusing new look. The sudden influx of thyroxine into my system resulted in a lot of new hair sprouting, which grew, straight upwards, through the threadbare remains of my old hair. I now had two different crops of hair on my head, which looked quite unusual! As thyroid hormone is also important in physical growth, I eventually began growing taller – and assuming a more curvaceous shape. To prove this, Mum drew my new height measurements on a door-post. I continued growing taller right through to my thirties, with Mum's pencil marks as evidence. And the presenting problem, the very low energy level, was cured.

Now that I had all of this information, it also explained (in the absence of any other explanation) why I had had that embarrassing mega-mucus problem in my high school years. Before the thyroid treatment, I had an excess of mucus; after the treatment, I have never had it again – not in those astounding quantities, anyway. Hypothyroidism is often signalled by jaundice in infancy, which was a sign not followed up. Nowadays, newborn babies are routinely tested for hypothyroidism, but this was not the case in 1955, when I was born. The thyroid treatment is life-long, so I am still taking the daily tablets.

On a physical health level, I had a new lease of life. I revelled in my new-found ability to run, instead of dragging myself around. Life had definitely improved for me in the energy department. I now experienced another new and unfamiliar phenomenon: a keen appetite. Unaccustomed to such a thing, I had to learn, for the first time, how to monitor this. I eventually found, however, that the "new me" made no difference to my social world, or lack of it; I still did not feel as though I belonged to the same world as other folks did.

While getting on reasonably well with my workmates, who were, for the most part, friendly and kind-hearted, I found one colleague difficult at times; she could be very abrupt, I thought. Part of it was, I suppose, that I did not know how to deal with her kind of personality. The example which springs most readily to mind was that of the brown wrapping paper. The Interloan system involved posting books – borrowers' special requests – back and forth, and, for this, we needed sturdy, brown wrapping paper. When I was engaged on my learning period with this, we were running out of wrapping paper, so, after being denied a new supply of paper, I was joining up several pieces of second-hand brown paper to make parcels. After some weeks, this particular colleague informed me that there was a letter for me from the National Library. I was excited about this, until my colleague added, grumpily, "You won't be so pleased when you see what the letter is about." The letter was a complaint about the state of my patch-work book parcels; I gathered that at least one had not survived the journey intact. I was removed from Interloan duties. What hurt the most was that the new person to be given this duty stated, straightaway, that she needed a new roll of brown wrapping paper – and got it, no questions asked. This had been the cause of my unsatisfactory parcels in the first place. I felt upset that there seemed to be two different rules: one for her and one for me.

As the years went by, I felt increasingly that I did not know where my life was going, and whether I had the know-how and personal power to make it go anywhere at all. My week-in, week-out routine that had previously pleased me seemed to have become a rut, and I did not know how to change it, or even exactly what I would prefer instead. Had I been able to pinpoint the source of my malaise, (which, at the time, I could not,) I would have been able to see that it was not really my job, but, rather, my lack of a social life outside of work hours. I had only one friend of my own age – but we were not close, and I did not know how to become so. I was socially awkward, and no longer wished to visit the kind families at every dinner-time, but I did not know how to break out of this routine without causing offence. As I knew no ways of altering any part of my everyday life in the small ways that could have helped, I did the only thing I could think of: I handed in my notice after four years.

On the home front, Mum had been gradually becoming friends with Eric – without my being able to read the signs. Finally, marriage and a merging of the two families was announced. I liked Eric, but I was not so sure about living with a step-brother and -sister; (two older step-sisters lived elsewhere). As it happened, the change did not impact hugely on my life: I still had my own room, and I continued with my own life as before. My step-siblings were more sociable than I, and enjoyed their own separate social world. They did not explicitly exclude me: it was I who was unable to join in.

In the other direction from my home at Karaka was Patumahoe, a farming and market gardening district. The main crop was onions, and I joined the staff of SMI Dehydrated Foods as an onion top 'n' tailer. There were two of us in this role, working on a two-person automated machine which had moving knives for slicing onions. We wore rubber gloves, aprons and hats. We were instructed never to run in the factory, because a piece of raw onion in contact with the concrete floor is better than a banana skin for slipping on. My work-partner and I got on quite well. The supervisor also told us that we must always work on the machine together, never singly, for safety reasons; if either of us got caught in the machine for any reason, the other partner would switch the power off immediately. Also, if we felt our rubber glove becoming caught and dragging our hand with it, we must let the glove be pulled off and thus keep our hand safe.

The cut onions fell down a chute into a huge wooden crate. To keep them from simply stacking themselves higher and higher in one place in the crate, my partner or I would use a long stick to prod them down to an even level. Leaning over the crate of cut onions certainly made our eyes water and our noses run. On first arriving for work, one's nose and eyes would have the onion-response for about 20 minutes, then one would not notice it for the remainder of the shift... until the next day. To ensure that no one took away my indispensable onion-prodding stick, I brought it home each day in my car. My Mum said that that stick sure stank, and that on my arrival home I could be *smelled* before I was seen!

The supervisor thought it desirable that I should learn how to operate the fork hoist. After my two training sessions, however, he did not seem to want me on this task permanently. Whilst I was trying to adjust the lever just right, the huge crate of onions first hit the ceiling, then the floor, then the ceiling again – to the accompaniment of my onion-partner's doubled-up, hysterical laughter. Yes, I can laugh at this too!

The work shift of the top 'n' tailers started mid-afternoon, whilst the supervisor and a few other work-mates were there, after which we two continued on into the evening. It was therefore our job to lock up the building when we left. The door was an electric roller-door, and the method was to press the "Down" button, then to get out before it closed. Part of the procedure was supposed to be to check, beforehand, that nothing was in the way of the door's closure. One night, we forgot to check this, and we were, of course, already outside when we heard the crunching and groaning of the door trying to close on an object in its path. By now, the object was well and truly jammed, and the door only trying all the harder to jam it. There was not much room to get back under the door to the inside, in order to reverse the switch. I stood there "oohing" and "aahing," not brave enough to crawl under the groaning door, in case it suddenly came down full force on top of me. My partner, in spite of her much fuller figure, did the heroic thing and scrambled inside.

One dark night, I did not discover, until my partner had already disappeared out of sight, that my car was stuck in the mud. My stomach did a somersault, as this was a lonely country district, with no public phone, and cell-phones had not yet been invented (I still do not own one, in any case). Luckily, I remembered some advice which Mum had given me long ago: find some flat objects – lengths of wood, a sack, anything – and place them right behind the back wheels; then, try to reverse on to these, and, from there, on to any firmer ground which is available. The factory was already locked up, of course, and I was in the dark, but I managed to find some pieces of junk which would do. I was hugely relieved when this plan worked – I was able to back on to a gravelled area and drive off from there.

After four months of this job, the novelty had well and truly worn off. I still did not know how to steer my own life. As the onion work was seasonal anyway, I left, not knowing what I would do next. My cheerful, friendly partner gave me a farewell box of chocolates, with a card saying "Thanks for been a good mate" (*sic*).

Around this time, Mum and Eric separated, with my branch of the family moving to the township of Papakura. This meant that my poultry menagerie had had to go – I left the hens with a friend at Karaka, but later heard that they had been disposed of and, I feared, eaten. I was lucky to find another good job, that of a clerk in the Education Board's bookroom, in Auckland City. I could catch a bus from Papakura to there, and had already taken this journey a number of times. On the morning that I had to arrive for work, however, I got confused over which bus to take. The workplace was situated a little way before Grafton Bridge, and the commuter buses were labelled "First Stop: Newmarket" and "First Stop: Grafton Bridge." I got on the latter before realising that this bus would take me too far, so I should have got on the other one. Becoming anxious, I alighted, and caught a bus with the other destination. Perhaps, in my increasingly stressed state, I had still got it wrong – for the bus sailed along the motorway to Grafton Bridge after all, before stopping. That meant that I had to back-track to the Education Board. The distance was an easy walk, but – I was supposed to be there by nine o'clock, and my mistakes had wasted precious time, so I ran back in the rain, arriving dishevelled and agitated. Fortunately, no one seemed to notice anything amiss, and I began my career as a bookroom assistant.

The bookroom was set apart, down a very steep slope, from the main building. For morning tea and lunch, one had to climb the hill to the tea-room; but, for anyone with a sweet tooth, it was well worth the trip. There was a mouth-watering selection of cakes for sale, but my staple diet became the rock cakes – at twelve cents each.

The administrative person who had interviewed me had been very friendly, and so was my boss – the manager of the bookroom. The other assistant, however, who was supposed to train me, was sombre, cheerless and somewhat hostile. Perhaps she simply did not like me – I have no way of knowing whether she was like this in all areas of her life. Anyway, it made things difficult for me at times, which increased my anxiety. This young woman habitually ate her lunch at her desk, wrapping up her banana skin in a sheet of office stationery before throwing it in the bin. At lunch time, she was then free to go on her own secret business, somewhere up the hill. Early on, I felt that there was insufficient work for me to do, so I asked the administrative person who had given me the job whether he had any extra work for me. The next thing I knew, my boss – Stanley – told me that I should not have done that, as it made our department look bad. Stanley started to show me some of his own work, to teach me extra skills. Before this could progress far, the other assistant took me aside and flew into a fury – I was not supposed to be learning Stanley's job, etc., etc.; I was supposed to be learning my own job – which, I now realise, I probably was not learning adequately. The fact that this assistant obviously disliked me, and, therefore, did not spend the necessary time teaching me, did not help my learning process. This situation created stress and dislike of my job, and I began to succumb to nausea attacks. It was a great disappointment, for a bookroom would ordinarily be my ideal place. The fact that my job was going wrong added to my other concerns about fitting in to the world –

where could I be successful, where could I make friends? Again, I dealt with the problem in the only way I knew, by handing in my notice after one year.

Chapter 7

Feathers with Everything! Part II

At first, I simply kept every fowl that I bred, whether it turned into a hen or a rooster; but this, as every poultry breeder knows, results in one being overrun with spare roosters. Eventually, I accepted that I had to do something about the situation, if only because the spare fowls ate masses of food. We could not eat the culls, because I could not (and still cannot) bring myself to kill them, and my mother, who will do most things for me, drew the line at killing, cleaning and plucking birds.

In those days, Chadwick's hardware store, in nearby Papakura, held an auction every Friday morning, complete with a set of poultry pens for the feathered merchandise. I began the routine of taking my spare fowls there to sell. This meant catching them the night before the auction; Mum and I would go to the chook-house under cover of darkness. One night, at the beginning of the moulting season, Mum carefully caught a magnificent red rooster, with one hand around his legs, and her other hand holding his tail in order to steady him. Her grip on his legs must have been insufficient, as he got them free and took off on his great escape – with Mum's other hand holding his entire supply of tail feathers. Due to fowls' regular moulting season, the tail must have been loose and waiting to fall out on its own – but our botched catching episode had helped the process along. He had avoided this week's auction, anyway. Next morning, we expected to see a crestfallen red rooster, but, no: there he was, strutting and showing off as proudly as usual, seemingly unaware that he was displaying a completely bare, pink backside.

When my bantam hens went "clucky," that is, they were taken over by the mothering instinct, and wanted to hatch eggs, they would be given eggs of my choice, if I had any I wanted hatching. If I did not require their services at the moment, they would have to be removed from the communal chook-house, otherwise they would start incubating any and every egg that the other hens laid. The place to put them – as taught to me by my father, and his father before him – was in a wooden crate with slats, and hung by a wire in a tree. This crate was called the "cluck box." This would keep them cool, which would, in turn, put them "off the cluck," whereupon they would be returned to the flock. One day, when we were taking the cows to be milked, a nosy cow put her head through the wire loop, then pulled the cluck box off its branch. This meant that she now had a large ornament, the cluck box, hanging around her neck, which she decided she did not like after all. She took the only action that she knew, that is, running and shaking her head until the box fell apart. The resident hen fell out, unharmed; we don't remember whether the experience put her off being clucky!

When I passed the School Certificate (the fifth form exam of those days, taken at around the age of fifteen), Aunty Freda gave me $15. Most girls of my age, (as I now realise) would have bought clothes, make-up or a hair-do, but I bought three geese – two females and a gander.

The geese had a different demeanour from that of the fowls, a certain poise, and a gaze which made them look all-seeing and wise. They were prolific breeders, and the downy goslings were very cute. My cat could not help herself, and would stalk the last baby straggler in the line – until the gander noticed her activities, and charged at her with outstretched neck and a ferocious hiss. Because we could not keep all of the offspring, I sold a few for Christmas eating.

One day, during Mum's renovations to the house, workmen were busy laying a large expanse of concrete. They had just got the wet concrete smooth and tidy when they decided to shoo the geese out of the way. Instead of herding them quietly, someone startled them, with the result that the whole flock took to the air, landing heavily in the wet concrete. The geese paddled around with their big, webbed feet, and the more they were chased, the more excited they became and the more of a mess they made of the concrete.

When we moved off the farm to live in the township of Papakura, I sold the geese to a man at Huapai, North-West Auckland. That was quite a drive from rural South Auckland, but Mum and Eric kindly arranged to transport them in Eric's station wagon. Not knowing what to put them in, they opted for poultry pellet bags, made of thick paper, cutting a hole for their heads to poke through. On the way, the birds created so much body heat and excreta that their feet came through all the layers of paper. When Eric had to stop suddenly for a traffic light at Mt. Eden Road, all 25 geese were jumping up and down in their paper bags in the back of the station wagon – with nearby motorists staring in shock. They were duly delivered, however, with quite a to-do on arrival – not only did they have to be removed from the car, but they had to be extricated from what was left of their paper bags. Poor Mum and Eric – the things I put them through. I think Eric resigned as goose carrier that day!

With earnings from my first job, I bought my first camera: a small pocket variety. I used up my first couple of films on taking photos of my poultry – close-up portraits a speciality. On excitedly rushing to the chemist to pick up these masterpieces, I opened the packet and was shocked and horrified to find – pictures of the Taj Mahal! "Oh, please, please find the right photos for me!" – I begged the chemist. This took a few more days – until the tourists back from India had opened their packet, I suppose. I wonder if they were any more pleased with mine than I was with theirs!

Chapter 8

Some Social Situations

Social situations occur every day for most of us. Even avoiding people is a social issue of sorts – it is the individual's response to a social expectation. I have singled out a few incidents for the purpose of making a separate chapter. As my life cannot be separated neatly, however, into exclusively "social," "cognitive," "communicative" and "feathers with everything" segments, some of these spheres of experience overlap.

Throughout my childhood, teenage years and young adulthood, I had been very shy; at least "shyness" was what people called it. I could more or less speak with my mother and brother – on some topics, at any rate. With other people, my communications were very restricted. Regarding the topics which were of most importance to me, for example the fears and the identity issues which I had, I stopped talking about these early on (even with my closest family members), or had never started. I had, from my early years, a sense which told me that others would not be able to under-stand my innermost experiences. This sense has proved to be correct, because even in my adult years, when I eventually became more eloquent in my communication skills, the situation was no better – especially when dealing with the helping professionals. Therefore, I can only be thankful that I did not expend a lot more energy and adrenaline than I already did, trying to get such people to validate that which they could not.

Relatively "natural" family contact was, and is, for me far preferable to "forced" family contact. Into the latter bracket come birthday parties and Christmas Day. The very thought of a large number of excited people gathering together in one small place can be off-putting and threatening to me. As my closest family members and I have frequent contact in any case, the compulsory "family togetherness" of Christmas Day feels artificial and overdone to me. It is as if someone else – the "higher authority" of social custom – is dictating terms to my family members and myself, and I do not approve of this! I realise that I could completely opt out and go somewhere by myself for the day, but I also feel that this would sadden persons such as my mother, who does not deserve to be made upset by inconsiderate behaviour.

Throughout my life, whenever I have been with one or more individuals I have often felt overwhelmed. Some types of persons overwhelm me more easily than others, for example, the bossy and aggressive types. On other occasions, prolonged contact with even my closest friend can become overwhelming. This is a feeling of being "swallowed up," of not being able to hold my own space, or my own personal power ("power," according to my own definition, has taken me a lifetime to more-or-less acquire, and it refers to my own ability to act, not to a desire to control others). The "overwhelmed" feeling saps my physical and mental energy so that I find it very difficult, if not impossible, to make decisions or to do anything. In this state, it is all the more easy to be carried along by what the other person decides, as I am unable to "stand on my own two feet." As I do not like this situation, I can try to avoid at least some incidents where this seems likely to happen, especially if it has already happened with the same person, or I can try to work out a few strategies beforehand, for example think of which decisions or plans I know that I prefer already, before I become "bombarded" with a lot of other stimuli. Such strategies may or may not work on the day, but, afterwards, at least, I may be able to hold on to the feeling that I tried something instead of nothing; and, over time, repeated experiments of this kind may start to reveal patterns of other people's behaviour to me. As other people are all different – a concept which I find quite troublesome at times! – I tend to study each person individually, especially in some areas of life, such as humour (with humour being one of the most complicated phenomena in life).

I have been bullied and taken advantage of by various persons during my life, and, although I have recently learned a number of "safety rules," this situation is ongoing. I realise that I will probably never be completely free of this source of stress, though I am now in a safer life space than formerly.

Starting school was a scary time for me. I remember hiding behind the piano. Fortunately for me, my local school was a small rural one. Our first activity for each day was matching up identical pictures, something which I could do easily. The infant teacher informed my mother that I was awkward and cautious about climbing up and down stairs. During my first year I began playing rough and tumble games with some of my classmates, until the teachers put a stop to this, insisting that I play with the little girls instead of the little boys. As stated in Chapter 5 "Identity and Boundary Issues," I never felt like a "little girl," and had little in common with them, so the instruction to play with the girls was no solution to my social awkwardness. In my second year, a little girl who would become my best friend started school. I then became part of her circle of friends, which was the group of girls who were one year behind me at school. I did not usually interact with the whole group at once, preferring (then as now) to interact with one or two individuals at a time. Also, some of my time was spent in solitary pursuits such as walking round and round the school's perimeter, and digging repetitively in the ground with a stick. I still had some social difficulties, e.g. the occasional bossy schoolmate, and the catch-22 situations when two school friends both insisted on sitting beside me at the same time, which was impossible on a two-seater bus seat. They would force me to "choose" one of them above the other, thus causing the other to be upset with me, whatever I chose! I never had any idea what to do in order to avoid the inevitable conflict, and I still find impossible situations like this very stressful.

I have always been a bit of a "dreamer," often away in my own reverie, not always inhabiting the same world as everyone else. It has been other people's comments which have made this clearer to me; for instance, one teacher who recognised my above-average intellect, but who added on my report card that I would often "be off on a tangent!"

Primary school was a breeze, however, compared to high school (secondary school). My small country school had included Form One and Two pupils, those who would ordinarily go to Intermediate School. I was unfamiliar with urban settings at the best of times, and on my first day at Papakura High School, after a lengthy bus ride, I was confronted by an enormous number of school buildings, a roll of 1200 students and an army of teachers. This was long before the modern innovation of students having familiarisation days before the actual starting day! As I had been one year ahead of my primary school friends, they were left behind, and I was on my own in this new environment, disoriented and scared. I could not even find my way to my classrooms for the first week or two, much less cope with all these new people.

When I did find my first two "friends," it was the completely random matter of who was sheltering under the same porch at the same time as me. I was relieved to find anyone who would smile and speak to me. After a few days, however, I realised, beyond doubt, that these two students had habits which were incompatible with mine, for example, the four-letter swear words which they were continually using. I did not use bad language, and I did not like hearing it, either. As for the factual content of their conversations, I had very little idea of what they were talking about. I then faced the problem of how to break away from them, when they had at least offered me their friendship. Over a period of days, I managed to fade away, out of their company.

To add to my feeling of displacement at high school, I had an embarrassing problem which no one else seemed to have. When I got a cold, and then sneezed or had to blow my nose, I had gallons of mucus, which no amount of blowing my nose could get rid of. It was thick and yellow, so that I would have a big, thick "rope" dangling out of each nostril, ropes which would forever keep coming out, whilst I tried to hide the situation with my handkerchief. If I just kept blowing in the attempt to get it all out, it just kept on coming – so that the hanky was full to overflowing, and I would then have to fish around for another, whilst still using one hand to try to cover my face. I could use up several hankies this way, and still have the endless "ropes" of mucus – which I would eventually have to break off clumsily, as best I could, and even then the stuff would be on my face, requiring another new hanky to wipe that off. This added to my feeling that I was some kind of freak. A seemingly related phenomenon was the wispy strips of something which would be attached to my lips – a white, glue-like substance which I would pull off with my fingers. This, I worked out by observing cause and effect, seemed to be a chemical reaction between toothpaste and saliva, but it would not be noticeable straightaway; it would take until I was at school, in the classroom, before the "glue" would set. At least, this was easier to cope with than the "yellow ropes." Yes, I have told you all this for a reason!!! Five years later (as I have described in Chapter 6), I would find out the cause, and the cure, for this.

Joelene was in my class, although she was at least a year older than me. As everyone took two extra "optional" subjects, it was surprising that we were together in all of our classes. We began talking to each other and sat together at lunch time. Having a friend was very important to me; I think a lot of what we talked about was our school life. It turned out that we each had a younger brother of around the same age, and no sisters. One morning, I turned up at school with a badly grazed elbow; Joelene kindly took me to the sick bay to have this attended to.

I had already started the year sitting next to other students in some of my classes, and Joelene now wanted to change places so that she could sit next to me in all of them. I felt uncomfortable about this, as I had grown to enjoy sitting next to my various classmates. I told Joelene that I did not agree with her idea, but she was very determined. As I would not ask my neighbouring classmates to shift, Joelene asked them herself, and they shifted. Now Joelene was the only person with whom I could fraternise. I now faded out of the company of my other classmates, because I had no opportunities to sit next to them.

Joelene had visits to our house, and I to hers. Her complexion was very fair, and on one overcast day at our place, she became badly sunburned; my mother and I felt bad about this. During Joelene's first overnight stay at our house, she commented on the total silence of the countryside, which made it hard for her to fall asleep! Total silence, that is, except for the night when the cows were in the paddock right outside our bedroom window: I had to explain the sound-effects of cows chewing the cud and belching. Joelene's father worked for the New Zealand Army, stationed in Papakura. By the end of that year, he had a transfer to the other army base at Whenuapai – North-West Auckland – as far away as any other suburb could be from Papakura. Joelene would be leaving Papakura High School... unless, she suggested hopefully, my family would take her in. This was a double shock. Although our day-to-day friendship would be ended by the move, I did not like the idea of living with her full-time: all day at school, and every minute at home. Away from school, I needed my own space and my solitary special interests. Fortunately, my mother realised this. Besides, Mum was by now a solo parent, and taking in another child would not have been a sensible decision for her. So Joelene left my school; and, by then, I had no other friends to fill the gap, as she had prevented me from spending time with my other classmates.

I was a studious young person, mostly enjoying my studies, except for mathematics. Though I had had a long, slow struggle during my primary school years coming to terms with "ordinary" maths, I had more or less mastered it. My first year at high school, however, marked the significant changeover in the curriculum to the "new" maths. No one in my family could help me with it, as it was all too different. My tenacious mastery of maths disappeared "down the gurgler." As soon as I started to get behind in my understanding of it (which was at an early stage), it became a lost cause, as I could comprehend nothing in my maths lessons from then on. I had never enjoyed maths in any case, so I had no motivation to engage in the effort which extra remedial sessions would have entailed. This situation was happening at the same time as my attempts to adjust to all other aspects of high school life, so I have to admit I gave up on the maths. From then on, it was a waste of time my being in the maths lessons, as I was too far behind to understand anything. I failed my tests and exams in this subject, which I still find upsetting, as I dislike seeing Ds on my report card.

On the other hand, I had an instant love affair with German. All Form Two pupils had been given a list of extra, optional subjects, from which one had to select two, in preparation for starting high school. I had not even heard the German language in my life before, so my choice of it was a complete gamble. In Form Two, at the rural primary school, we had studied a little French, which I had not much liked. In the monocultural place and time in which I grew up, I had had no contact with any other languages, except for a few Maori songs, so I had no data on which to base my choice of German. Maori language was not available as a subject option at that time. Luckily, as soon as I heard German spoken by our teacher and on the language tapes, I loved the sound of it. At home, I would walk around the place reciting sentences learned by heart. We were given frequent tests, of which I was often top of the class. My only serious rival for this position was a boy who was also studying French, and who was of the likeable, high-spirited type. My most immediate concern, after each test, was which one of us had secured the top mark!

Regarding my language skills, although I had always been able to write to an above-average standard, I had trouble carrying on a conversation in English. This was because of such factors as my marked "shyness," my usual inability to understand the social situation into which the conversation fitted, and my relative slowness in mentally processing the rapid-fire nature of conversation, which in turn was partly due to my thinking processes being carried out via pictures, rather than in words. However, the fact that in German class we were encouraged to memorise sentences and whole conversations meant that I was, for the most part, more able to converse in German than in English... as long as I possessed a stock of sentences which would fit the required topic. Decades later, still unable to talk freely and easily in English, I would return to this foreign language teaching method for the purpose of teaching myself to speak my native tongue! Thus, it can be said that, in some ways, I taught myself English as a foreign language. The facts which I have given in this paragraph show some important features of my social (as well as cognitive and communicative) development: for instance, I was "learning how to talk by numbers," so to speak. These spheres of development will overlap in other chapters, as they permeate all of a person's life.

The next person who made friendly overtures was Sharon; we were both in the Fourth Form. This relationship soon developed into a very dominating one, with Sharon dictating where, when, and with whom I would meet – the "with whom" being her, of course. Again (as has been a recurring theme in my life), I did not know how to deal with a domineering person, and remained caught up in a situation which I did not like. The problem was, and is, not simply one of being too cowardly to stick up for my own rights: I sometimes did protest, and did try to break free, but the more dominant individual knew how to thwart my attempts, how to "run rings around me." Therefore, although high anxiety levels have been a constant feature of my life, my timidity was only part of the issue. The other part was that I genuinely did not have the social know-how to understand what was going on and what to do about it: the brain circuitry for this side of life seemed to be missing. Another interlocking factor was that my mental processing speeds seemed to be slower than average (for certain subjects only, such as social understanding), so that I could never "keep up with the play" in a social situation, especially when the other person was of the bullying or manipulative type. In addition, bullying and manipulative types could easily identify me as someone they could dominate, and so I appeared to involuntarily attract such persons. This was something I could not help, no matter how much I wished and tried for things to be otherwise. Of course, I did not know, at the time, why I was having so much difficulty in social situations; it was just a part of the general confusion I felt about the world and how to live in it.

As my high school years continued to the Fifth and Sixth Forms, I became increasingly aware that I was not like my peers in some ways. I had difficulty making friends, and, after making them, would have trouble maintaining them, or would make an unsuitable friend who would then dominate or bully me, so that I could not escape the relationship. More noticeable than this, however, was the fact that the others all seemed to have opposite-sex friends, were going to parties, and were dating. Added to this was the girl students' interest in fashion, hair-styles and make-up – things which still left me completely bewildered and bored. I overheard one female classmate exclaiming, "Fashion? Who *isn't* interested!" I knew that the answer to this was "Me." My lack in all these areas caused me to wonder if something was wrong with me.

Finally, some time in the Sixth Form (I was fifteen or sixteen years old by now), a boy in my Geography class suddenly asked me to go out with him on Saturday night. He seemed to be a nice, friendly boy (as far as I could judge such matters), not too much of a rascal, and also happened to be Maori. My first date! What a surprise this was – so much so, that I was flabbergasted, scared, and did not know what to say. I finally mumbled something about having to see my Aunty (this was, in fact, a prior arrangement) and that was the end of my first date! I don't know how Reg felt at being "rejected," although I did not mean it as a permanent state of affairs. In fact, a few days or a week later, I hesitantly approached him and asked "You know about that outing – perhaps another time." But maybe Reg had already had his feelings hurt, or had changed his mind by that time, for that was my first and last chance of a date during my school years. In hindsight, this was probably a blessing in disguise: if I could scarcely cope with a conversation, or with the power dynamics of social situations, then I was not socially and emotionally ready for boy–girl encounters and all that they might bring, that is, an introduction to the romantic and sexual realm.

During my last year at high school we older students had a careers information day. One of the careers I chose to investigate was that of the printing industry. On approaching the man in charge, he announced "We don't hire girls!" These days this sounds very sexist, but there was, unfortunately, a valid reason for his statement. At that time the printing was still done using metal trays full of metal pieces which had the letters embossed on them. Working in the industry meant constantly carrying and lifting these very heavy trays around. Until my thirties, I was small and light-weight for my age, so I would neither have looked capable of, nor actually been capable of, such a job. I found that quite disappointing. There did not seem to be any careers on offer which would use my writing skills. Besides, I felt apprehensive about leaving school (which was, at least, my "known world") and entering the big unknown of the working world.

With the end of the Sixth Form, I would have been out into this unknown world, except for a good idea of Mum's. I could have stayed and done the Seventh Form, but as this was meant as a stepping-stone into university, and I did not wish, at this stage of my life, to go to university, Mum offered me the suggestion of going to Manukau Technical Institute. There was a year-long secretarial course available, for which I enrolled. I needed to learn some practical job skills, and – even more importantly – Mum realised that I was still "too young for my age" to enter the big wide world. She and I had no way of knowing why this was so, but we knew that it *was* so. Taking the secretarial course would postpone, for a year, the moment at which I would have to enter the working world. Besides, I had little idea, as yet, of which career I should pursue.

In the all-female milieu of the secretarial course, I had no opportunities for meeting males, but I was kept so busy with my studies, and my own hobbies on the side, that I would have had no time for dating. Nor did I have any close female friends at this point in time, although there was a sort of classroom camaraderie which gave me the feeling of at least belonging to a group.

When I did finally graduate into the world of work, I was lucky that this was at a time when jobs were not too difficult to come by. After a few attempts, I found myself a library assistant position at Papakura Public Library. I loved this job, for the first years at least. It was my own malaise over having very few friends, no romance on the horizon, and increasing unhappiness about the way my life was going, which prompted me to leave this position – as if leaving a good job would solve my problems! – but, possessing very few problem-solving skills, I could not work out any better plan of action. My adventures as an employee are outlined in the chapters called "In the Workforce."

During the end period of "In the Workforce: Part I," when I was 22, I tried a new method of meeting eligible males: the personal column. The only men I knew were older, with wives and children, and I had no idea how else to meet anyone. It might not have been so difficult if all of my acquaintances had not been getting themselves engaged and married; but being "on the outer" of what I thought was normal life caused me to worry that there was something wrong with me. One particular letter and photo which I received via the personal column led to a meeting and friendship. Lindsay worked in a chainsaw shop, and, like me, was of the more reserved type of temperament. He had three brothers and two sisters, and he was a big fan of the Bee Gees.

Lindsay and I enjoyed a number of "quieter" sorts of outing, such as a drive to Ramarama, whereupon we walked and climbed around a picturesque spot with fields and crags. At this stage, I had not so much as let him help me scramble up a piece of rock! I was happy with this relationship plateau: although I could now tell myself that I had a "boyfriend," it was a platonic arrangement so far (and, in hindsight, probably not enough for any man).

The next stage was when, one day with a freezing, howling gale, Lindsay suggested taking me to a place he knew, called Ihumatao. Although near the Auckland International Airport, where we ended up looked and felt like the Arctic tundra or the Russian taiga (not that I've ever been further afield than Sydney, I must admit). Nestled under a partial canopy of wispy shrubs, I soon found out that we were there to explore the tactile realm. Lindsay slipped his hand under my jersey – the chilliness of the day made that a breathtaking experience! My long-starved tactile sense gave it an immediate ten out of ten. He invited me to do the same to him.

And so on from there – the hours flew by as we shivered with the delights of icy human touch.

Our outings – dates – courtship – progressed along a continuum of physical intimacy. Having had all those years of missing out on the affection which my Dad would have given me, I was all the hungrier for the experience of love with and from a man. Whilst I enjoyed this new-found pleasure, I had some concern over how far it was all going to go. It seemed to me that in order to keep a man, one had to keep him happy by whatever means it took; though I still held on to the idea of keeping my virginity until marriage.

On another day in the country – another of Lindsay's well-known haunts – we had a lush paddock to ourselves, fringed by trees and a stream with a little bridge. We opened our chilly-bin and ate our picnic lunch to the sound of birds twittering and insects humming. Lindsay then suggested that we take off our clothes. It felt exciting and free to cavort with the sun and the breeze on our bodies. Our feet felt the rough concrete of the little bridge to nowhere. Not for the first or last time, I lost my balance. The tumble downwards seemed to take a long time, terrified as I was. I did not know how deep the water below was, and I could not swim. I could have grabbed Lindsay in the hope of arresting my fall, but decided against it, as that would probably have caused him to fall in as well. I think of myself as a not very brave person, so that split second of choosing not to grab him seemed just about my bravest moment.

Having plunged underwater and with my head now back up for air, I yelled for help. That was probably unnecessary, as Lindsay had seen the whole thing, and was standing directly above me on the bridge. When I ascertained which way was up, I realised that I was sitting in only a few feet of water. That water was, however, green and grimy. On scrambling out, it was apparent that I had several large grazes on my back and elsewhere. Lindsay helped to wipe off the slime and to dab at my wounds with a clean cloth. We had nothing in the way of antiseptics with us, of course, so we headed back to my Mum's place, where I then lived.

It was a Sunday night tea, with an elderly aunt for company. Proudly relating, by now, the events of the day, I told of my misadventure and subsequent injuries. My aunt enquired "And did you have to take off your clothes, for Lindsay to wash your grazes?"

"They were already off!" I blurted out.

After Aunty had left, Mum spoke to me sternly: "Don't say things like that in front of your Aunty!"

I was happy for this courtship state to go on forever, but Lindsay wanted to settle down, to have a wife and family. At the age of 23, I was already somewhat behind schedule for engagement and marriage, compared to my acquaintances. The thought of marriage was not particularly appealing, but it was what "normal" people did. In order to appear "normal," to others and to myself, I could see no alternatives. Besides, I enjoyed the company of Lindsay, and, if I declined his offer of marriage, he would look for someone else, and I would be back to square one: with no friends again. On asking an older relative, I was given to believe that if I did what other people did, i.e. get married, that act alone would make me "normal" like everyone else. I had long been desperate to appear, and to be, like other people. This was the magic formula! We set a date.

According to my wishes, Lindsay and I had a small wedding with close family members only. We moved into a flat in Manurewa, and soon afterwards bought our own house in the same suburb. The sloping section gave the house three levels. Two sides of the section were made secluded by the neighbours' trees. A spacious circular garden within a concrete wall gave me an ample flower bed, and I began planting native trees in another spot. It was a quiet corner of town, yet it was close to most necessities, especially after I discovered a handy walkway. At the end of the walkway was a block of shops which included a sumptuous bakery and a scrumptious fish 'n' chip shop.

I learned to make bacon and egg pie and lamingtons (Lindsay's favourites), and roast lamb with vegetables (my favourite). We built a concrete block wall together, with me pushing full wheelbarrows full of cement and poking the air bubbles out of the cracks with a stick. (Since then, I have enjoyed doing small-scale concreting projects, using a bucket and trowel, by myself.) We converted the plastic swimming pool into a goldfish pond, and Lindsay started breeding fish. One day, Lindsay brought home a day-old duckling, who became our household pet. We frequently visited Lindsay's family and my family. His parents were very warm and kind towards me, and I loved their cooking (as well as my own Mum's cooking: the two cuisines were just different, that's all). I still did not have anyone with whom to share the academic side of my self; but this was partly solved (as far as time would allow) by my starting a Maori language night class.

Due to starting on thyroid hormone at the age of eighteen (prescribed for an underactive thyroid), I was still growing taller throughout my twenties. On visits to Mum, she would make a new mark on the door-frame where she recorded my height.

The physical intimacy side of Lindsay's and my relationship, which had seemed so promising, now took a nose-dive. Now that we were free to "go the whole way," it became a problem. As I had had no previous partners, I had no experience in love-making; and, it became apparent that Lindsay, too, was far from experienced. Our less-than-successful efforts were causing pain for me, and I lost interest. As well as this – or interwoven with this – I lost interest in being married at all. It probably did not help the situation that I was also in a job which was very stressful (the hospital), and would come home overwrought. Lindsay sometimes "punished" me with silence, refusing to speak to me. This was something unknown in my family, and it made me feel panicky. He was also, I felt, impossible to please as regards my hairstyle and my clothes. No matter how hard I tried to achieve what he wanted at the hairdresser's, it would still not be right. Although I had, at that time in my life, some very pretty dresses, he did not like them and made me give them away. At some stage I began to have attacks of frustration and rage, and would hit out at something. One time I broke a place mat which Lindsay especially liked; in retaliation, he broke my favourite salt shaker. Another time, I found that the bath surround could not withstand my pounding. In my worst such incident, I threw a concrete block into the plastic fish-pond – which made a cut in the side, creating a big problem for Lindsay, as he had to try to fix it without emptying out all the water and the fish. I am so ashamed of this incident that I am disgusted to admit to it. However, I am trying to be honest at all costs in this book, and I want to be fair to all parties.

Underneath it all there was still some caring friendship left. One day in the basement, Lindsay was cutting enthusiastically with a hand saw – until it jumped out of its groove and into his hand. Fortunately, I was nearby when it happened, as I saw his face go white, and – knowing Lindsay's propensity for fainting at times like these – I knew I had to get him into the car before he did so. I drove him to the doctor's, where his hand was stitched up. The generous amount of bandages that he had to wear for weeks afterwards made it difficult for him to get dressed, especially with pullovers, so at times he needed a helping hand with this.

Lindsay let me keep the duckling until well into its adulthood, when he became a large white drake. We did find out that we had to keep him out of the goldfish pond, as the fish would decrease in number after a visit from Mitchell. We also had to ensure that the duck was outside when we locked up the house each day. One morning, I was sure that I had checked his whereabouts – for a day in which we would be away not only all day, but part of the evening as well. On finally returning home and opening the door, who should be inside but a jubilant white duck, flapping and quacking to greet us. "Oh no!" I cried, imagining a houseful of ducky-doos. I rushed into every room, to check the state of damage. To my relief, Mitchell had not deposited his usual daily amount – because, I assume, he could not obtain any water that day, which caused his digestive system to slow down.

Perhaps through the frustration of remaining a bachelor, Mitchell gradually became bad-tempered. Lindsay and I could cope with him, but Mitchell had the run of our cul-de-sac, and we had to concern ourselves with what he got up to in our absence. One Saturday, I saw a little child from the next-door unit toddle over with its bottle of milk. Mitchell and the child met on the boundary line; the duck was the bigger of the two. The toddler, in a touching display of generosity, offered Mitchell a drink from its bottle, touching the teat to Mitchell's beak. Mitchell appeared to misinterpret this gesture, lunging at the child and knocking it down amid screams of terror. I rushed to the rescue, later telling the tale to Lindsay. We could not let Mitchell terrorise the neighbourhood children. He was already banned from the fish-pond area; now he had to be banned from the top boundary, the entrance to our section. However, we did not want to fence off our entrance, as it would be awkward for driving in and out. The obvious answer was that Mitchell would have to go. Whilst I was still thinking about it, one day I came home and Mitchell – and the pet-carrying cage – were gone. Lindsay told me that he had given Mitchell to his Vietnamese workmate – for duck chow mein. It still upsets me to think about this.

After five years, Lindsay and I decided that we had had enough. Lindsay now wanted children, and I knew that I was not the right person to provide them. Still waiting to become "normal," I could see that the "instincts" I needed and wanted were just as lacking as before. The only instinct I have about babies is with feathered and furry ones. Better to let Lindsay find someone else and have a new chance, I thought. I took some of my things and went back to live with Mum for a while. Lindsay and I sold the house, the proceeds allowing him to start a new home purchase, and me to buy a little unit of my own in Papakura. Not long after, Lindsay did find a new partner, and, the last I knew, they had two children. I am happy that his life has now gone in the direction he wanted.

In the ensuing years, my confusion over most things in life led me through most of the available options in the field of sexual orientation. As described in Chapter 5 called "Identity and Boundary Issues," I came to the conclusion, at one point, that I was Gay. After six or seven years identifying this way, I then felt that this was no longer correct, and that I was, instead, Bisexual. This unleashed another set of issues, as, at that time at any rate, Lesbians had a policy of strong disapproval of Bisexual females. As I understood it, Lesbians would not have minded Bisexuals as long as the latter kept well away – but Lesbians became very upset if Bisexual women tried to attend Lesbian events. It may have been, however, a case of the more radical Lesbian elements having the loudest voice; in which case, perhaps the "rank and file" Lesbians did not necessarily feel the same way.

So, I now entered my Bisexual phase. In order to meet others who identified this way – so that we could discuss the concept of Bisexuality – I again consulted the Personal Column. I was to find out, however, that those who responded to me had a very different agenda. Whilst I wanted to explore the theoretical, the academic, side of Bisexuality (and sexuality in general), the people who responded to me wanted simply to *do* it! Two different married couples contacted me – for my present purposes, I will call them "Couple A" and "Couple B." The man and woman of Couple A offered me anything money would buy – including luxurious holidays – if only I would agree to sex with them. No, this did not appeal to me, so I did not contact them again. They did follow up with a further phone call at a later date, and, while not wanting to hurt their feelings, I told them my answer was the same.

Couple B and I met several times, and this contact was even more of a case of mis-communication and misunderstandings – caused, I can see only now in hindsight, by my trying to call myself Bisexual. Talking about sexuality was not high on *their* list of priorities, either – yet this was what I was still, in my social naivety, trying to do. Looking back on it, I see now that they must have thought that I was "playing hard to get" – because, in this field, I was "all talk and no action!" Finally, the man of the couple made a grab at me and shoved his hand down my pants – this was definitely not what I wanted. Miraculously, in the next split second the phone rang. With this sudden sound breaking the spell of what was happening to me, I extricated myself from the man in order to answer it. Then, I was more able to find my own power, sufficiently to tell Couple B that I wanted them to leave. By then they had worked out that I was a waste of time anyway, so that was the end of this "relationship."

I experienced quite a number of other unwanted sexual encounters along the way. I was no longer calling myself Bisexual, as it was by now apparent that this was getting me unwanted results. Even advertising for a flatmate to live in my spare bedroom was enough to get me a lot of unwanted attention from males who saw me as something more than a potential flatmate. One flatmate frequently harassed me for sex; another potential flatmate tried to pressure me to have sex on the spot; another, I realised just in time, intended to run a prostitution business from my spare bedroom; a fellow student at university suddenly and unexpectedly grabbed me and tried to kiss me, but I managed to pull away before our mouths met; and other men, who invited me to their places for "a cup of coffee," proved sooner rather than later to have something more than refreshments on their minds.

Other people have told me, at various times in my life, "Listen to your feelings about a situation; feel the vibes; trust your instincts – and thus be forewarned about dubious situations." But! – I did not *have* any feelings, vibes, or instincts in the sphere of social relating, so I had nothing inside me for guidance. Therefore, I had no "alarm bells" available to warn me of impending danger – where people were concerned, at any rate. I was also "slow on the uptake" in these matters, and unable to learn what had gone wrong from one time to the next. I usually had to make the same mistake a number of times before I could work out that it was a bad idea, which meant that I was getting into risky situations over and over again. I was lucky to escape from most of them relatively unscathed, but I was not so fortunate with the encounter which I describe in Chapter 15, "Married to a Mole."

By now I had discarded all my previous orientations of Heterosexual, Gay and Bisexual… So, when I heard a female friend call her own sexual orientation "Unlabelled," I adopted this with delight and relief. With this solution, one no longer has to waste time and rack one's brains trying to work out what one is!

Chapter 9

Co-ordination Issues

During my infancy, the first hint of possible motor skills (movement) problems became apparent when I failed to learn to crawl. Instead of crawling, I propelled myself around the floor by "swimming" on my stomach, using my limbs as flippers. Next, walking was significantly delayed: I did not begin until 22 months of age. (Walking at one year of age is considered average or late-average, with early walkers starting at around nine months.) Until the walking milestone was achieved, Mum's Plunket nurse was concerned, wondering if the problem could be Cerebral Palsy – the only possible contender, apparently, in those days, for motor skills delay.

There is a saying that "you can't walk until you can crawl," and this may have some scientific validity. At least some people think that the co-ordination which a baby learns in order to crawl is important in later learning to walk, and in all movement skills. When I did learn to walk, it seems that I had an unusual and somewhat ungainly gait. I can say this using the evidence of my teen and adult years: other people made occasional comments about the way I walked, so, in order to check this, I sometimes watched my reflection in a shop window; also, a friend has been able to see for years that I walk with an odd gait. For one thing, my legs do not straighten out fully; in fact, even when lying down to rest, my right leg (in particular) has a permanent kink and will not lie down flat. As my walking style is still like this now, it seems logical to say that my gait as a young child was also unusual. Adding to the picture is the statement made by my second teacher to my mother: that I was awkward and unconfident about climbing up and down steps. To that can be added – was awkward and timid about any task involving gross motor skills (the large movements, such as walking, running, jumping, climbing, and riding a bike).

This situation did not really improve as I grew older – judging by my performance in physical education at school. I loathed and feared the school sports days every year. My small rural primary school competed against all the other rural primary schools within a certain radius; and all pupils had to compete, not just the physically skilled ones. I was always in such an anxiety state about the sports day that Mum would give me an aspirin that morning, to try to settle my nerves. When attempting the long jump, I would not even make it into the sawdust landing area. (Mum recalls that I commented to her, "If I could only get into the sawdust, I would be happy!") On attempting the high jump, I was afraid of touching the steel pole, so, in spite of my good intentions, I would always stop short just when I reached the pole, without even leaving the ground. Besides, I had no idea of how to co-ordinate my body in order to stop running, and start jumping, at the correct moment. Points were given out for coming first, second or third in any event, and these were recorded by the officials on a card which was pinned to one's shirt for the day. While most other pupils had points in the tens to twenties, I would be walking around all day with a card which proclaimed that I had two points – (and I don't know how I got *those*, unless they were handed out for "trying!") A few pupils would scamper around checking everyone's points card, seemingly searching for the highest and lowest scores, because when they got to me they called out, "Look! Here's one with two points!"

Mat exercises were no better, so that I was the pupil who took years to work out how to do a forward roll. The other gymnastic feats were too much for me. I was too afraid, and too confused as to how to do it, to vault on to the wooden horse. The gymnastics teacher wrote on my report card that my effort was somewhat lacking.

At high school, one phase of the girls' physical education was a kind of dancing to music whilst throwing and catching a ball. This was nightmare territory for me, as stepping to music was already challenging enough, but adding ball-handling skills as well meant multi-tasking and failure. Even worse, we had partners, and had to throw and catch the ball with our partner – whilst stepping to the music! The result was that I spent most of the lesson chasing the ball the whole length of the gymnasium – and it was a very long gymnasium. This caused me to feel bad on behalf of my partner, who could not participate in the exercise whilst I was off chasing the ball – and, as the other girls appeared to enjoy this exercise, I was inadvertently spoiling my partner's fun. No matter how hard I tried, the result was the same. We had to do this exercise in our physical education time-slot for weeks on end.

Another phase of our "Phys-Ed" classes was ballroom dancing. This also required more co-ordination than I could muster. In addition, as I was behind schedule in some areas of social and emotional maturity, I did not see the point of ballroom dancing, as it was not my scene: I was into my solitary pursuits of catching water-beetles, digging for kauri gum, rearing chickens, reading, and so on. To my dismay, the high school then offered ballroom dancing lessons one night a week after school, and Mum enrolled me for them. On the odd occasion that I did start to get the idea for one particular type of dance, then the teachers would stop that one and move us on to the next type – so that I could never master any one type. If I had been allowed to repeat and practise just one type of dance, then I would probably have eventually mastered it; but the frequent changing to a new type interrupted and thwarted my learning process.

Mum also believed that everyone should learn to swim, so when I was twelve – and having failed to learn to swim thus far – I was enrolled and taken to a course of swimming lessons. I hated this so much, because I was (and am) afraid of swimming lessons. Every day, I would start crying when it was time to go there. This was not just plain naughtiness – it was fear and distress. The swimming school gave a guarantee that any pupil who failed to learn anything by the end of the course would be given another course for free. Just when I had got to the end of the hated course, I was told of the extra free course – and had to go through it all over again. During the second time around, however, I finally learnt something: how to take my feet off the bottom of the pool. This was mega-progress for me. This meant that, for the first time ever, I could float and "swim" a short distance. I say a short distance, because to keep on swimming one has to learn the breathing technique. Therefore, I could swim for only as long as I could hold my breath. Learning the breathing technique was another huge step, and one which I have never managed, due largely to fear. My swimming ability has remained at this point. I do not feel that I am in much danger from drowning, however, as I stay out of the water for the most part. Probably my only chance of drowning is if a tsunami engulfs Auckland.

Ice skating was not exactly my idea, but I tried it once. It felt disconcerting to have my legs flying out in all directions, so I held on to the hand rail for most of my time on the ice. My companions then suggested that I try to let go of the rail. As soon as I did so, another skater came hurtling towards me, face-on, and collided – with the result that I did some kind of a backwards flip on to my head. The ice felt rock-hard, and moments later I had an egg-sized lump on the back of my head. The man in charge of the rink came out and gave me a free cup of tea. My companions then thought it best that I end my skating session.

To go back a few years, learning to dress myself was a difficulty, involving not only co-ordination, but also the understanding of which way round things went. It seemed to take me longer than other children to grasp that looking at the front of a garment is *not* the right way round for putting it on; one must turn it around so that one is looking at the back. I would often put my clothing on the wrong way round on my first attempt, and sometimes with multiple attempts, even into my teen years. Tying my hair back, when I had long hair as a teenager, was a similar difficulty: as I could not see behind my head, I could not see how to do the task. Looking into the mirror was even more confusing, as the mirror image is a different way round from reality. It took me years before I could tie my hair back by myself.

I was often cumbersome at ordinary practical tasks, which was, of course, more obvious at Manual Training lessons. It did not help, I am sure, that I also had no interest in these types of work! When helping to iron tea-towels, I burnt my finger on the iron; my sewing never progressed beyond sticking a row of pins in the fabric; and working in pairs for cookery lessons confused me even more than working by myself (which indicates problems in co-ordinating with another person, as well as any awkwardness I had for the task itself). In these lessons, I also suffered from having very little cognitive idea of how to perform the tasks, as well as the physical difficulty of carrying them out. One day, I stood patiently beside the stove for most of the lesson, waiting for the pot of water to boil – but I had forgotten to switch the stove on. When the teacher arrived to check my progress, she appeared quite frustrated with me. At least, on this occasion, I had some sort of an excuse for my behaviour: as one of my classmates explained to her, at my house we had an Aga cooker, which ran on coke and which was always "on" – hence it had not occurred to me that other stoves operated differently.

One evening, as an adult, I went to a new acquaintance's house for a coffee and a chat. Although I wanted to do something sociable, I was very nervous. I was handed my cup of coffee and then sat down. Alas – the sofa was very different from ours at home, going down much further before my bottom stopped – so that the long descent and the unexpected jolt at the end caused me to spill my coffee. I don't remember what we talked about, but the person I was visiting – Tania – did her best to be friendly. When it was time to leave, it was dark. Going down the front steps, which I could not see clearly because of the darkness, I misjudged a step and fell sprawling. By now, full of embarrassment, I was glad to get away!

Another time, going to lunch at a relative's place, I had brought a bag of tomatoes. Bounding lithely up the wooden front steps of the patio – or so I intended – resulted in my landing with a belly-buster on top of the tomatoes! Oh well, it could happen to anyone! (Couldn't it?)

At university, going to one particular class meant leaving the level footpath and suddenly descending down a sloping paved area. I did this every day at a walking pace, but one day, having fitted in a toilet stop between classes, I was in a rush. At running speed, I did not register the sudden slope in time, falling head over heels. I was too dizzy to get up immediately, and someone kindly asked me if I was all right. In the process, I had skidded on one knee, tearing my track trousers and grazing my knee. The blood was welling up to the surface, and I was somewhat in shock, but it would need to be more than this to stop me attending my German Literature lecture. At the end of the class, I went to the Student Health Service to have the wound attended to. For the rest of the day, I was able to bask in "punk" notoriety, due to having ripped trousers.

When I entered the poultry show fraternity, there was a new variety of co-ordination and multi-tasking to master. It was my first show with the Auckland Poultry and Pigeon Association when I took my prized Black Australorp rooster out of his carrying cage and placed him in his show pen.

The rooster noticed before I did that the back of the pen was not attached, and disappeared out the other side. As I soon learned was common practice, the call went out to "Close the doors!" – whilst the chase was in session. The most nimble of the poultry fanciers on the day would, eventually, gain kudos for catching the misbehaving bird. I moved to the task of penning my next bird, an Old English Game hen. Just at the moment when I had opened the carrying cage and was about to grab the hen, a group of poultry friends came in and called out "Hello, Jen!" I turned to look at them and to reply – whilst the hen took this opportunity to escape. It was another case of "Close the doors!" – until she was caught. Having caused this ruckus twice in quick succession, I was highly embarrassed by this time!

The poultry show example is exactly the same as another, decades later, but taking place in a printing centre. My task was to collate a large number of pages into books – a task I enjoy doing – except that the pages on this occasion were high-gloss and very slippery, especially when I had to keep handling the collated but unbound, and very slippery, books. Using all my concentration, I managed not to drop any of them over a period of hours. As soon as a colleague came up and asked me a question, however – at the same time as I was picking up one of the completed sets – the distraction caused me to drop the book to the floor. As it was unbound, the pages went everywhere – and they were unnumbered. I was unable to sort out the mess, and it took my supervisor half an hour to do so. When handling "slippery and difficult" objects, then – like glossy pages or hens – any distraction calling my attention away may cause me to let go of the object. This fits in with the multi-tasking difficulty I have always had – because handling an object and answering a question adds up to *two* tasks.

In another workplace, I had been highly amused by the sight of a colleague accidentally getting caught up on a trolley as she walked past, which caused her to be pulled backwards suddenly, almost flipping over. She did not fall over, nor sustain any other injury, so there was no harm done. Later, I was excitedly trying to tell my other workmates what had happened. In my enthusiasm, I performed a replay of the event – except that, this time, I got carried away and accidentally *did* a backwards somersault, landing heavily on the floor. Luckily for me, there had been no objects in the way, on which I could have hurt myself. I had not intended to go the whole way with this gymnastic feat – and I am amazed, to this day, that I managed to do a backwards flip for only the second time in my life (the first time being at the skating rink) – yet, when *trying* to do anything of this nature, I have never been able to do it!

In my thirties, I wanted to have another go at learning to dance; it was a variety of folk dancing which interested me, (not ballroom dancing). I had come across a small group of people who performed this special dance tradition, complete with a highly skilled teacher. I attended all of the practice sessions and tried my hardest. It was obvious to me that I was having trouble, however; as soon as I stopped dancing the steps, I would be unable to re-start, due to having forgotten how to do it. It was also obvious to the teacher that I was having trouble, but he seemed to attribute it to lack of application on my part. His instructions were to keep practising the steps at home; alas, I could not, because I could not remember the steps, as soon as I had ceased doing them. That is, by the time I had returned home, I had long since forgotten how to do the dance steps. In order to assist myself in learning, I arranged to visit another member of the dance group, for practice between lessons; by the time the day of the lesson came around again, however, I had still forgotten the steps. The teacher did not seem able to understand that I was, in fact, trying very hard to learn the dance, and became impatient with me. Over time, I was unable to cope with the teacher's frustrated reactions to me, which were by now causing me stress. Therefore, I ended up leaving the dance group, feeling sad, disappointed, and with a feeling of having failed again.

In my thirties I also started a t'ai chi class. Again, I had problems copying the complicated movements, even when we were learning these singly. Part of the lesson was to combine all of the movements into a sequence, for which I was lost completely. My earlier failures at learning similar activities probably contributed to my feeling that this was not going to be a success; this time, I became discouraged relatively quickly, and gave up.

I had always wanted to try indoor bowls – reasoning that, as I had been skilled with my childhood skittle set, I should be able to do it. However, when the time came, it was a lot more complicated than I had anticipated. Our team leader showed me how to do it – and showed me, and showed me. It required the co-ordination of "left leg forward – right arm forward –

right leg forward, left leg back – right arm back, left arm forward" – etc.,etc., or so it sounded to me. In the end, everybody else in the crowded bowling alley seemed to be staring at me!

When John came into my life, although we have never lived together, we seemed to do a certain amount of furniture shifting. Shifting of furniture is another "major" in my co-ordination inventory. Whenever engaged in this task, I seem to be grappling the furniture in the opposite direction to my partner, or I jam him or her in a doorway. It is very difficult for me to co-ordinate for two people at once – him or her, as well as myself. John would become quite annoyed at times, because I did not know what he wanted me to do – as if I could read his mind, I told him! He still thought that I should be able to see what to do, or "intuit" from him what I should do. Both of those requirements are mysteries to me.

For me, there is an element of needing to look at my body part in order to use it or to do something to it. For instance, it can be difficult for me to apply ointment to the correct place on my body without looking at the place. This state of affairs has improved over time, however. The top of my head still seems to have this special position, as I am unable to see it in the normal course of events. This means, amongst other things, that I forget I have hair (which needs to be combed) unless I happen to look in a mirror. I suspect this is why I used to have trouble with walking into cupboard doors, until I made it a rule that all cupboard doors have to be shut immediately after use. It seems to be the reason why I frequently knock my head on the upper door frame of a particular chicken coop – because I have trouble gauging where the top of my head is, in relation to the top of the door frame. One day, when brushing away a stray hair, I felt that there was something sticking out of the top of my head. It was a large wooden splinter, which must have got there the last time that I knocked my head on the chicken coop. Fortunately, I had John on hand to remove it for me! On another occasion, after being in that coop, I felt something moving in my hair. I tried swishing at my hair with my hand, the movement would stop for a minute, then start again. Finally, I dislodged the culprit – an earthworm!

Although my fine motor skills such as writing and drawing were not delayed – in fact, I had ability in these areas – I still had some fine motor problems in other areas. One teacher who noticed this gave me the task of arranging apple slices on a pie, "to give me practice in using my hands." One other significant issue was, for years, the use of keys. I was terrified of being put in charge of the key to a door, because, when the time came, the key would often be difficult to turn, and I did not always succeed. Nowadays, I am aware that many keys and their locks have idiosyncrasies such as needing an extra twiddle this way or that. I am now able to use this knowledge to (usually) succeed with this task. Another fine motor skill – though this one is also combined with cognitive difficulties – is tying one's shoe laces, and this is a task which I was late to master. Because I still could not achieve this by the time I entered secondary school, I had to wear shoes with a strap instead of laces.

Even eating can be an occupational hazard, as I have "phases" of accidentally biting my tongue and the inside of my mouth, drawing blood. After the first such bite for a while, I am so carefully trying to avoid the same spot in my mouth that I accidentally bite a different spot. It often goes in threes. I have noticed, (as with other items mentioned in this chapter), that being asked a question while biting my food can cause this to happen. Perhaps a survey will be able to find out if this or any other co-ordination issue is widespread.

Chapter 10

Other Special Skills and Interests

One of my biggest, life-long interests has been that of poultry-keeping, but you know that already – this topic is covered in my chapters called "Feathers with Everything!" My other special interests and skills will be mentioned here.

Right from my earliest days – as soon as I could propel myself to the bookshelf – I was hooked on books (as well as hooked on chooks). Before I could read, I could easily find the book I wanted, just by the look of its spine. I still find the book I want in the same way, if it is a book which I have seen before. This makes me faster at locating a particular book than people who have to read the titles on the spines.

Luckily for me, I was blessed with parents who believed in the benefits of reading to children. I presume that this had a lot to do with producing my lifelong passion for books, and I am grateful to my parents, grandparents, and Aunty Freda for reading to me. As is the case with some children, I memorised stories word for word just by listening to them. When poor Mum became tired of the same story over and over again, she could not skip a page or two to shorten it, because I protested at the loss of even one word.

My love of books and of language meant that, on entering my school years, I was keen to learn reading, writing and spelling, and was always at the top of my class in these subjects. Following on from this, my written work was excellent. This contrasted with my poor ability, and lack of interest, in mathematics.

Being a country child, the only library I saw was the room at my rural school that doubled as a film room, which would be darkened for the treat of an educational film. I was at least half-way through my secondary school years before I realised that such a thing as a public library existed. Not that I had been deprived of books until then – far from it, as I had many books at home and at school.

As a teenager, I joined the public library of our nearest town, Papakura, which I could visit after school, meeting and going home with Mum if she was in town. Although I was entitled to borrow from the Young Adult section – and my small, young looks would have enabled me to pass as a Child member as well – I was still recalling the comments of "babyish," "immature," directed towards me by a schoolmate. This meant, unfortunately, that I missed out on reading the books which would have been of most benefit to me, as I tried to convince myself that I had "grown-up" tastes by borrowing only from the Adult section – fiction which I could not understand. On one occasion, I saw what looked like an interesting novel – judging by the cover. Having developed a taste for anthropology, I chose the book because it had a picture of Inuit people (previously known as Eskimos) on the front jacket. Even I – not one to register subtlety – could not help seeing the frowns and disapproval of the librarians as they checked the book out to me. Later, on trying to understand the story, I realised why – because *The Night of the White Bear* by Alexander Knox was known more for its sexual content than for its anthropological merit.

A few years later, on completing my education, I would obtain a position at this public library; this matter is described in Chapter 6 "In the Workforce: Part I."

My rural childhood allowed me the opportunity to observe plants, insects and birds, which became an ongoing interest in nature study. As a primary school child, I knew more about the huge variety of animals in the world than, probably, a roomful of adults would have collectively known. I have forgotten a lot of these facts nowadays, as I have cultivated other interests and activities.

Allied to my passion for books and words was my interest – once I discovered that the phenomenon existed – in other languages. My upbringing in rural New Zealand in the 1950s and 1960s, was, unfortunately, deficient in this regard: it was a monocultural time and place. Even the indigenous language, Maori, was not in evidence, except for the occasional song and haka learnt at school. Had I been exposed to other languages at an early age, I may well have blossomed into bi- or multi-lingualism; but lessons in languages other than English did not begin until part-way through Form Two. At this stage, the only available language for study was French, and somehow I did not thrill to this subject. During a holiday with my aunt and uncle in the Bay of Plenty, I felt the excitement of seeing and hearing two elderly Maori ladies, with moko on their chins, speaking to each other in Maori. At this point of my life, Maori language study was not available at school.

On reaching the age of enrolling for secondary school, I wanted to study Latin, but this subject had been phased out in the previous year. On the options form which Mum and I had filled in prior to starting secondary school, we had chosen German for me. This was a complete "gamble," because I had never heard any German in my life, so I had nothing to guide me in this choice. It turned out to be a happy circumstance, for, as soon as I heard it spoken, I fell in love with the sound of it – and have loved the sound of it ever since. The method of teaching at my school – Audio-Lingual – although deficient in some respects, such as grammar, enabled me to memorise and recite sentences from the first day, which added to the delight I felt about the language. In this way, it seems that I did achieve an inner grasp of German word order – which, I was to realise much later, does not always happen with every learner.

The panorama of the world's languages began to unfold before my fascinated eyes. I began what would become an ongoing interest in the names of languages, who speaks them and where, and which other languages they are related to. I began to care passionately about the uniqueness of each language, and whether it would live or die. I still feel that each language is a treasure-trove of beauty and knowledge, containing a unique world view, which will disappear forever when its last speakers die. So what could I do about this? I started close to home, with the endangered Maori tongue; if I learn it, I reasoned, at least it will have one more speaker. By then, I had left school, and I studied Maori at evening class. Again, I found that I loved the sound of it; I also revelled in some of its grammatical patterns.

Late in my development in most spheres – except in my skill areas of reading and writing – I was rather late in discovering pop and rock music. Our house tended to be quiet, with no TV for many years, no radio on, and no stereo – and this was the way I liked it. When my schoolmates were talking excitedly about the Beatles, I thought them silly time-wasters. In my teenage years, Mum bought a small mono record player, and we bought our first records – The Seekers. Playing music was a new phenomenon for me, but I quickly became a Seekers enthusiast. My brother, who was learning to play the guitar, acquired records of guitar music: The Shadows, Tony Mottola, and Joe Walsh. As he played the same few over and over, the tunes ingrained themselves into my brain, whether I liked them or not. As it happens, my brother's "brain-washing" techniques were successful: I grew to love guitar music, and still do.

I was in my twenties, a bit late for a teeny-bopper, when I had my first crush on a rock hero; the object of my affections was Elton John. I found that I loved his early songs, for instance, "Daniel," "Grey Seal," "Madman Across the Water," "Tiny Dancer" and "Your Song," as well as most of his works on the *Goodbye Yellow Brick Road* album. Of course, I learned all the words, and could guarantee a bliss-out by playing one of his records. Gradually, I was also learning to appreciate the immense talent of the Beatles, Rolling Stones, and other rock groups (just somewhat later than did my peers).

In my thirties, the earlier brainwashing by guitar music began to take a stronger hold, in the form of a new rock hero, Joe Walsh. I still think his *But Seriously, Folks* album is stupendous, and hard to beat. I tried to find information on him, and pasted pictures into my scrapbook. This was the time when I was working at the Royal NZ Foundation for the Blind, and I started making the cassette aisles into "streets." I made posters – as artistically as I could – and fastened them up so as to make Tracy Chapman Street, Roxy Music Street and Joe Walsh Street. One day, imagine my excitement – when the deputy manager informed me that Joe Walsh was coming to Auckland. He was to play at the Powerstation, a music venue and night club. Wild horses would not keep me away.

I wanted to do more than merely see my hero, though, so I began to devise my plans. I had a pocket camera at the ready, so I would have to get as close to the stage as possible. I wrote a short letter declaring my devotion, and stuffed it into an empty plastic drink bottle. To make it less trouble for Joe to reply, I included a stamped, self-addressed envelope. To make it a good weight for throwing, I added a stone. I stuck a sticky label on the outside, which said "Letter to Joe Walsh." Trembling with excitement, I headed for the Powerstation.

Whilst waiting for the main musician to start, I sat on the sideline. Behind me, one man asked another, "Who is Joe Walsh, anyway?" His companion replied, "A burnt-out fuck-wit."

When the big moment eventually arrived, I wriggled my way to the front of the crowd. Joe was wearing a tie-dyed T-shirt in yellow, orange, red and green, and his trousers were red. His brown wavy hair hung shaggily to his shoulders. I saw the movement of his arm muscles as he strummed and picked the guitar strings. The lighting was an added thrill for me, as I had never before seen such special effects: green phosphorescent crickets seemed to throng the walls and floor; lances and arrows speared the crowd, though no blood was shed.

Unsure whether one was allowed to take photos, I knew it was my only chance, so I did it all the same, then sliding the camera into my pocket. Repositioning myself a little further back, I hefted my plastic bottle containing letter and stone. With no opportunity to practise my throw, it would be a hit-or-miss effort, I knew. Finally, I flung the bottle; to my joy, it landed on the stage. A very burly security guard called out, "Who threw that?"

I continued to have the night of my life, jumping up and down (I can hardly call it "dancing") to my rock hero's songs. Afterwards, he walked past me so close that I could have touched him; but I didn't want to push my luck any further in one night. Tripping on ecstasy (the natural high, not the drug), I found my way home.

The photographs came out well: one, at least, was good enough to be enlarged – one copy for "Joe Walsh Street" at work, and one for my bedroom wall. I used the experience to write a poem called "Night at the Powerstation," which was then printed by a music magazine. Two days later, what should arrive in the letter-box but my self-addressed envelope – containing a reply from Joe Walsh! He, and his bass player, had written on the back of my letter. The first letter read: "Hi, my name is Rick, the bass player, and Joe and I are sitting around here in Auckland – what a wonderful place. Thanks for your support." Underneath that was written: "Jenny, it's really me. Thanks – All the best – Joe Walsh."

For one rare occasion in my life, I had dared to break the rules – and won! If you, too, would like to "air-mail" a letter to your favourite musician, just follow my guidelines written above (no responsibility is taken, however, for any subsequent arrest and jail sentence).

Although I had always loved libraries, going there deliberately to have ecstasy attacks is something which developed during my thirties. Not only was there the thrill of constantly finding interesting books – more than one could read in a hundred lifetimes – but there was the sensory aspect as well. The rustling of pages, and the scuffling of people rummaging in their pencil-cases, makes my hair tingle in the most pleasurable way. I suppose this is how a cat feels when it purrs. (People eating apples or potato crisps has the same effect, but one does not normally hear those sounds in a library.) Looking back beyond four decades, I can identify the first time I responded this way to sound: when I was a preschooler, and my grandmother was teaching me how to make scrap-books – with the sound of her mixing up and stirring the flour-and-water paste being my ecstasy trigger. As long as I don't have any urgent reason to leave, I can just bliss out to these sounds. My brain unfocuses and my body goes weak. It's the best way I know to unwind from stress! If I should have to leave before the sound trigger finishes, it is very hard to get moving again – because I feel like a jellyfish. I feel lucky to have discovered something simple (and free) which gives me so much pleasure; the only drawback is my developing a dependence on it, and having "withdrawals" when all the libraries are shut!

Different libraries have different smells, too. The basement – reached by going down a stepladder – of the RNZFB Library (Braille Section) – had a peculiar smell all of its own, of sweetness and mustiness; not surprising, as it contained hundreds of very old Braille books. I maintain that I can identify the German Literature section of the University of Auckland Library by smell: a sort of spiciness. One day, posted up on the library notice board, was a complaint addressed to the Head Librarian: "Can't you do anything about the *filthy* German books???" – As many of the German titles are very old, obscure, and rarely used, they become covered with a layer of dust, which, I presume, accounts for both the smell and the "filthiness." I would rather that they stay this way, however, so as to keep intact the familiar welcoming aroma.

Chapter 11

Aunty Hazel: A Story[*]

There was a contrasting shape on the trimmed grass, following the gentle rolling slope, far wider than the ginkgo tree itself, a fan-shape of canary-yellow fallen leaves. He continued along the path of white and brown pebbles stuck in concrete. He wanted potato fritters in a sandwich with pickle. The purple stucco cottages clustered in the foreground of his mind again. Chartreuse and apple-green rambled together on the hills behind, in this painting he'd seen and captured. Vineyards and rough roads exposed the orange earth.

He stepped into a pot-hole and lurched. The red ants were still commuting to where he'd left the empty honey pot. The stalks spearing their way up in the garden looked good to him. He hurriedly placed something that was in a brown paper bag inside the brick barbecue, unused at this time of year. Between the compost bin and the lemon tree, he reckoned, there's room enough here. The ginger pig with black spots had had a cute face.

"Leave those jandals outside," came the voice of Uncle Colin. Aunty Hazel was stirring something in the wok. What was it about the dress that

---

*   I wrote this story in the 1980s, then put it aside and forgot about it for at least a decade. My recent rediscovery of it stunned me. I had written insights about my inner, different world, yet without knowing the reason for them. Though the characters are fictitious, the social dynamics and dialogue style are replicas of the real-life situation in which I once found myself.

hit him in the diaphragm? Not the style, certainly, with twenty years between them.

"Did you have a good day, Raf?" Aunty Hazel smiled, put down the stirrer and started holding her arms out for a hug. Inside him laughed in joy as he murmured, "Yes, thank you," smothered against her. Ah, it was this same print but in yellow, he remembered, when I last saw this material. On Mum.

In his room he had wires set up, and tin cans. Luckily there was already a nail in the wall, and a hook in the ceiling. If I twist this bit of rubber around here, maybe it'll work... No. Maybe this other way. He bit his lip as he experimented. I'll just get another piece of wood. Outside his door in the back porch he saw a rough scrap of wood about two feet long. It was leaning against his wall and had two nails stuck in it. He fetched a different piece.

They used to encourage me to practise hitting nails into wood. We walked along the beach one day, Aunty Hazel and me. Aunty Hazel said, "Ten is a good age to be, probably the best." She let me arrange the rows of cut apple on her pies. They said it would help me with manual dexterity.

"Tea's ready, Raf," called Uncle Colin. He had already taken the rocking chair. Raf sat between the potted palm and the ceramic panther.

"Just the right amount of seasonings, dear," said Uncle Colin. Raf bit into a lump of ginger too awful to chew. He swallowed it. Uncle Colin got up to fetch a beer. Raf pulled out of his pocket the shell he'd found on the way home and walked across to show Aunty Hazel, carrying his plate. She saw him coming.

"Put that fork down!" she exclaimed, backing away. She nodded at the shell.

"You know, Raf," said Uncle Colin, "you shouldn't be wearing shirts with flower patterns. It's not, you know, macho."

We found lots of shells at the beach, not just ones like this. Uncle Colin picked up a long stalk of seaweed and hit me with it, playing, you know. So I got one and flicked his legs with it. He whipped his seaweed in the water and at me, so that it splashed my clothes. Aunty Hazel laughed. I whacked my seaweed in the water, aiming for Uncle Colin, but he dodged and got me twice. We all laughed. Soon I was drenched. I think that was the day I got pictures for what it was like with them. They are the blue sky, I am the sun. Blue and Yellow, where we meet, where we intersect, together we make Green. Green forests, green waving cornfields, green tropical isles. The wind and sun slowly dried my clothes on me. Aunty Hazel declared Uncle Colin the winner.

"Hey Raf," said Uncle Colin, "don't eat your dinner with your fingers!"

"You don't get any better with age, do you, Raf?" said Aunty Hazel. "I'd like to see your heaven and earth, your light and dark in a bit more equilibrium than they are now. You know that book I gave you." Turning to Uncle Colin she added, "At least since he's been with us he's had balanced meals. Even if that's the only balanced thing about him."

Raf recalled the first time he told someone – wearing good clothes at an important function – what his aunty did for a living. "She's a Yin-Yang Professor, and before it became a fashionable subject, too," he'd added proudly. Uncle Colin chuckled: "I think they know that, Raf, since this is a book-launch in Aunty Hazel's honour."

"I thought I'd paint the garage this weekend," said Raf.

"With what?" enquired Uncle Colin.

"That tin of purple paint in the back porch."

"Oh no you don't," grinned Uncle Colin. "If you had your way, everything would be purple." Turning to Aunty Hazel, he said, "We've landed a big contract at work. Might get some overtime."

Raf watched Aunty Hazel. She didn't smile.

"I was given a special privilege at work today," Raf announced. After a pause, they looked his way. A white-and-tan bull terrier romped through the doorway. "Any A and B mould copies, if they're exactly the same, I'm allowed to – " Splosh! Over went Raf's milo, aided by Tex's exuberance.

"Get a cloth! The dish-cloth!" cried Aunty Hazel.

"You shouldn't have had your drink there," growled Uncle Colin.

Dabbing away at the chocolate-coated sofa edge, Raf said, "Where should I have put it, then? Tex knocked it over, not me!"

"That's bound to leave a permanent stain," scolded Aunty Hazel.

"If we have to get it professionally cleaned, you'll be paying for it," said Uncle Colin, running a hand through his silvery hair.

It wasn't time to wash up yet, going by the household rules. Raf retired to his room. The Kenworth truck, purple with cream secondary colour, idled reassuringly from the window, where its intended use as a towel gave way to that of curtain and decoration. Raf reached under the bed for his cache of dried fruit. Mmm, this is a good batch of figs this time. Rummaging in the wardrobe, he rediscovered his old suitcase, dusty and with the label still tied to the handle from when he first came here: "Rafael Whittaker, To: Herne Bay, Auckland." Luckily they had the same surname. He put on his *Fine Young Cannibals* tape. That was when he seemed to fall into a ready-made gang of mates, Kevin and Mark and the rest. It had helped a lot. Last October Kevin had got engaged, and the others moved away or lost interest. "Conrad, you're my best mate now," he murmured, seizing the foot-long model of a rig he'd painted to match that on the towel. He munched on a fig. Ah, this is my favourite song that's on now. He fingered the contours of the model truck. The seeds crunched loudly in his head. What should I do with this sculpture, Conrad? Try weighting it a bit more over that side, you reckon? Just one more fig.

He was back with Mum and Dad again, in his dream, and Beth, and Rajah sneaking off into a mud puddle whenever they took their eyes off him. Mum and Dad were sort of taking turns wielding the axe, and he and Beth were vying to find the most and the best bits of timber. Mum in her yellow print dress with the small flower pattern again, oh why does she keep wearing dresses for this kind of job, maybe they're wallflowers like in her part of the garden. Wallflowers, my favourite flower, though it's hard to choose. Some of the steers wandering through the clearing were black, some were white with brownish-red markings, and the same tree standing sentinel still had its long black streamers hanging down. With all this sand you could pretend you were at the beach. He flung himself at a dune. With a rude awakening he opened his eyes to a lone star peeping around the edge of the Kenworth towel. Oh gosh… he could feel those figs slowly and deliberately forcing their way through every inch of his internal plumbing. How could I have made that same mistake again?

And so it went on until six o'clock, when – better hurry, he realised, this is the moment we've been waiting for, as he scrambled out of bed. On his way back he noticed that the wooden board in the porch had four nails hammered into it now.

In the park, moisture drizzled down on his straight black hair. The canary leaf shape had shaken its shimmering wings and flown away. In its place was mud, leaves mixed with mud, rent by wandering cracks, fissures, which apportioned the mud into islands. Like William Holman-Hunt was here, thought Raf. My favourite painter studied for years in the Middle East to get the landscape right. The mountains were behind, and this sort of wet lifeless plain in the foreground. With those chasms in the treacherous-looking terrain, where is safe to step? And yet the shaggy-haired goat is trying to step! Raf shuddered at the memory. A pinky-purple dahlia unfurled its first petal skywards, blithely unaware of the horror it bordered. Further down the track, a long narrow band of apricot-gold snaked its way out of the grey dawn cloud. A fiery snake-god, a worm-god! Watching as he walked, a grey glass tower obscured it. A lemon-geranium bush lent its fragrance to the crisp open air. A red flashing sign offered Breakfast but they didn't have it ready, you had to wait, he remembered. Out the other side the serpent was regurgitating, hatching, giving birth to, a great ball of gleaming molten gold. A creation myth re-enacted before me, for me! Grinned Raf in delight. Bet you've got a guts-ache too. No one else is looking at you; it's all for me! All that side of the sky became awash in apricot juice.

It was Pirates Day at work, and Raf walked in with a red polka-dotted scarf knotted around his neck. He rolled his trousers up around his knees and sported the widest belt of Uncle Colin's he could find. Geoff appeared rather startlingly with a cutlass between his teeth! The back of Raf's neck prickled slightly. The supervisor had a green fabric parrot clipped to his shoulder. In the Mouldings Department Geoff showed Raf how to set up a template. The diagram was there in black and white painted lines. It seemed straightforward enough until Raf tried to do it, and found that he couldn't tell whether what he'd done was the same as the diagram or not.

"Follow the diagram," encouraged Geoff. But Raf laughed, because he couldn't tell if they were the same. In the afternoon he borrowed the cutlass and holder-thing for his belt. He wanted to wear it home to show Aunty Hazel, but Geoff said he'd have his sister to answer to if he showed up without it.

They were playing with Tex on the lawn, throwing a rubber bone for him to fetch.

"Why do you wear jandals in this weather?" asked Aunty Hazel, though it was more of a statement by the sound of it.

"Saves my shoes getting soaked," replied Raf.

"Yes, and then you traipse your muddy feet inside," said Uncle Colin. "Now, what have you been doing in the garden over here?"

"These are my corn plants," explained Raf, "and those are turnips."

"Corn? You mean sweetcorn?"

"Popcorn."

"Popcorn!!" gasped Aunty Hazel. "I didn't know that popcorn grew on – er – plants!"

"Popcorn!" exclaimed Uncle Colin. "Turnips! Who the hell eats popcorn and turnips around here?"

"I do," said Raf.

"You haven't eaten any turnips since you've been here!" protested Aunty Hazel.

"Only because you haven't cooked any," said Raf. "When these have grown, we can cook them."

"Oh no we won't!" declared Uncle Colin. "Aunty Hazel and I don't like them! Why didn't you put in some proper vegetables!"

"You told me –" Raf's voice was faltering – "that if I cleared the weeds out, I could plant whatever I liked."

"But this is ridiculous!" maintained Uncle Colin. "I should've known you'd do something like this. You'll have to get some of that out and make room for some silver beet and brussel sprouts."

"What about what you said–" Raf pleaded.

" – on the weekend."

Raf patted Tex absently. A gust of chill air sent them towards the kitchen door. Pork chops! The aroma told him. My favourite!

"Here, have this big one," said Uncle Colin, putting it on Raf's plate. "And this nice bit of crackling. Don't forget the gravy. Here's the apple sauce. There's enough for a second helping. You look as though you need fattening up."

"Mmm-mm!" was soon the only sound to be heard in the living room. Raf reflected again on the three sisters who wanted to go to live in Moscow, who seemed to be always meeting army officers and crying. I know Anton Chekhov was brilliant and subtle – 'cos it says so in the preface of the red book of plays. So why is it just a whole lot of nonsense strung together and called a "Play"? Why, I could write a play myself, in that case, Raf decided. That's what life is, after all: a whole lot of nonsense strung together and called "Life."

Uncle Colin belched. "We'll have to have these more often, Hazel."

"Uncle Colin, can we have a pig?" They turned towards him. "At the back, between the compost bin and the lemon tree?" They looked at each other and smiled. Yellow and Blue, he felt without words, make Green.

"Raf, you're all the pig we need around here!" He supposed it was a joke, so he smiled.

"Speaking of which," piped up Aunty Hazel, "I hope you're up to date with all your washing. Do you do a load of washing every week? I hope you haven't got piles of dirty laundry heaped around in there." She got out of her chair and made for the passage. Raf leaped up. His door was thrown open.

"Oh my God! What *is* all this!"

Uncle Colin marched along the passage. He was too startled to say anything for a few moments.

"It's my kinetic sculpture I'm making," explained Raf.

"Sculpture!!" cried Uncle Colin. "What an almighty fucking mess! Are you off your rocker?"

Raf drew himself up for his delivery of enlightenment. "The aim of most kinetic sculptors is to make movement itself an integral part of the design of the sculpture, and not merely to impart movement to an already static object. For example, Len Lye – "

"That's enough of that!" Turning to Aunty Hazel, he said, "You can tell he's got *that* out of a book! He who can't normally put two words together."

"This is *our* house!" said Aunty Hazel, "and while you're living here you have to live by our standards. What would people think of us if they saw inside your room?"

After washing-up he sat quietly, he hoped unnoticeably, between the palm and the panther. Uncle Colin was eating an apple, a Braeburn, and it was too good to miss.

"Ugh, I can't stay in the room with that noise," said Aunty Hazel, making for the kitchen.

The crunching, munching, chewing and slurping stroked the inside of Raf's head into an ecstasy, a purring that lasted the duration of the apple.

This is better than eating it, even. Please eat another one, Uncle Colin, he prayed.

"Oh, there you are, Raf," said Uncle Colin. "Did you get that – " he lowered his voice to a whisper – "African violet you were going to get for Aunty Hazel's birthday?"

"Yesterday," Raf whispered back conspiratorially; "or was it the day before? Anyway, I hid it in the barbecue first, then smuggled it into my room. Just as well I got it when I did, 'cause I went back to the shop today and it wasn't there." Uncle Colin looked at him as though trying to work something out. Raf felt the Green – the forests, waving cornfields.

"Think about what you just said," suggested Uncle Colin, rubbing his aquiline nose. But there wasn't time. The slightest hint of a chug and Raf was at the window.

"A T400! Four hundred horse-power Cummins engine! Fifteen-speed gearbox! Seven hundred litre tank! Don't you want to see it, Uncle Colin?" By the time the older man got there, it had gone past. Aunty Hazel must have come in, because she was watering the palm.

"If you love those trucks so much, how come you can't make head nor tail of a car manual?" she asked, rhetorically.

"Aw, Hazel," reasoned Uncle Colin, "the same way I can love a woman without having intimate knowledge of human biology – "

Her gaze locked his eyes still and cut him dead.

"Yes, that's exactly the trouble with you, isn't it!!" she ground out. "You hit the nail right on the head!"

There was a sudden loud crunch and Uncle Colin leapt up to save the pot-plant stand from Tex's over-playful molars. A sharp slap on the muzzle put a stop to that.

Raf's eyes lit on *The Listener,* which in a moment was rolled up and offered to Uncle Colin. He hesitated a few seconds, looked as though he couldn't be bothered, and then with a twitch at the corner of his mouth he took it and stood up. Raf delightedly grabbed the *Suburban Weekly.* Aunty Hazel gave a sigh as the two ducked and dodged and landed a series of spirited thwacks on each other. Or rather, it was, as usual, Uncle Colin managing to hit home, while Raf's wholehearted lunges seemed only to place him perfectly in the firing line. After a minute, and with the late news just coming on, Uncle Colin grabbed Raf's wrists and with a deft kick –

Thud! Raf was flat on his back.

"Oh, Colin, don't hurt him!" cried Aunty Hazel. "Raf, are you all right?
– You know I can't stand – "

Uncle Colin was half-bent over him, surveying the situation.

"He's a bit dazed, aren't you, kid?"

"He just missed hitting his head on the coffee table, can't you be a bit
more careful, Colin?"

Raf tried lifting his head up, but wasn't sure which way was up, yet. He
was so dizzy he started laughing. The Green forests rustled to join in the
fun.

"See, he likes it," said Uncle Colin. "It's him that starts it. Come on…"
Raf staggered to his feet and went with Uncle Colin to the kitchen sink.
"Bend over." The cold tap was turned on his head. He burst out laughing
again. "There, is that better? Serves you right, anyway."

The patterns on the brown-and-gold carpet were interesting to watch
as they swirled around. The sliding door breathed in and out in time with
Raf.

"He still looks pretty stunned to me," said Aunty Hazel. "Like after he's
had two beers. He's so much smaller than you, you should take that into
account, Colin."

Conrad parked snugly against his pillow, Raf was just nodding off
when his whole body jerked awake. The voices in the living room were
getting louder and fiercer.

" – why I've stuck with you this long, I must be mad!"

" – anywhere better to go? You'd better do it, then!"

" – pushed to my limits around here!–"

Raf's stomach always shrivelled inside him when they fought. He
curled into a ball. Just as he was pulling the covers over his head came a
near-shrieking from Aunty Hazel,

" – that little blighter! Nothing but a nuisance around here! – Stupid
things he wastes his time on – does nothing to help himself or anyone else!
How long is he going to be allowed to keep upsetting things around here?
How am I supposed to keep my own equilibrium that I need for my work?"

His entrails went cold inside him from hurt and fear. Then they must
have shut the living room door, for all was too muffled after that.

Next morning they all slept in as it was Saturday. Raf went quietly to the kitchen and gave Tex half a weet-bix to keep him quiet. He measured out the rolled oats and put the pot on the stove. He tried this way and that on his wooden maze puzzle they'd brought him back from Wanaka. No, not quite. Aunty Hazel came in, wearing her blue dressing-gown.

"What are you doing?" she demanded.

"Making some porridge."

"That's not the way to do it! You've spilt some on the stove! You should've asked us first!"

"I was doing it for a surprise – "

"Well, don't! We don't like you meddling with things when we aren't here to supervise! What with having to keep a constant eye on the things you get up to, how are Uncle Colin and I supposed to get any peace? Just because you don't care about your own yin and yang, you have to make sure the whole household is kept on an uneven keel! It's not fair on me! You don't know when you're well off! If it weren't for me, I reckon you'd have been down the road long ago."

A new wave of horror swept over him, combining with last night's "bad dream." Aunty Hazel put the pot on the back element.

"Now leave it 'til I'm dressed and I'll do it," she said. Raf wandered in a circle around the living room before he found the doorway to the passage. Uncle Colin spotted him.

"Hey, Raf, are you going to go down to the bakery for me this morning and get those pies? It'll save us a lot on Tex's food bill. I'm giving him a pie each morning and dog food at night."

"Yeah, sure," exclaimed Raf, glad to be important and useful. "Just going."

Aunty Hazel was suddenly there, nuzzling Uncle Colin's neck. "I'll make us a really nice beef stroganoff for dinner tonight dear."

On the footpath he pondered anew on the concept he called Plane-Logic – different self-contained logics operating at the same time in the same person. As if on separate planes. Nothing seemed out of the ordinary if the logic that said $2 + 2 = 4$ won the battle; nobody noticed. But if the logic that insisted that $2 + 2 = 5$ came out on top, people commented and looked at you funny. You couldn't tell beforehand which would happen. He wondered if it was the same for everybody.

Beside the Industrial Park the lushness of the almost biliously green grass had a slightly unnatural air about it, he thought. Were the industrial genii training the vegetation, complete with resident pukeko, to grow up and camouflage the towering chimneys belching smoke?

"I've got some extra pies for you today," said the bakery man. "I guess the wet weather we've been having kept some of my customers away." Raf supposed so.

On the way back he explored where that hole in the macrocarpa hedge went to. The back of a rugby field, now a sea of mud. He decided to see how far he could creep along inside the hedge. A grapefruit lay on the dry leaf mulch. It was still good. My library books are pretty good this time, he mused. The plays of pre-revolution Russia are fascinating, even if they're hard to make sense of. I'm liking the story of Joshua's Mother more now. It's been heavy going. I don't think they knew I was crying in my room over one chapter. The best way to read it was in bed with Conrad, T400, American Cummins diesel engine, aerodynamically designed cab and bonnet. There's a delicious smell of cheese coming out from this paper bag. Mmm, tastes like steak 'n' cheese. – He hadn't had breakfast. One pie only made him hungrier. – This one's bacon and egg. No it's not, it's bacon and savoury mince. Who cares, it's still scrummy. Better get home, Uncle Colin will be waiting to feed Tex. He made sure he wiped his mouth.

He gave the white and yellow jonquil he'd picked to Aunty Hazel.

"H'mm, very nice," she said. "Didn't you put on a clean shirt today? What's all this?"

Oh no. He looked down. Uncle Colin came to take the bag.

"Gravy all down your shirt! Have you been eating those pies?"

No use trying to get out of it, Raf knew.

"Those pies are mine, according to an agreement I made with the bakery man," said Uncle Colin sternly. "That means you stole them. How many did you eat?"

There was no way to escape. "Three," murmured Raf. There was an agonising silence.

"Three stale pies!" tut-tutted Aunty Hazel. "You deserve to be sick!"

"And there's something else Aunty Hazel wants to talk to you about," added Uncle Colin.

"You know we don't have people in to this house," began Aunty Hazel. "If we ever do, they stay in the living room. The doors are always on the safety catch. You're the only one who has free range of this house. Fifty dollars has gone missing out of my purse."

His legs felt like water. Sounds seemed to ebb and flow in volume.

"This is very bad," said Uncle Colin. "All this time we've trusted you and treated you as our own son. Where is the money?"

All he could do was shake his head numbly and dumbly.

"It'll be jail for you at this rate," said Aunty Hazel, "so you'd better get that straight now. If you return the money immediately and if you apologise for the way you've treated us, we'll consider the situation and maybe Uncle Colin will be lenient this time; it's not for me to say."

"I – didn't – do it!" gasped Raf through chattering teeth.

"You heard what Aunty Hazel said." This was Uncle Colin's no-nonsense tone. "No one else can even get into this house. So that makes you a liar as well. Why, you've already proven you're a thief by eating those pies this morning."

His legs shaking uncontrollably, Raf sat down on the floor. There was a pain in his stomach.

"Well, you might as well admit it here and now," said Uncle Colin. "If you don't, we certainly won't go on putting up with you. You can start by admitting to us that you took that money. That you're a thief."

"And a liar," added Aunty Hazel. "That you're not trying to be a normal, decent sort of person, that's what makes us angry. You don't do what you know you should be doing. Have you kept up with your t'ai chi? Obviously not."

How do you know what I'm doing or not doing? Raf's thoughts protested. I glean as much as I can, from all sources, and sift it all for clues. I read what I understand, as well as what I don't. I pray to my Higher Being daily – 26 tonnes carting capacity, aluminium and fibreglass – and do my yoga every day, at your own suggestion, Aunty Hazel. I try my best. But if all I do amounts to "nothing" with you, what's the use of saying anything? Anyway, his thoughts consisting of colours and patterns, the immediacy of the moment didn't allow for translation time.

And the bog picture was back again, William Holman-Hunt, the long-horned goat was back, a garland festooning his ears and horns.

Perched, standing room only, on a shaky mud-crust, fissures all around, he didn't know where to step, and his bleats echoed back from the purple mountain range. Next step the quagmire. Nobody was there to hear him. I know how that goat feels, thought Raf.

"We're waiting," said Aunty Hazel.

"TELL US THAT YOU'RE SORRY FOR BEING A THIEF AND A LIAR!" shouted Uncle Colin. Something was shaking Raf from the inside out, and tears careered down his face. The yelling and accusations went on and on. Slash and burn culture, the geography lesson came to his mind. The pain of it welled up inside until it reached his throat and came out as a scream.

"Slap his face, Colin," commanded Aunty Hazel. Uncle Colin took a step towards him. Raf's guts shook with a contrary spasm of mirth: Do you think that would be as painful as this, Aunty Hazel?

"Christ, we've wasted all morning dealing with you and your problems," scolded Aunty Hazel, "and we haven't even got anywhere! I hope you're satisfied! No wonder you've got no friends any more! Nobody wants to be near you! You don't deserve to have any friends – or anyone! Come on, Colin!"

"Right then!" ground out Uncle Colin, marching after her to the kitchen.

He wasn't sure how long he huddled there. They – his elders – were having milo in the big brown mugs. There was none for him. Out of the corner of his eyes and ears he perceived they were talking animatedly and happily, not a glance for him. They were all in the same room together, he observed, but no Green was being made. He started to gradually edge his way backwards towards the door and out, still unnoticed.

Coming back from the bathroom, he couldn't help seeing that the plank leaning against his outer wall had a cluster of nails whacked into it now, at least eight. A dread fascination forced him to squat before it and examine it closely for markings. He could see only the grain of the wood. Whatever is there is on the inside, he concluded. I would have to break it open – but not right now. I know what they're doing. The haunting question returned: Does the goat *know* that the people have deliberately sent him out to die?? Some preservation instinct made him pick up his house key before he went out, he didn't know where.

After lunch, Aunty Hazel was humming as she dusted, picking things up and putting them down. These are Raf's library books lying around again. As she picked them up she felt a sneeze coming on, her eyes watering, so she dashed off for a tissue. Now that she was in their bedroom she couldn't help tidying up. Her busy fingers knocked the special hair brush Uncle Colin had given her and it fell behind a cupboard. Tex came bounding in, but she yelled at him to get out. With a grunt and a groan she shifted the cupboard to reveal the hairbrush and something red, a fifty dollar note. She placed the shell-inlaid gift from Uncle Colin on the bed, and quickly replaced the cupboard.

What rubbish was Raf reading this time? She spread the books out on the eiderdown. *The Complete Plays of Chekhov, Volume II, Practical Pig Keeping*, and *Joshua's Mother Leaves Town*. She opened the last one.

> For about three months after my mother went away, I didn't talk to anyone. I'd just go to my room and lay down and stare at the walls after I'd done my homework. Sometimes my grandfather would phone…

She swallowed. She sat on the eiderdown.

> When it seemed true that Mum was never coming back, there were some things of hers still in the house and we put them in boxes and took them up to the attic. I keep some of her perfumes on my dresser for decoration. They remind me of her – the way she used to smell.

The room was getting blurry, behind eye moisture and she didn't know what else. Inside her chest wasn't feeling too good either, all of a sudden.

> My father says that when I grow up he's going to give me some of her pens and some good framed photographs.

Pain shot through Aunty Hazel's chest and rage engulfed her. An arm lashed out and her hand hit a small ceramic pottle of dried flower petals, orange and azure, the yin-yang colours, sending them flying and scattering. That little shit Raf, everything he does, how am I supposed to keep an even… She directed her efforts to the pillows, until a few particles of foam rubber started popping out the end. That little bastard, next time I see him I'll wring his fucking neck!!

After walking the city streets until dark was coming on, Raf again felt the joy of seeing the 005 bus approach the stop. Herne Bay, my home by the sea, where I am loved. Snuggling into the seat, he had time to contemplate the matter of plane-logic. It's also like when Uncle Colin first got the remote control switch – before I realised what was happening, I'd be watching the second programme still thinking it was the first. Only if I happened to make a comment or ask a question would the others put me straight. Tonight I'll gift-wrap the African violet – tomorrow is the day to give it to her. So now that he was on the azure wooden doorstep, why was he trembling? His body knew already what his heart and soul had yet to accept: that there would be no more Green made, not ever again.

Chapter 12

The Psychiatric Hospital

All names have been either changed or deleted. International publishing law prohibits the use of certain data, so I am limited in the details I can give here.

I was an inpatient in a New Zealand psychiatric hospital three times, the longest stay being for eight months, in the mid-1980s, when I was 29 to 30 years old. At the time, I was not coping with my job, nor my life in general, so I took the medical advice I was given.

For the first month I was in the acute ward, (or "villa," as the buildings were called). The acute wards were relatively pleasant and harmless, in my experience. The hospital was set in farmland, ten miles from the nearest township, with established trees and cosy old buildings of red brick. Towards the end of my first month, I was assessed by the consultant psychiatrist, who considered that I would gain more by being transferred to the "farm ward," the set of buildings which was placed separately, on a farm across the road from the main hospital. Referred to, by some, as the "Neurosis Ward," it specialised in intensive group psychotherapy, with the patients living in. Vehicles could enter via a driveway, but people coming and going on foot used a raised pathway over a creek verdant with watercress. The cows were not quite under the bedroom windows (as in my farm upbringing), but were often pastured only a few metres away.

There were certain rules attached to admission here: a patient would have to promise to complete a minimum of three months' therapy. Any less time than this, one was warned, would result in one's being left uncured, and one would remain a hopeless case for life. The patient needed to stay in the ward for at least three months, or until the staff told him or her that the cure was complete. We were warned that nowhere else would be able to help us: this ward was our one and only chance. Therefore, every patient had to guarantee to "try one's hardest to become well," and to co-operate fully with the staff. We were also told that we were not allowed to discuss what went on in the ward with outsiders, and we were discouraged from mixing with patients from any of the other wards. All of this meant that there was a lot of emotional baggage even before setting foot inside, because of the warnings of what would happen if one "failed."

I had done what the medical experts had advised: I had entered a "therapeutic community" in order to get well and stay well. I was always a very conscientious person, which meant that I took a promise very seriously indeed, especially after the warnings about what would happen if I did not. Also, I trusted the medical experts to know what was best for me; I had no other information with which to make the decision.

For the first few weeks, I sat silently listening during the group therapy sessions, trying to understand what was going on. I had had little previous experience of discussing my feelings, and never in a group situation. Fortunately for me, during the first few weeks the staff were fully occupied with the life issues of the other patients, and left me alone. I sometimes felt uncomfortable about the interpersonal relating style which I observed here, both in and out of therapy sessions. After the attentions of the staff and other patients turned to me, I changed, forever, from being an observer to being a participant... whether I liked it or not.

Living in a dormitory with all the other female patients, I found the complete lack of privacy oppressive. Some patients specialised in reporting anything one did to the next "therapy" session, in front of all patients and staff – so that the person reported on would be subjected to a "feeding frenzy" by everyone in the ward. This happened frequently. As far as I could see, the bullying tactics of the more powerful patients were, in fact, encouraged by the staff, as a form of "punishment therapy." With our whole lives revolving around these "therapy" sessions, finding anything to report there – no matter how trivial – seemed to be most patients' main preoccupation. Once reported, even the smallest detail became a matter of huge importance, its meaning to be "interpreted" at length by the staff and most patients – until it was turned into something which I, for one, no longer recognised as my own.

Piece by piece a concept has formed for me: that the staff had a few ready-made formulae which they applied to very nearly every situation, seeing most behaviour as deliberate non-compliance, "attention-seeking," or "game-playing" – to all of which they reacted strongly. Looking back, it seems to me that these three categories were a mental short-cut for the staff, thus saving them from having to think. I found it next-to-impossible to ever do or say "the right thing," as very nearly everything (including doing nothing) would elicit responses of the sort which terrified and crushed me. Often retreating in fear and distress, I found that this, too, was construed as "playing chase-me games," with the punishment for this consisting of the whole ward turning on me as psychological torturers for days at a time.

Entering the ward, as I had, with differences in cognitive processing, communication, and many other areas, I soon realised that I was at the bottom of the ward's power hierarchy. I felt more and more powerless, and mentioned this in a group meeting. I did not want power in order to dominate others; I wanted it simply so that I would be able to hold my own space. I felt so annihilated in such a place that I could not achieve the feeling of simply "being." This rekindled existential issues as to whether, for instance, I was even actually alive, or living in the same dimension as other people.

One day during my stay, we were taken on an outing to a beach. I did what came naturally to me, that is, I started walking along the beach in the sand. To my surprise, I was stopped by a staff member, who herded me back to the main group. Later, back in the ward, the staff said, in front of everyone, that my behaviour had been like that of a handicapped child. They added that, if this were the case, then I was not a suitable person for this ward, and I would have to go elsewhere – with all the threats that this implied: forever on the human scrap-heap, incurable. In retrospect, I respond with the comment that, indeed, if I was "handicapped," then I should not have been in that particular ward, and this would mean that the initial assessment must have been flawed. The staff's comment shows that they noticed I was not behaving "normally." They did not, however, act upon this observation, except to criticise me for it, and to label it as "game-playing" on my part. On a number of other occasions, the staff criticised me for a lack of spontaneity. Yet, when I did something on my own initiative, such as the beach walk, that was, to them, a sign of being handicapped!

An activity in which all of the patients had to participate was an obstacle course: a sort of Outward Bound exercise, I think. This involved climbing quite some distance up a tree (to a height well over our heads) and then walking along a tight-rope with the aid of two other ropes as hand-holds. Naturally, some patients were afraid to do this, but all activities organised by the ward staff were compulsory. One female patient was screaming in terror for the duration of this exercise, and she also became frozen with fear whilst high up on the tight-rope. Finally, the registrar (a doctor in training) climbed up to rescue her, but the patient still had to continue walking along to the end of the tight-rope, screaming all the way, as there was no other way of getting down. I, too, was terrified of this exercise, but my terror manifested itself as shocked silence instead of screaming. I do not feel that such extreme activities are suitable for patients who are already in a nervous state, and especially after they have exhibited such very high fear levels.

The staff members' office was situated in the middle of the ward complex, with windows overlooking the main thoroughfare. We had to walk past the office on the way to each group meeting and activity. Some patients developed a dread of approaching the office windows, and found a lengthier detour to avoid them. When the staff found out about this – as they invariably found out about everything – they put these patients on anti-paranoia medication. Additional patients were put on these pills, or had their dose increased, during my stay there. The medication had a side effect called "tardive dyskinesia," (a motor skills problem,) which at least one patient disliked intensely. The underlying reasons for why patients might be afraid of the staff appeared never to be addressed.

To add to my other stresses and anxieties, my special interests of reading and writing – indeed, my necessities of life – were taken away. Henceforth I was not permitted to be seen with a book or writing materials, except for one writing time-slot per week, and with stringent restrictions placed on what I was permitted to write. As mentioned, the total lack of privacy meant that I could not secretly flout the rules; and, in addition, my promise, on admission, to obey the staff, ensured that I would steadfastly do as I was told.

This prohibition had major repercussions for me. Writing, although an intense interest for me, was far more than that: it was one half of my thought processes. The other half was thinking in pictures. I had an original, creative way of understanding everything via mental images in moving technicolour.

Speaking was, for me, often slow and hesitant, as I had to translate from my pictures to words, but this became a problem only when I was pressured and rushed by other people to hurry up. As soon as anyone put this kind of pressure on me, my mind would freeze and I would be totally unable to do the translation into words – which is what happened constantly in the ward. Up until then, the other half of my communication strategy had been satisfactorily achieved through writing (as opposed to speaking,) because writing allowed my words to flow out unhindered, whereas speaking did not. Now that there was a ban on writing, I could barely communicate; and it also had an adverse effect on my thinking, as I needed to have my thoughts in visual mode in order to have full use of my cognitive capacities. I now felt intense frustration, and also experienced greater difficulty in my ability to think…which did not, of course, help me with my progress in the ward.

The one exception to the writing ban imposed upon me was Thursday evenings, when I was instructed to write down my thoughts and feelings about my life in the ward. I therefore made a written record of some of my experience. The rule was that what I wrote would be submitted to the staff members, to be then read out at the ward meeting next morning, to all the staff and patients.

Thus it was that the staff and my fellow patients heard the following entry: "It's been a hard week for me, in which I felt hopeless against the bonds of fear which hold down my doing and thinking processes. I feel just as anxious with females as I ever did. Being able to find and use what abilities I might have beneath my fear is my big (? surmountable) problem. I wanted to go out next Friday. But since I'm still reading and sending messages incorrectly, thereby causing reactions in people, I must not be ready. Whether I will ever be any readier, though, is the big question."

The word "messages" was commonly used in the ward, and the other patients appeared to understand what was meant. I did not understand, at the time, that it referred to facial expressions, eye contact meanings, body language, and all indirect, "between the lines" communication, which is used constantly by most people. Within my most recent years, I have read estimates which say that between 50 and 90 per cent of all human communication is done via these indirect messages. At the time of my hospital stay, however, I could neither send nor receive these correctly, if at all. I would not have even known this use of the word "messages," had the staff and other patients not mentioned it. As it was, I noted the word when I was told it, but still did not understand what was meant. Such a person is in big trouble in the communications department: he or she is in Misunderstanding City.

The question mark in front of the word "surmountable" indicates that I had serious doubts and anxieties as to whether I would ever be able to surmount this fear problem. Certainly, living in an environment in which I felt near-constant fear, confusion and powerlessness did not help the situation.

Then there is the issue, as revealed in my written comment, that I was the one to blame for my deficits: it was, supposedly, my fault for "causing reactions in people," thus justifying harsh treatment from others. Living in this place and therefore being unable to get a "reality check" with the outside world, I was being moulded to see myself as others around me did. From this one written comment, I recall three layers of suffering: first, I had symptoms which meant that I could not fit in with what was expected of me; second, these symptoms "caused" other people to react harshly to me, thus inflicting more suffering; and, third, I was also "to blame" for all of this, which produced confusion, fear and misplaced guilt.

Another issue revealed in the above excerpt is my anxiety around females. This was exacerbated in the pressure-cooker environment of the ward, where, in addition, females outnumbered males. It is also strongly connected to my comments about "messages:" I now (at the age of 47) realise – intellectually, at least – that females are said to be more prone than males to using constant indirect communication. For me, a person who could not understand this unspoken language, the result was that I was constantly unable to understand the social life of the ward, often behaving "inappropriately" as a result, which produced more negative reactions from others, and, in turn, increased my confusion and anxiety, thus creating an on-going cycle. At the time, I had no idea what was going wrong (except that it might have something to do with this memorised word "messages") and all I could work out was that I seemed to be getting into less trouble with the males than with the females.

Accordingly, I wrote on the same day: "Matthew, I feel close to you; closer to you than to anyone else in this group, I'd say. You feel like a brother to me. I enjoy going for walks with you and it was neat when you named the stars one night."

As Matthew and I had entered the ward at around the same time, and as we had some characteristics in common, I felt that I had more of a friendship with him than with any others. We were both loners in some ways, preferring to get away from the crowd whenever we could, which was not always easy, as patients were not permitted to go further than the gate without accompaniment and permission. Also, Matthew and I were both of an academic bent, and had grown up with intense, off-beat interests, which we preferred to talk about rather than to socially chit-chat. Matthew and I also shared the problem of our minds "going blank" when asked to speak in the group meetings, which was incorrectly taken to mean non-compliance, with the negative reactions that that brought. I found his company a refreshing change from the fraught atmosphere surrounding the other patients.

The nursing sister, however, did not like the sort of personality that Matthew and I had, and made no secret of the fact. On one occasion she referred to us, before the assembled group, with the statement "Passive people are very difficult to treat!" Her prescribed treatment consisted of repeatedly goading and provoking us, seemingly in an attempt to make us react. If we did respond in any way, however, that, too, was used as a weapon against us – and as an open invitation to the rest of the patients to join in the verbal attack.

My preference, at this time, for male company (because it was proving to be less problematic than female company) was also part of my life-long feeling of androgyny. As I wrote at the beginning of Chapter 5 "Identity and Boundary Issues," I had never felt like a girl...so how, therefore, could I fit in with girl-only groups? Again, in hindsight, it seems to be a matter of the "secret language of indirect communication" which was at least one component of my deficits in all-female company – I could not decipher the code. Also, I have, for a lifetime thus far, lacked the "feminine" desires to dress prettily, use make-up, wear jewellery, follow fashion, style my hair, or have babies. When, in adulthood, I learned the word "androgyny" – that is, neither male nor female, or having equal amounts of both – I was glad to have a word to describe how I felt. Constantly prodded to say something in the ward meetings, as we were, I thought my claim of androgyny to be a valuable piece of information for others. Instead, the nursing sister responded that this way of being was not allowed, and that I would have to renounce it!

The ethos of this ward, known over the road in the main part of the hospital as well, stated that this ward was one's only chance of getting well. To get well, a patient had to obey the medical staff. If one did not obey, one would be expelled from the ward, with no further chance of recovery during one's lifetime. The fear of this outcome meant that we had to comply at all costs – sometimes even having to "live a lie" about who we were. I found such lies very painful and unpalatable, but the dilemma in which others placed me was a no-win scenario: either be untruthful (when necessary,) or be "on the psychiatric scrap-heap" for the rest of one's life. My trust in what people told me, added to my literal way of thinking, meant that these two scenarios were, indeed, the only choices available – with both of them being undesirable. To this day, I still feel "yucky" about the few times when I was manoeuvred into saying that I was something that I am not.

By this time, the mid-1980s, the world had already experienced the Hippies, Women's Liberation, racial equality movements, and the Sex-Drugs-and-Rock'n'Roll era, and was well on the way to embracing Gay Rights and the Green movement as well. Therefore, I was shocked and puzzled that androgyny could be an unacceptable concept. I was required to renounce it, in order to have my only chance in life of becoming "well." What, then, is the point of group psychotherapy, I wondered – if not to provide a safe space in which I can be honest about my feelings?

The ward staff's way of working seemed to be an alternation between telling patients, in no uncertain terms, what (according to them) the patients' shortcomings were – and leaving the patients to work out, for themselves, what was going on. Both methods were particularly unsuitable for me, as I was terrified of the aggressive communication style of the staff members, but when left to work out social relating insights by myself, I was hopelessly unable to do so. The latter scenario often resulted in my feeling distressed for a week at a time, unable to understand, nor to cope with, the group dynamics. For example, one day I was told of two (female) patients' negative feelings towards me, yet I had no idea what I had done wrong. I was told that their negativity towards me had been going on for a long time. Due to my own style of thought processes, the only way I could respond to this was to wait until Thursday night, at which time I was permitted to use pen and paper. My written comments ran: "And since I still don't know what caused their reaction then, nor why they are being so nice to me now, I feel completely confused about my relationships with them. I felt at the time that my hurt at being rejected was made out to be my problem entirely, by Erica. I disagree with this and feel the incident has not been dealt with as far as I'm concerned, hence my confusion."

This, too, was taken by the staff to be read at the ward meeting of staff and patients. My repeated statements that I was in a continual state of confusion did not prompt our caregivers to address the issue of why this was happening to me, however, so I was left floundering.

This same entry continues: "Percy's [Percy was a male nurse] 'challenge' to me on Monday afternoon came as a demolishing blow because the subject, my not talking enough in group, (WAS that the subject?) is already my number one sensitive area without being told off about it. It made me feel upset that he and others think what I already feel in most groups – that I'm a lump of lead. I couldn't prove that I do try to think of helpful things to say. But the harder I try to think, especially when I feel I should be saying something, and most of all when I'm asked to say something, is when my mind freezes and there aren't any thoughts in my head to say. It is intensely annoying to say the least, especially when people think I'm not trying."

As mentioned, when I DID find something useful to say, I could be made to renounce it, or it could be (and often was) used as a target for a barrage of disparaging remarks from the others.

That same day's written commentary continues: "Next day, when planning the psychodrama [a compulsory exercise], I had no such trouble and in fact felt dominant, having to hold myself back lest I hog the whole session. I was NOT trying harder. For some reason the exercise was much easier for me than normal. The reason involves static subject matter as opposed to the constantly changing flow of ordinary groups. If true, this would also explain why I have difficulty scoring table tennis and playing basketball. I get so despairing about this problem that I often wonder if there is something mentally wrong with me."

And, again, on another day: "Table tennis scoring [which I was repeatedly pressured into doing] can be a terrifying, paralysing, and humiliating experience. Contrary to what people probably think, I AM concentrating my hardest. Translating what I see into what I have to say, it gets lost somewhere in between."

These writings go a long way towards describing my thought processes, and why I had major difficulties in an environment of constant pressure. I was, and, to a large extent, still am, unable to cope in a pressured, fast-moving, or emotionally fraught situation: all of which were constant in the ward. Any deficits in my coping ability were responded to as non-compliance, adding much more frustration and distress to my already over-loaded state. In the second to last paragraph, I explained that "static subject matter" is profoundly easier for me to deal with than "the constantly changing flow of ordinary groups" – and this is why I performed at extremely different success rates, depending on the type of activity. My writings from this time (the mid-1980s, when I was 30 years old), show that I had a high level of understanding about the nature of my difficulties (although not WHY I had them) and that I was trying to get the medical staff to understand as well…though the latter effort was in vain. The main reason why I was getting so despairing about it was that the staff did NOT understand, nor give any sign of wishing to, and made no allowances for my different thought processes – instead making them the subject of repeated adverse comment. They could have chosen to pay attention, from a medical point of view, to what I was writing – thus learning about a different way of being, and how to assist such a person – not to mention celebrating difference. Instead, however, the more I told them of my differences, the more they seemed to act as though their only interest was to eradicate them…which made me feel as though my very person-hood was being eradicated. As I already had so many fundamental identity issues (see Chapter 5), these additional assaults on my identity made me feel as though I was being subjected to a slow form of murder.

I have always been a very non-sporty person, and, in particular, have avoided team sports and swimming. When left to organise my own keep-fit activities, I opt for walking. The compulsory sports in the ward, though, were usually basketball and swimming. Team sports were, from earliest childhood, problematic for me in several ways: I had trouble understanding the group dynamics, the principles (and the point!) of team play; and my co-ordination was not up to standard. In addition to this, the indoor basketball games of the ward were very rough-and-tumble, which made it all the more unpleasant for me. It seemed to me that it was happily accepted by the ward staff that someone might get injured during sports – whilst I found this to be an unacceptable prospect, especially for something which I did not want to do in the first place.

Playing the sport was not, however, the worst aspect for me: worse was the humiliation and ridicule to which I was subjected for my lack of skill in this area. It seemed to me that the staff – as in every other area of ward life – roused the emotions of the majority of patients against one other, singled-out patient – which was often me, due to my deficits in a variety of areas. This is usually referred to as "scapegoating": one person (usually the most timid and least powerful) is set upon by everyone else; and the leader of the pack is the one who deliberately starts and maintains the attack. The nursing sister was in charge of the ward, answerable to no one, and so she could get away with it. Being isolated away from the outside world, with no reality check, and not permitted to leave unless we wanted to lose our only chance of being "cured" created a situation similar to jail, in which getting on with one's fellow inmates was the difference between heaven and hell.

To continue with the topic of indoor basketball: one day, I was nominated as the person who would pick the teams. As with everything else in the ward, I had no choice in the matter. Remembering how, in my childhood, my peers had fought over NOT wanting me in their team, I saw my chance to ensure that this task be done fairly: I picked the patients for whom I felt the most compassion; the patients who, I thought, might not be other people's No. 1 choice for a basketball team, and I placed them in my team. For this, I was again set upon by the staff, who also tried to excite the other patients into joining in: I was labelled an inept and irresponsible team leader, who picked unsuitable team members, thus making things harder for the few decent members who were in my team. I had failed at the task, and was worthy only of scorn. As would often happen to me in the ward, whatever I said and did seemed to be twisted around to make it turn from a positive to a negative. It seemed to me that the staff – especially the nursing sister – kept changing the rules as they went along, thus ensuring that the patient in question could never succeed at the set task. Over time, I also felt increasingly that the staff members only wanted to make patients feel bad and worthless, not positive and encouraged in a way which would help them to get well. It seemed to me a very strange agenda for a therapeutic community.

On one solitary occasion, the weekly sports session turned out to be an activity I enjoyed: a sort of harriers' treasure hunt. As I was reasonably fit where walking and running were concerned, I was able to race from Point A to Point B as required. Moreover, it was a sport involving individual effort, as opposed to team play – thus enabling me to concentrate on the task at hand so much more effectively, without struggling with the group dynamics I always found so baffling. Because of these differences from our usual activities, I succeeded quite well with this one, and no one could find fault with my performance.

Again on the subject of physical exertions, one of the main features of the therapy was the "psychodrama," which was practised on two afternoons per week. In this activity, scenarios were nominated by the staff, the parts of which all ward members (patients and staff) would act out, as in a play. This was intended to be therapeutic, as various social and emotional situations could be played out. The staff also set up a video camera each time, so that the completed psychodrama could be replayed and discussed. Some of the psychodramas were enjoyable for me, and some seemed pointless, while others could become quite physically rough. In one of these, I was being repeatedly dragged along the floor, so that my jeans were dragged down; as I could not move to correct this situation, a male nurse repeatedly pulled my jeans back into position and re-fastened them. Under present-day sexual harassment laws, this would be a questionable state of affairs. Yet the same staff found the word "androgynous" unacceptable! For certain other patients, the psychodramas were far worse: anyone who had suffered childhood sexual abuse (for which this ward was recommended as suitable treatment) experienced terrifying memories from being roughly manhandled in this way.

The video replays afterwards were, for me, usually a far worse ordeal than the activity itself: the staff would make seemingly endless negative comments about what patients had done during the psychodrama. And nothing could be denied – after all, there it all was, recorded on film! As mentioned elsewhere in this chapter, one's motives and behaviour were usually interpreted by the staff in the worst possible light, so that they would then be "justified" in humiliating and verbally attacking the person.

Regarding the compulsory sessions in the unheated hospital pool, worse than the actual water was changing back into my clothes afterwards. I have always been slow and awkward at manual tasks, such as getting dressed, but, in my adult years, my prowess at dressing myself was of no concern to anyone else – until I entered the ward. I didn't even notice, after the first swimming session, that I was the last person to finish getting dressed, until it was harshly pointed out by the staff. As usual, it was said to be an attention-seeking device. This was a ridiculous statement, however, because I greatly feared and hated this cruel sort of "attention." Therefore, the next time we went swimming, I tried very hard to dry and dress myself more quickly. Alas, I found that I was again last. More reprimands followed. And so on each week: I was not allowed to get out of the water until instructed, so I was prevented from having a "head start" in my frantic efforts to dress quickly. The harder I tried, the more anxious I became, with the result that I became more awkward, and slower, in my efforts. The ward staff repeatedly criticised and ridiculed me (in front of everyone) for what I genuinely could not help: my innate co-ordination difficulties. In hind-sight, one can see, again, how the staff set up the situation: by not allowing me to leave the pool a few minutes earlier, they ensured that I would "lose the race" every time. This recurring situation is one of my worst memories of life in the ward: even writing it now, the sweat of fear is pouring down my body.

The matter of "attention-seeking" behaviour deserves further elucidation. Most behaviours – and especially those which the staff did not understand – were labelled as such. The other side of this equation was that the ward ethos did not allow "attention-seeking" behaviour, which elicited highly distressing consequences from the staff and from the majority of the other patients – who were under the sway of the staff. Whether or not one had actually been guilty of "attention-seeking" behaviour, the results were the same: nobody would talk or interact with the patient thus labelled, except to express hostility, and the group meetings would deal with nothing else but one's "unacceptable behaviour." After a day or more of this, each time – remember, I was trapped amongst these people with no outside input – I was always completely traumatised. Yet, I was still expected to carry on with the daily life of the ward…as though nothing had happened.

Although my weekly written commentaries had to be carefully worded – taken, as they were, to be read out to the staff and patients next morning at the ward meeting – I sometimes managed to deliver a home truth. One entry reads: "…getting more than one's share of attention is the cardinal sin amongst other group members." Add to this the fact that the type of attention I usually received – that which emphasised my shortcomings, no matter how hard I tried – was the opposite of what I wanted and needed! Even getting the unwanted type of attention, however, was seen as "the cardinal sin" by the majority of the other patients…and one would be treated accordingly. With very few entertainments available and allowed in the ward, complex and unkind varieties of social control had become THE entertainment for a large number of patients, which was known and encouraged by the staff. Each morning, the more dominant patients would bring complaints about other patients (usually those at the bottom of the pecking order) to the ward meeting of staff and patients, there to be discussed and "interpreted" at great length. When I say "the majority of the patients," the occasional patient who was very timid, or who seemed to be operating on a different wavelength (like Matthew and myself), were on the outer of this activity – making us all the more likely to be targets for the more dominant personalities. Someone who had no ability to even understand indirect communication, as in my case, had no chance of emotional survival.

The worst incident which happened to me in the ward is still too painful for me to write in this account.

Towards the end of my stay, a new young male patient was admitted to our ward. I am omitting any description of his appearance due to privacy issues, and I have changed his name to "Jesse." The ward staff told the rest of us, before we even met him, that Jesse could well be leaving us again very soon, that is, after two or three days. By now, very subdued and dejected with my own difficulties in the ward, I did not have much interest in getting to know a new patient who would probably be leaving in a few days anyway.

However, what is important here is the staff members' explanation. They told us that Jesse had a condition which would be likely to cause him to become a scapegoat in the environment of this ward, so that it might not be a suitable place for him, in which case he would be taken out again. I remember thinking at the time, "Well, aren't I a scapegoat, too? How is it that I am not taken out of here, then?" Sure enough, after two or three days, Jesse was taken away and that was the last I heard of him. Obviously, I have no way of knowing what his problems were or what his diagnosis was.

After eight months, and preparing myself to leave the ward and re-join the outside world, I felt no more capable of this than before. In fact, I was, in some ways, even more confused about social life than before, due to living in such an inexplicable environment. Because of never having a moment's privacy – and never being allowed even a private thought in one's head, it seemed to me – I now had increased feelings of paranoia, with which I have struggled ever since. Also, the treatment had programmed me into incorrectly thinking that being constantly overpowered and out-manoeuvred was "normal relating," and I was to have years of undesirable relationships of various sorts as a result. I have had to work on "un-learning" a lot of what I learned there.

Another result of the treatment was that I had been moulded to think of myself, and my very thought processes, as inadequate. Feeling hounded, every day, because I was communicating differently from others – and, moreover, because my differences were responded to as though they were wrong and undesirable – I misguidedly put all my efforts into learning to speak as other people did. Having had the experience of learning German at school, I brought examples of these language-learning techniques into use for the purpose of teaching myself how to speak English…even though this was, officially, my mother tongue. I studied correct English sentences in the same way that I had learned German ones…and because this visual approach suited my way of learning – and because I have a natural ability with written language – after ten years of effort, I achieved a result. Finally, a switch in my brain switched from pictures to words. Now, at last, I could think in words, which enabled me to speak like a native speaker of English. There was a cost attached to this, however: I can no longer think in pictures – this creative side of my being is gone. Now that, very late in life, I have discovered that certain other people DO think in pictures, as I did – and that it is, therefore, a valid (as well as an original and inventive) way of thinking – I feel cheated that I was made to feel that I had to change my very thought processes in order to become "well," and "normal." It feels like another "sell-out" into which I was manipulated by this hospital experience. Knowing what I know now, if I could go back and reclaim my previous cognitive individuality – that stolen part of my soul, my self – I would.

In order to get out relatively safely and in one piece, I wrote a "Thank You" clause to the staff in my last piece of writing. It makes sickening reading now, but, at the time, it was necessary for my survival – for antagonising the staff at that juncture would have further jeopardised my future life. That is because, if one needed future follow-up assistance, one would have to see the same staff all over again; and I had found them difficult enough to cope with the FIRST time around, without providing them with provocation.

Because the staff did not take a medical interest in my own description of what was going on for me, they could neither learn new facts, nor compile correct information about me. Had they kept themselves informed with knowledge from overseas, or even paid attention to what I was telling them through my written commentaries, they would have been able to see why certain patients formed a "pattern." The staff had already noticed that Matthew and I were two of a kind – and they would have seen many others of the same kind (for example, probably, Jesse) – yet did not investigate what this might mean. Their assumptions – relying, as they did, on ready-made formulae – resulted in incorrect data being passed on to whichever professionals I was to see in the future. Whenever I was, later in life, to turn up at a different psychiatric hospital for support, it might be all right for an hour or so, until the nurses obtained my previous hospital records. From that moment on, it would be a case of being treated abruptly, being told that they could not help me, and being told to go away and stop disturbing the unwell people with my presence. Due to this happening several times, I can only surmise that something very negative seems to have been written in my previous hospital records by the "farm ward" staff;

for why else would the appearance of my previous records trigger such a change in attitude? As I could not, therefore, obtain the understanding and help which I needed, I was on a downhill slide into depression and other mental health problems, perpetuated and compounded by my "farm ward" admission.

In the above ways, the psychiatric hospital experience was not merely an eight-month stay, but has affected my life for far longer – giving me additional difficulties which I am still working through, as well as taking away my most creative attribute.

At least, I was luckier than one particular fellow patient: soon after leaving the ward, he was found to have terminal cancer. He entered a hospice and died shortly afterwards.

Only recently in life did I discover that there is a complaints process available to patients who have had unsatisfactory hospital treatment, and I sent a fully detailed account to the appropriate body. The investigator decided that "no further action will be taken," with the rationale being: 1. "that Medical staff and not nursing staff are responsible for diagnosis of mental health illness and initiating treatment modalities;" and 2. "the considerable time lapse [sixteen years] since the treatment was provided to you."

I am not necessarily opposed to the existence of psychiatric hospitals. Properly run by caring and competent staff members, they can be a useful resource for people in their time of need. My own experience illustrates, however, that staff and treatments need to be monitored and made accountable, otherwise they can do more harm than good.

I feel very sad that I was made to feel all of this "despair" over my differences, when I should have been allowed to enjoy and celebrate these. Using the reasoning that at least half of my differences must have been positive ones, what strengths could have been encouraged and built upon! What could have been a very happy, fulfilling and rewarding young adulthood was made, instead, into a time of rejection, failure and hopelessness. Now, in my late forties, and with some recent radical life changes for the better, I am able to appreciate and enjoy my own uniqueness. I can not go back and recapture my lost "despairing" years, however, and to remember this is to experience grief.

Chapter 13

Asking for Help

1. A Day Clinic of the Auckland Hospital Board: I described my developmental delay (no crawling, late walking, slow growing, looking very young for my age as a child, thyroid disorder), and said I thought there could be something in this; these facts were ignored.

   At another time, seeing the same therapist, I said that I thought a girl's sexual development is affected by the presence or absence of her father. At this, I was angrily met with "But you don't have sex with your father!" Thus, I was invalidated, humiliated, and had my comment turned into something "dirty," which I did not intend.

2. An Endocrinology Clinic at a public hospital: I saw Dr – regarding my thyroid condition. He asked me to contribute to his experiments, which involved running up stairs, then having my reflexes (ankle and knee) tested. He was delighted, "amazed;" I took it that my reflexes were on the very slow side. I asked for clarification as to what the tests were for, but he declined to give any facts, saying that it was just for his own interest.

   Yes, this finding would certainly tie in with my own perceptions of having slow responses (too slow for activities like driving,) and slow processing speeds in general.

   Had he followed this up, or sent me for follow-up to the appropriate specialists, I might have had the appropriate investigations done (and the correct conclusion reached?) 20 years earlier. Also, it was unethical of him not to get my informed consent, and not to explain the results of the tests or answer my questions. Therefore, I am upset that he was irresponsible on all counts.

3.   A ward of a psychiatric hospital: See separate Chapter 12.

4.   Another Mental Health Day Clinic: On telling a counsellor, (who looked young enough to be a Fourth Former), that I had grief issues, involving terror, she responded by saying something similar to:

> "No, I've read the text books on grief, and terror isn't one of the symptoms. Try again!!!"

I was horrified, (and still am), at the total invalidation which I received at her hands. So much for getting grief issues handled: there was no chance of this, after such a comment.

5.   An advertised Social Services Workshop: Some of the "exercises" were way beyond what I could do, notably the one where I had to "see beyond" my partner's façade and see his real self; my futile attempt left him feeling worse.
        Then, in small groups, we had to recall memories of each parent; the grief burst out and I was sobbing uncontrollably; no one, including the leader, seemed to know what to do. I maintain that this type of workshop may sometimes be harmful, as they can stir up a person's most painful memories, and then leave the person stranded without proper support. If a leader is going to have such a workshop, then they should be careful what they do to participants, and be properly prepared for what can happen when they rekindle a person's trauma; otherwise, the leader is acting irresponsibly.

6.   A registered psychologist, M.A. (Hons): When I spoke of thinking in pictures, she responded angrily: "I'm a registered psychologist, so I know that people don't think in pictures! Do you think you know more than I do about psychology!"

7. Another psychiatric hospital: I was very scared and had a migraine from stress; when I got to the reception desk, it was a doctor I'd seen previously, Dr – , who was (again) very scornful and disrespectful of me. She refused to take me seriously or ask me any questions, telling me that I could sit in the chair, (totally ignored), until closing time at 5 p.m., when I would have to go home.

    Later on, back at the flat, she phoned to ask how I was! I found this distasteful, as she had not cared how I was when I was there in front of her. As she had not believed, face to face, that I was not all right, I now said that I was all right, and she believed it! I found this even more distasteful, as she had caused me to tell a lie (that I was all right), then she had chosen to believe the lie, but not the truth when I told it. As I had not been able to endure her (or anybody) not believing me when I told the *truth*, I had, the second time around, told a *lie*, in order to be believed!!! Then (and evermore), I have felt very yucky about this incident: I rarely tell lies, hate doing so, and hate the knowledge that I "sold out" to her demands to say that I was "all right."

8. A Psychiatric Ward of another public hospital: Having another anxiety attack, I entered it as a place of refuge and place to "get help." However, a doctor told me not to come in here and disturb the unwell people (I was assumed to be perfectly well.)

9. The same psychiatric ward: Another anxiety attack, it was also my Christmas holidays, with insufficient support system; I entered hospital for "help." As soon as they had my name and therefore my medical record, they said: "We cannot do anything for you, you will have to go." As it was already nearly night-time, they allowed me one night there, then sent me out, crying, next morning.

    It was obvious to me, from this and other experiences, that there was something detrimental written in my medical records, for as soon as someone would get my file, or recognise me from a previous time, I would be treated with abruptness, disrespect and told to leave. Recently, I have met someone else who is an ex-patient from the same hospital ward, and she has been labelled as having "Factitious Disorder" – i.e. fictitious, malingering – I suspect the same might have been on my file. This then ensures that the person asking for help can get no help, but instead gets a "boot up the backside" whenever they ask for help. So much for asking for help!!!

10. One organisation offered a Buddy System for the intellectually handicapped: I read about this in the paper and that it was available for adults too, so, feeling strongly that I also needed the life skills buddying that they were offering, I rang the number. I politely explained that I was not intellectually handicapped, but that I needed this type of service, and so would they please put my name on the bottom of their list of clients, for, when all their existing clients had buddies supplied, then my name would finally come up?

I was treated to a lecture from the woman on the end of the phone, about how I was bad for trying to take services away from valid clients. I probably started to plead by then, and I think I recall that I started to cry, whereupon the woman sternly told me that all I had to do was to "choose to be happy." If I did so, then I would have no problems, according to her.

Well, how about all the intellectually handicapped clients, then? If they "chose to be happy!" would they suddenly become normal, have no problems, and therefore not need a life-skills buddy any more? The woman's reasoning seemed to be lacking in this respect, but she was very adamant that I was bad for asking, and I would certainly not be getting any help from that quarter, and my name would not even be put on the bottom of the list. I felt desperate, as finally I had been "so close" to getting the sort of help I needed – a lifeskills buddy – and now I was not only not allowed it, but was reprimanded for asking.

Postscript: Very recently in life, I again saw an advertisement for this support service, which, this time, stated that I *would* have been eligible for this support, as a special category, after all. This gave me a very painful jolt, as I had been desperate when I asked and pleaded for help the first time around.

These ten incidents (although there were more than ten such incidents in my life) show what can happen, and what did happen, to an adult who asked the "helping professionals" for help: one is treated with rudeness, disrespect, and invalidation; one gets no help, and one is sent away in even more of a state of despair. No wonder I was having suicidal thoughts, and no wonder that some others carry out their suicidal thoughts.

In at least nine of these cases, the professional concerned was in a position to investigate what my difficulties consisted of, yet did not ask the right questions, if any questions. If he or she did not know how to investigate my difficulties, then he or she should have sent me to someone with more knowledge, who could have followed up my case. The fact that all of these professionals (and more) chose to do nothing about this shows a great amount of irresponsibility on their part. They hindered my receiving any help, in some cases, for a further 20 years.

This list also asks huge questions about the gatekeepers in our society: the powerful individuals who decide whether to give, or withhold, services. Such persons hold the power of life and death over us lesser mortals. As such, at least some of them develop (or had in the first place) a power complex, perhaps even deriving pleasure and satisfaction from making powerless people squirm and sending us away unassisted.

I have recently seen lots of yellow posters on shop windows announcing, "It's OK to ask for help!" To this, I must ask: in that case, have the "helping professionals" been better trained in the meantime – since I was the one asking?

Chapter 14

In the Workforce: Part II

I obtained a job at a plant nursery at Drury, near Papakura. For my first day of work, I made myself an enormous cut lunch, imagining that the physical work would make me ravenous. Inside the shelter of a plastic house, that is, a glasshouse made of plastic instead of glass, I joined many other workers in the task of transplanting seedlings. A tractor would bring a load of vegetable or flower seedlings in large trays, and our job was to transplant these into the small punnets in which they would be sold. We were standing up all day, working at a bench. Having been a gardener all my life, I treated plants as fragile living things, and handled them gently. I quite enjoyed the work. Each worker fetched her own large tray of seedlings from the supply area, and was expected to record each tray as these were emptied, thus keeping a tally of her work output. I found that I did not need such a large lunch after all.

On one of my first days there, the rain fell heavily on the plastic sheeting which was the roof. A large pool of water collected in one place where there was a dip, and, eventually, the whole lot tipped out on to one particular woman. I have to admit that I couldn't help laughing. She shrieked, and left the job in a soaking state.

It was my fourth day, I think, when the supervisor walked over to me and said that my work output was not good enough. My gentle plant-handling methods were, I now understood, too slow. I could not bring myself to go any faster if it meant rough treatment of the plants, however. I responded to the supervisor, in a shaking voice, that I would like him to make up my wages, because I would leave as soon as possible. Before I received my pay packet, I heard one worker telling another that someone was "writing wrong numbers" on her output tally. I did not know what that meant until years later: so that was how one could ensure keeping one's job there. If one did not mind writing wrong numbers, that is.

I don't recall how it happened, but I found myself in a clerical job in a public hospital. My position was that of Booking Clerk, sharing a side room with three others, a few steps away from the Admitting Office. That was in the days of using typewriters, stencils, and the narrow strips of cardboard that I think were called kalamazoo files. My job was to receive patients' referrals on to the hospital waiting lists, making files for them, and recording their details on these narrow strips of cardboard, which were then mounted on to metal holding frames.

Outside my side room, the Admitting Office contained three or four more clerks. Through another door was Accident and Emergency, with another two clerks, except for the "Graveyard Shift," when there was only one. Booking, Admitting and A & E clerks were all responsible to the Office Manager and Deputy Manager. I felt pride and fulfilment in working for such an important service. We each had our own locker, and down the corridor was a cafeteria serving mouth-watering meals; my favourite was crumbed cutlets. The hospital had its own Post Office, and the Railway Station was right outside the door. In my own scheme of things, what more could a worker want!

The other clerks in the Booking Office were friendly when I started work there. Nell, who was seated at the central desk, made all the phone calls which gave the more fortunate patients – the chosen ones – their admission dates. Somewhat older than me, she was warm-hearted and jovial. The woman on the other side of Nell typed up a list each day of the patients who were booked, some days ahead of time, so that the Medical Records clerks could find their previous records. The fourth person in our side room was the Registration Clerk, who put together the complete packet which was to go with the patient, containing medical records, forms, personalised labels and a wristband.

I found that I soaked up medical terminology, with its Latin and Greek names, like blotting paper. I had never consciously studied Latin or Greek, but, as medical terminology was a language-based skill, it fell within my sphere of special interest and ability. Early on in my job, I diagnosed my mother as having carpal tunnel syndrome. I was able to do this because of the patients' orthopaedic files, listing presenting symptoms and subsequent diagnoses, which would find their way on to my desk. My reading of these had to be very fast, as my work kept me busy and I could not afford the time for "non-essentials." Mum's general practitioner confirmed that she had the wrist condition.

There were lots of phone calls to be answered, both from hospital staff and from patients waiting for their turn for surgery. The latter calls were, I soon discovered, very stressful: the patient was phoning because he or she was in pain, and wanted the hospital to hurry up and make the arrangements. I sympathised with his or her predicament, but the problem was that I had no power to do anything about it. I could not perform the surgery myself, so the best I could do, and did do, was to put the patient's file in a special display rack for the doctor to see, with the note that the patient had phoned in distress. If and when I saw that particular specialist, as they would come into my office from time to time, I would also tell them that the patient had rung, and indicate that the file was in the special rack for the doctor to see. There was no more that I could do, as I had to await orders from each doctor, yet I suffered mental anguish for the patients when they begged me for an admission date.

The time when the phones were busiest was early morning, for the booked patients were instructed to phone the Booking Office to check that their bed was still available. We had a typed list of who was booked for each ward, but the ward sisters would have to cancel some of these due to emergency admissions overnight and early in the morning, and this situation was ongoing as we were taking calls. This couple of hours required fast thinking and very fast-moving responses as the bed situation in each ward changed by the second, at the same time as the patients were phoning in. Every time one of us finished a phone call, we would have to recheck and, if necessary, rewrite, the state of play on the booked patients list. Leaving the room, to go to the toilet, for instance, would have meant a big gap in one's understanding of the situation by the time one came back. It would be very easy, in spite of one's best efforts, to "lose the plot" and give the wrong information. In spite of trying my hardest, one morning I did just that: I instructed a patient to come in, but, alas, her bed had been taken already, in one of these quick-fire changes to the arrangements. By the time I realised my mistake, the patient and her family were seated in the Admitting Office waiting room. Aware of the full implications of a patient making all the necessary arrangements and "psyching" oneself up for a hospital admission, I was horrified at having to tell her the bad news. Our Deputy Manager, knowing the difficulty of the morning phone routine, kindly told me that she would inform the family herself. I felt, however, that it was my mistake and that I should own up to it, so I screwed up all my courage and marched into the waiting room, ending up crying tears of remorse in front of the patient. The Deputy Manager saw what was going on and took over; she never criticised me for my genuine error during the "crazy phone hour."

We had to wear dresses, skirts and blouses, or good-quality trouser outfits for the office environment. Something called a "sun-dress" was not permitted; I am not entirely sure what this was, but it included a lack of sleeves. Office dress was not to my taste, although I chose the simplest clothing possible. Even then, I had trouble with keeping all of my garments on straight, correctly and "ship-shape:" adding petticoat, pantihose and bra to my usual attire caused me to feel constantly in a tangle. Perhaps my shoulders are too sloping to hold bra straps up, because they were always falling down – but if I tightened the straps, they cut painfully into my shoulders. Every time I went to the toilet, the struggle to get my skirt, blouse, petticoat, pantyhose and undies back into their correct positions seemed to take forever, and afterwards I was still not satisfied with the results. This even caused comments from at least one workmate, who marvelled at how long it took me to go to the loo! – which made it even more embarrassing.

I had started the job not long before Christmas, and after this day there were big changes in the office. The Manager, Deputy Manager, and Nell all left within a short time of each other, and new people filled these roles. The benevolence of the previous Manager was a thing of the past, and in its place was a new type of person: small and wiry, with a sharp, high-pitched voice, and with something called "management skills."

Back in the Booking Office, without Nell, the clerk on the other side underwent a personality change. When I continued to talk to her in the same way as before, she responded to me grumpily and critically. At a time when this co-worker was out of the room, the new Manager came in, and told the rest of us something about how we should and shouldn't do our work (the exact details of what she said are now forgotten). Reporting this information back to my colleague on her return, I made the bad judgement call of using a phrase which I did not fully understand: I said that we (in the Booking Office) had been "hauled over the coals." Little did I expect, however, that my colleague would go immediately to the new Manager and tell her exactly this! About five seconds later, the Manager was standing in front of me, demanding to know whether I had said these words. I replied "Yes." My boss was furious, and I was in trouble with her already. In retrospect, it seems that my fellow clerk had no concern for what would happen to me if she "told tales" to the Manager; she would have known that doing this would result in trouble for me. I was usually a careful person in what I said and did, but this slip-up made me even more cautious about anything which came out of my mouth from then on. My "new-style" colleague also made a fascinating study in something I had previously heard of only in my sixth-form history lessons: the Balance of Power. Mr Fletcher had spoken of it with regard to the countries in Europe before the First World War. Now I could see it operating for myself: with Nell gone, the whole balance of the Booking Office had been upset; for example, my previously cheery co-worker was now unpleasant to work with. The whole office atmosphere was also to work its way to world war status, figuratively speaking. From that moment on, I had a new tool with which to study group dynamics.

The new Manager, Rosie, also told the hospital doctors her new rules of how they were to interact with the Admitting Department. Soon we were all treated to scenes such as angry altercations between Rosie and the specialists, and, on one occasion, an impressive tug-of-war as Rosie and Dr Parry fought over the possession of a large exercise book. In turn, the doctors were often angry when they visited us in the Booking Office, resulting in greatly increased stress levels all round. Rosie elected herself as Union Delegate – so now nobody could ask the Union Delegate to check on the activities of the Manager, as they were one and the same person.

A new staff member in the Booking Office, although pleasant in many other ways, had the habit of making frequent racist comments against Maori and Pacific Island people. As someone who strongly dislikes unfairness in all its forms – and who categorises prejudice and racism as types of unfairness – I found this very upsetting. At the time, I was also learning the Maori language at night class, which was a most rewarding activity for me. I expressed my disapproval of this person's remarks, but, as has happened before and since, as soon as the perpetrator learned how I felt about it, she took pleasure in doing it all the more. (I now recognise this behaviour as "baiting," and now know that it is useless for me to try to argue with it or to respond to it: it is all just a game for the perpetrator.) A few other staff members would agree with her attitudes, and, at the time, I could not emotionally disentangle myself from the distress it caused me.

A health policy was instigated in the Admitting Office: henceforth no staff would be allowed to smoke in any area which was visible to the public. This meant that all of the Admitting Office and the A & E counter were out of bounds to smokers, as these could be observed by patients. Quite a few of the office staff members smoked, and their solution to the new situation was to pop into the Booking Office – a sideroom away from the public gaze – in order to light up. The trouble was, the Booking Office was very small, and I – someone whose body reacts badly to cigarette smoke – had to work there. On top of that, all my co-workers insisted that the windows be kept closed; I had constant complaints from them if I opened my window so much as a crack. A fine rule this is, I thought: while the public sees us as keeping a "healthy" image, I am choking to death on second-hand smoke.

At some stage during my four and a half years there I was given a role change to that of Admitting Clerk, which I found that I liked better, at first. It involved asking questions of newly admitted emergency patients, then returning to the office, typing up these details, photocopying them on to sticky labels, preparing a wrist-band, ordering any previous files from Medical Records, and so on. The patients were sometimes in A & E, or in some other waiting area. I often felt compassion for the plight of patients, who were unwell, in pain, and frightened. For a long time I felt guilty about making them answer questions when they were already sick or hurt; later on, I thought that maybe answering the standard questions might help to distract them away from their fear. Some patients actually liked to chat, and some would ask me for a bed-pan, or some painkillers, or something else. As I was not in charge of bed-pans or pills, I would have to find a nurse and ask for the required item. This would extend the time that I was away from the Admitting Office, and, it became apparent, this was a blot in my copy-book. One day the new Manager told me that I was taking too long, with an implied threat to my job. What am I to do then, I wondered anxiously, when patients ask me for something? I was not able to turn away and ignore them. Rosie continued to find fault with me; I knew that my blunder when she first started would not have helped, and I could not undo that. One day, she called me into her office, along with one of her colleagues, and told me that she wanted me to resign. She added that, legally, she could not *make* me resign, but she would like me to do so "voluntarily." I received a nasty shock from this, and felt very frightened. Nevertheless, something inside me felt that giving in to her tyranny would not be the right thing to do, so I refused to resign.

In retrospect (what a marvellous thing is retrospect!), I would have been better off to resign and to have got myself out of a bad situation. Rosie and the whole office environment only became more and more stressful for me, turning me into a nervous wreck. Every morning, when I arrived at work on the train, I made straight for the public phone in the foyer, and, in tears from high anxiety, phoned my Mum. This was a necessary ritual in order for me to get enough courage to enter the office. By now I was suffering from severe bilious attacks every second Monday: the combination of a painful right eye, avoidance of light, great desire to lie down, diarrhoea (and sometimes vomiting) marked these out as a form of migraine, to which my Mum was already prone. Overwhelming levels of workplace stress, together with being forced to breathe too much cigarette smoke, were bad for my health. It seems that it took my body two weeks to work its way back to the start of the migraine cycle. Nevertheless, such was my sense of responsibility to my job that I arrived anyway, feeling like death warmed up. After making enquiries, I discovered a sofa, in a locker room, at the other end of the hospital; to this I would retreat, every tea break and lunch time, in order to have the lie-down for which I was desperate. In the case of tea breaks, the walk there and back meant that I had only a minute or two in which to lie down, but I considered this to be better than nothing.

On the other hand, we office workers were encouraged to study for the NZ Health Records Association examinations, and, at least in the medical

terminology category, I excelled. When we had our first test, as a prelimi-
nary to the examination proper, I scored a very high mark, perhaps the top.
It turned out that my colleagues did not all find medical terminology as
easy as I did.

I had a period of working afternoon shift in Admitting for two
evenings a fortnight. Two clerks did this shift together, taking turns to
interview patients so that one was always in the office. The time flew so
much faster at night, and no one could explain why. Part of the thrill was,
for me, that every night an orderly would bring our dinners on a trolley!
There was a main course with meat, and also a dessert, with metal lids over
them to keep them warm and hygienic. My work partner, Miriam, never
touched her dinner, but neither would she cancel her dinner at the kitchen.
I thought it a terrible waste. One evening, whilst she was the one out of the
office, I was ravenous and ate hers too, replacing the metal lid so that no
one would notice. Miriam returned; I tried to look innocent. For once, she
made a bee-line for the dinner trolley, saying, "I'll just see what the dinner
was, anyway!" She lifted the lid and we both stared at the empty plate.
Neither of us said a word about it.

The months wore on and, finally, the "Management Skills" Manager
worked herself up into such a state that she collapsed in her superior's (the
Hospital Manager's) office, and had to be given mouth-to-mouth resusci-
tation. Soon after this, she left, and a new manager came to lead us in
Admitting, Bookings and A & E.

I was given the slightly different role of Registration Clerk for a while;
this clerk was part of the Admitting staff, although the actual desk was
situated in the Booking Office (the side room.) Prior to this, I had heard
some staff members complain about their turn on this job; for one thing, it
was an extremely busy role. I already knew most of the components of the
position, due to the overlap of my previous duties. As soon as I had learned
the routine, I found that I enjoyed this position very much, as there was a
set order to the tasks, and once one had reached the end of the sequence,
one started the same sequence of tasks all over again. In this role, I was not
expected to answer patients' queries all day long, which allowed me to
really "get into the swing" of my relatively predictable work day. The high
point of the sequence of tasks was, for me, allocating new patient numbers!
Having ascertained that a patient had never been admitted to the hospital

before, I would then write his or her name in the big red book with numbered lines. Oh, the power I had – to issue a number to a person! The Admitting clerks stopped having turns at being Registration Clerk after I took over the role, because I liked it so much, and they did not, so why change a good thing?

I felt very friendly towards some of my Admitting Office workmates, and our Samoan colleague sometimes brought us taro with coconut cream to share. Sepela also invited me once to her home, and to a prestigious Samoan entertainment evening presided over by her father, a chief. One day she told me that she was being subjected to racism in the workplace, and from our superiors at that. Unfairness in all its forms has always been extremely distasteful to me, and invoking the word "racism" was, for me, like waving a red rag at a bull. I didn't hesitate in writing to our workers' union, asking for help with this matter. I had never contacted a union before, so I did not know the procedure. I thought that the issue of racism was the important part, and did not give my name, just "a concerned colleague." In about a week, a visitor arrived at the office: someone from the union. I neither saw nor heard any of the proceedings.

When the management brought the matter to everyone's attention, the only important point was "Who wrote the letter?" The existence or absence of racism in the workplace was never mentioned – the hot topic was now the letter-writer's identity. As usual, the new situation took me by surprise. Always needing to assess a situation slowly and thoroughly in order to come to a decision, I waited whilst I thought what I should do. Besides, I was now frightened about what would happen to me. I asked a colleague for her opinion; she replied "You could always apologise!" This told me that no one, not even my equals, supported the letter-writing action, so I was on my own. The tension in the office was unbearable, so I ended up going to the Deputy Manager and "owning up," in a flood of tears. In all of this, the original topic of possible workplace racism had seemingly been forgotten.

My reputation now in tatters, I struggled on in my job for a while longer. I did not want to have to admit "defeat" and "failure." I now feel that this was rather misplaced heroics, but, at the time, I had no way of knowing what to do. One day, sick from "passive smoking" due to the office health policy, I stuck a notice on my side-room door: "Do not come in here to smoke." In about two seconds, the Manager was upon me, demanding that the notice be taken down and that the situation remain the same. On another day, for the first time in over four years, I finally completed all of the work which was on my desk. I had sometimes seen the A & E clerks leafing through magazines when their work was all done. For the first time ever, I picked up a magazine and opened it. I had not read a single word, however, before the Manager was at my side, brusquely asking, "Haven't you got enough work to do?" It seems, in hindsight, that I was now seen as the resident "trouble-maker," on whom a sharp eye had to be kept at all times. When I finally resigned, the pay clerks suddenly realised that they had been underpaying me for my whole four and a half years. If they had not informed me, I would never have been any the wiser. I left, therefore, with an extra cheque for around three thousand dollars. It was sad for me, however, to leave my work in the healthcare field, which had been so meaningful for me.

Chapter 15

Married to a Mole

Still desperately seeking "Normalcy," and "that special person" – yet, still having no idea of how to do this – I answered another ad in the "Personal" column of the newspaper.

I received a letter, phone calls, and then a visit, from an Englishman with long curly hair. He had a large old car containing two border collies, who went everywhere with him. He said he was an artist; he painted in oils, mostly landscapes. He ate only certain foods which were on his health food list, and he was a follower of the teachings of the psychic Edgar Cayce.

He was friendly enough on first meeting. His conversation topics tended to be unusual, which made him interesting company. Several times, he told me that he was listed in *Burke's Peerage*. As I did not know what this meant, he explained the importance of pedigree to the nobility. I found this strange, and remarked that I thought that pedigrees were for livestock only.

Soon came the day when I was invited to his house, the address being an isolated district of Northland. I booked a bus ticket to Whangarei, from where he would collect me. Part-way along the journey, the bus stopped so that driver and passengers could have a tea break: cups of tea and meat pies. Sure enough, at journey's end he picked me up with the car and the border collies.

His house was an A-frame, dark in colour, set amongst farm paddocks. Once inside, one could see that everything was yet to be finished: the floors were bare concrete, there were no dividing walls, no running water, no bathroom, no kitchen. The water needed to be fetched from the neighbouring farmer's tap; various containers served as chamber-pots. The dining facilities consisted of a table and chairs in the "open plan" design; the staple diet proved to be a packet of cereal and a chilly-bin full of goats-milk yoghurt. A wooden staircase connected the bare downstairs to the bare upstairs.

When bedtime arrived, I found that there was a single bed upstairs, with very dirty bed-clothes, and a mattress and dirty blankets on the floor for the dogs. Due to his bad back, he said, he could not share the bed with another person, so my place was on the floor with the dogs. At least one of the dogs would urinate on the mattress during the night. Far from happy with this arrangement, I was also too far from home – from anywhere – to do anything else.

He was not an early bird, his usual hour for rising being two in the afternoon. Inside his dark and gloomy house, I could look out the upstairs window and see sky, and sun; and it brought back to me a story on the Children's Request Session, Radio 1ZB, of Sunday mornings. It was the story of Thumbelina, a tiny girl who went through some difficulties due to marrying a mole. Once underground, she grieved the loss of the sun, light, sky, and warmth. Somehow, she heard or saw a bird flying overhead, and begged him to rescue her; she wanted to fly away on his back. Now in similar circumstances myself, I empathised fully.

Telling me at first that he had a temporary cash-flow problem that would be sorted out in a week or two, he asked me for a loan. This "loan" grew and grew, and he became increasingly pressuring and unpleasant if I tried to resist. All my savings from my bank account ended up in his possession, and I was never to see them again.

Although he maintained that he was not fit and well enough to perform any sort of work – even his painting seemed now to be only an occasional pursuit – he was fit and well enough to demand sex, all through the afternoon. I did not feel romantic towards him, and did not get much enjoyment out of these encounters – especially after I began to feel harassed and pursued for more. Without a toilet in the house, he filled up his plentiful supply of empty yoghurt containers with his urine, and lined them up in rows. He then forced me to drink some of it – and to eat his faeces. At some stage, in great distress, I whacked my head against the concrete floor, sustaining lumps and bruises. His only concern at this was that people might think *he* had hit me!

The next stage was that he wanted me to sell my home unit, which I had bought with my own money, and put the proceeds towards a new home with him. As he had no money to put in – except what he had already "borrowed" from me – I could see that this was not a good idea from my side of things. Here is where I have to thank my Higher Power for stepping in. Overpowered, long ago, by the mind-games of this man, I nevertheless managed to "climb on board" the back of the rescuing bird, around this time, and flew away. It was still not easy, as I had no other friends or social outlets to take his place.

I was never to be totally free of him, however: I had developed a burning pain "down there." It was a difficult task to get this diagnosed and treated, at the time, as there was no freely available information that I could find, some of the doctors I approached were unhelpful, and it was a taboo subject. One GP told me that I would have to boil all my towels and bed linen from then on, to avoid infecting anyone else. I have since been told that this was incorrect information. After some very painful tests which involved the sore parts being pricked and scraped, I was finally told I had herpes. It turned out that he had had an active outbreak of herpes during the time we were together, but had not divulged this fact to me. At the same time, I also had a rupture inside, presumably from a profusion of herpes blisters. It was painful for me to walk, and this went on for at least seven weeks (after seven weeks of pain, I lost count of time). I was still going to work during all of this time, with my job being a relatively physical one, so I was feeling very miserable, both in body and in mind. Another GP told me that I would have to be stitched up inside, to repair the damage, if the rupture did not heal within another couple of weeks. Fortunately, it healed up by itself by the deadline. I was in physical and mental anguish, but was getting insufficient treatment and support, as I had told only doctors of my plight; I had no close friends at this stage in my life, and no one with whom I wanted to share this problem. Herpes is, at the time of writing, still incurable, and would come back to haunt me many years later, bringing the bad memories with it.

Months later, I would also be crying out in the night from bad dreams of this man. I knew this only after I started getting invitations from female work-mates to stay the night in a spare room at their houses. Next morning, they reported on my night terrors. (When sleeping alone at my own place, I had no way of knowing that I was calling out in my sleep.)

Amazingly, this same man recently contacted my mother, asking for my current contact details! Thank goodness, Mum decided to ask me first. No way did I want to hear from this man, much less see him again! Mum had the impression that he was interested in rekindling our relationship! I wrote *him* a very stern letter, telling him what I thought of him, but without divulging my own address. We have not heard from him since.

Chapter 16

The Training Course

One year, I had what I thought was a brainwave regarding how to combine part-time university study with an income. I found out that I would be paid an allowance if I attended an approved training course, which I intended to take at the same time as a university paper. I discovered a training course that sounded good to me: Introduction to Teaching. Teaching students on a one-to-one basis is one type of career that I thought might be suitable for me, so this course seemed as if it would teach me useful skills. The training establishment, which taught several courses, was situated very conveniently in Queen Street, Auckland, thus allowing me easy access to the university. I went to see the person in charge, who was very friendly, and our chat persuaded me to go ahead with the course.

The staff, both teachers and administrators, were Maori, and were very warm, helpful, and approachable people. We students were even supplied with toast and jam for breakfast every morning! I was able to enjoy short conversations in Maori, a language I had studied as an adult, with the staff members. One of the students in my class had a baby girl, who was made welcome in every session. All of my classmates were enthralled to have a baby in the class, and knew how to talk to her in baby language and how to play baby games. I did not know how to talk baby talk; on the few occasions I had anything to do with babies, I talked to them normally as if they were adults. Right from day one in my new course, I was the odd person out when it came to the matter of responding to the baby.

Our first project was to choose a subject, prepare material on it, and present it to the class in three teaching sessions. One student chose "How to make chocolate eclairs;" I chose "Poultry Keeping." We had to give a background to the subject, changing gradually from the general to the specific, so that the Chocolate Eclairs student had to speak on nutrition and baking before giving the recipe. For the background to my teaching session, I gave an overview on what an animal is, worked through to general pet care, and finally to poultry. The grand finale of the project was to arrange a class visit to the subject in real life, so that the Chocolate Eclairs visit was to a bakery, and mine... I found myself being expected to arrange a visit to a poultry farm in Pukekohe. For some reason, I could not get away with a class visit to my house, where I kept my hens. It was rather tricky to locate the farm manager and make the arrangements by phone; however, that was the easy part, when I realised that I was responsible for getting my classmates from Queen Street to Pukekohe, and to a backblocks address at that. Driving scares me at the best of times, and being responsible for a carload of people added to the stress that was building up over this issue. Luckily for me, at the last possible moment the teacher decided that the training establishment would supply a van, to be driven by one of our classmates who felt happy about driving. I do not think that my classmates were as thrilled as I was about the sights and smells of the poultry farm, however.

Soon after the course began, we were told that the students of all three courses in the establishment would be going on a trip to Waiheke Island... for a number of days. This was news to me, and unwelcome news at that, as during my chat with the principal I had not gleaned this information. If anything about Waiheke had been mentioned before I signed up for the course, it had not registered in my brain; or perhaps I had assumed it meant a day trip, which would have been OK, in fact, enjoyable, for me. Now, class plans for food provisions and cooking were beginning. I did not (and do not) like the thought of lengthy stays away from home with people I do not know very well; and besides this, it would be no easy matter to arrange pet-care for my poultry, as pet minders are not familiar with chickens, and there would also be a sizeable fee attached to this. A date was eventually set for the trip, so I tried to come to terms with the inevitable. However, not long before the departure date, our tutor suddenly had to go into hospital, so the trip was postponed.

Wesley was soon back in front of the class, and the trip was rescheduled. Again, I tried to adapt to the situation, but felt anxiety about the change of plans, as well as about the trip and the pet-minding implications.

Over these years I was developing irritable bowel syndrome, which entails having extremely temperamental "guts," and frequent discomfort, with the constant situation of either "can't go to the toilet" or "living in the toilet," without ever being able to achieve a balance. For several years, and the year of the training course was one of them, my life was disrupted on a daily basis by this problem. I was prescribed medications, but, after prolonged trials, concluded that one of the medications was actually making the problem worse, so I discarded it. The other medication, on its own, was insufficient to treat the condition; so I had to learn to live with it as best I could. The much-promoted aloe vera treatment did not seem to help me, and it was also too expensive for someone living on a student allowance. I eventually found a herbal treatment which was the best solution I had tried; but the manufacture of this was discontinued soon after. Nowadays, I am sort of "muddling along" with the situation, with no ideal answers to it.

Another classmate's teaching sessions in front of the class were on the subject of ice hockey, a special interest of hers. I found myself being kitted out in a very heavy, all-enclosing protective suit, which I found oppressive right from the word go! At least, on this occasion we were not obliged actually to play ice hockey. On other days, however, we were taken to the basketball courts to play indoor basketball – another part of the course which I had not anticipated, and, as a very non-sporting person, did not want. To add to my anxiety around physical activities, I had developed pain in my right knee, which made it difficult, at times, even to walk – and walking is the one physical activity which I do enjoy. I had, as yet, no diagnosis for the knee problem, and I was awaiting a hospital scan. In the meantime, basketball was out of the question, so I had to tell the teacher that I would not be able to participate in sports – whilst lacking an official diagnosis, which caused me the stress of wondering if people believed that I really did have knee pain.

One of the many enjoyable parts of the course, for me, was the class visit to the Lion Brewery in Khyber Pass Road, Auckland. Although I had always been interested in flora and fauna, I had never before seen a hop plant; a shrivelled specimen was on display at the starting point of the tour. We were shown the barley, the mixing process, the storage and fermentation vats; it was all fascinating. Our tour guide gave us strict instructions about staying within the painted yellow line, as the brewery's fork-hoist vehicles would speed around without warning. Our next project, on returning to the classroom, was to write and draw descriptions of the brewery, as if we were explaining it to our own pupils. This, as well as the illustrated picture book project, was well within my capabilities.

My inborn academic skills made the book-learning part of the course pleasurable and easy for me. One day, for instance, Wesley was pacing the room whilst beginning the subject of the Maori pantheon of gods. On reaching my desk, he said "the god of earthquakes," whilst looking straight at me, so I promptly answered "Ruaomoko." Soon after, he was talking about geology, and asked me to supply the missing term – "tectonic plates" – which I did. On this day, at least, my quick-fire general knowledge ability was in top form! It was a different story, both then and on most other occasions in my life, when it came to practical ability: I would tend to become suddenly and totally inept. The change from one mode to the other has, I think, bewildered some people, due to my startlingly uneven repertoire of skills.

The proposed trip to Waiheke Island was "on again, off again" at least once more. This situation was extremely difficult and stressful for me to deal with; the sudden changes back and forth were anxiety-provoking enough on their own, but the uncertainty also meant that I could not arrange a definite date for a pet-minder, not to mention the worry of entrusting my beloved birds to anyone, and the matter of paying a fee for this service. Some of the other students had husbands and children; I wondered how they and their families coped with all these changes to the plan?

The obvious difficulty I experienced in saying the socially correct things to our classmate's baby was an ongoing issue. As all the other students knew what to say and do, and as the baby was being constantly looked after and cuddled anyway, I decided to leave it to them. One day, the baby's mother asked me (rhetorically, it seemed to me), "Do you really think you are suited to teaching?" No, I didn't really think it, not for more than one-on-one teaching, at any rate. Her comment caused me to feel more inadequate on the course than I already did. No longer could I even half-believe that I was fooling half of the people half of the time!

A trip to gather flax, for the purpose of doing craft-work, was another class outing. This would have been enjoyable for me but for the very hot sunshine that day. As is my custom, I wore my sun-hat, but this did not protect me from the general heat all around me, and the glare, with no shade into which to retreat. I do not subject myself to this level of heat and sun when left to my own devices, but on this occasion I had no choice. As has happened before and since, I ended up with heat exhaustion, which also gives me an upset stomach, and from which it takes me up to two days to recover.

Our singing sessions were a joy for me, especially as we were treated to songs from a variety of cultures: we enjoyed the benefits of our teacher's Maori heritage, plus many of us were originally from other lands, and I could even add a contribution from my German studies: "Weisst du, wieviel Sternlein stehen?" Each of us taught our classmates a song, which meant that we ended up with a song from the Maori culture, and one each from Sri Lanka, Iran, Samoa, England, and Germany. My lifelong interest in languages meant that I could pick up such knowledge relatively easily. For those songs which were accompanied by actions or dancing, however, I had difficulty with co-ordination. We practised our songs with a view to the end-of-course celebration.

One of the tenets of the training course appeared to be "Celebrating Diversity," which was totally in line with my own personal beliefs. Thus it was that one day Wesley began the subject of different sexual orientations, trying to make his students stop to consider how it would feel to be different in this arena. Finally I could stand the "theory divorced from reality" no longer, so I stood up and announced that I had been in a Gay nightclub! Not only had I done that, I continued, but I had identified as Gay for a period of my life. Though I no longer identified as Gay, I still empathised with Gay people, and I felt that I might be Bisexual. Soon after saying this latter term, I wound my mini-lecture down, as I was (and still am) considerably confused as to what Bisexuality entails, and as to which sexuality label

I should identify with in any case – finally settling for the happy term "Unlabelled!"

Wesley may have been impressed by this disclosure, as he ended the session with the statement that he fully supported anybody with such a "difference," and that he would tolerate no discrimination in the training establishment. I think I recall that it was then time for afternoon tea, as when the three classes regrouped, there was already a change in the air. By the end of the day I knew what it was: a large, sturdily built young woman from one of the other classes was glaring at me, and muttering and hissing comments at me. After some time I realised what the main words in her hissings were: "A man." I was a much smaller, less physically endowed person than she, and if either of us could be mistaken for the other sex... Out on the street after school was finished, this young woman spat at me.

During the next days on the course, the class was introduced to the young son, aged around four years, of our student from Sri Lanka. Afterwards, his mother remarked, in front of the students, that her son had not known whether I was a man or a woman. I supposed that, in the traditional culture from which he had come, he had not seen females with short hairstyles before. Whatever the reason, the student's comment started off another round of mirth and comments at my expense.

Too many things were stacking up for me now: the anxiety over Waiheke Island; the anxiety over my knee pain and having to excuse myself from sports; the "toilet trouble" of irritable bowel syndrome; the anxiety over not being able to talk "baby talk" to our classmate's baby; the stress of never knowing what new activity we might be having in the next day or two; the anxiety over my difficulties with manual types of activities; feeling unsuitable to become a teacher; and, now, prejudice because I had formerly identified as Gay. It had all converged on me now, and I could no longer cope. My anxiety levels were very high, and depression was setting in. Within the week I obtained a sickness form from my GP, stating that I had Manic Depressive Disorder, and that I would not be continuing the training course. (The Manic Depressive Disorder was not suggested by me, but the doctor had to think of something to write on the form, and this diagnosis was the one which it looked most like to him.) Then, as now, I hate leaving a meaningful project unfinished, and the training course had been a meaningful project for me. I am sad that it had to end this way, but I could no longer cope.

Postscript: The Sickness Benefit that I was now on allowed me to finish my university paper, so I could at least accomplish that. When I got the CAT scan at Auckland Hospital, it showed that my knee had a torn meniscus. How I could have sustained that I will never know: I have rarely played sports (and only under duress!)

Chapter 17

In the Workforce: Part III

I got myself a job as cafeteria assistant for one of the Auckland Regional Authority bus depots. The job designation was actually "Dishwasher," but that was only one part of it. As explained by the recruiting officer, I would start in the Mt. Roskill bus depot, but after a few weeks I would transfer to Wiri depot. As I was then living in Papakura (South Auckland), travelling to Mt. Roskill took two buses, but I knew that, when I transferred to Wiri (another South Auckland location), I would be much closer.

On my first day, I was given a pretty uniform patterned with brown checks, and everyone was friendly to me. The Mt. Roskill staff consisted of a mother and daughter team and, now, me. In the afternoon, I was whisked away to have my photo taken and an identity card made, so that I could have free travel on any Auckland Regional Authority (ARA) bus. At the time, however, the bus company which served Papakura was a different one from the ARA, so I could not use this card for my daily travel to and from work.

Next day, I found out what my working life there would entail. There were stacks of dishes, but that was not the hard part. For one thing, I found it extremely difficult to remove the burnt-on, rock-like rice from the bottoms of the huge cooking utensils; and the cooks did not have to worry about burning the food on to the pots, as they were not the ones having to clean them. This was taking me so long that I was becoming more and more anxious. Also, my pleasure trip the day before, in order to get my identity card, had prevented me from learning what my usual afternoon duties consisted of. I suddenly found out, when the younger woman on the staff let out an angry yell: "Jesus Christ!!!" it began. It then continued along the lines of: "Do we have to carry you every day? We cleaned the ovens yesterday for you, and you haven't done them again today! You won't be getting away with this!"

Fear clutched at my insides, as I hate being harshly criticised. I had not realised that cleaning the ovens was part of my afternoon duties, and, now that I did know it, I was well aware that I was unable to keep up with the workload – due, partly, to the pots with burnt food stuck to them. I could not see how I could also fit the ovens into my schedule, and, therefore, I was not able to perform the job adequately. As well, I knew that I would not be able to cope with being yelled at whenever the other staff were displeased. With quaking voice, I responded, "I'll have to leave, then."

At that, the older woman tried to tone down the situation. She said that leaving would not be necessary, and I don't remember what else, with the result that I decided at least to try going back next day. I tried my hardest to complete all of my duties satisfactorily, although kitchen work is far from being my forte. Seeing me struggling to clean the oven trays, the older woman said, kindly, "Take it easy! Otherwise you'll cripple yourself!" When it was my meal break, she gave me a delicious lump of boiling bacon, free of charge. I was at least getting better meals there than at home in my own flat!

One of my duties was to wipe down the tables and bring the dirty dishes back to the kitchen, where I would then wash them. One day, I saw a cup containing some dreadful-looking slops on the serving bench where the bus drivers picked up their cutlery. I'll be in trouble if my superiors see that sitting there, I thought, and hurriedly threw the mess down the plug-hole. A few minutes later, the cry went up: "Where's the mint sauce!" It was roast lamb day, and the "slops" had been the mint sauce. I tried to look invisible, as I had no wish to add this to my already questionable work record. Ascertaining that there was none left, the older woman sent me out with some money to buy more mint sauce, thus giving me a pleasant walk in the fresh air!

On another day, I was frantically trying to get the huge tea urn full in time for the drivers' morning tea break. No matter how much water I poured into the top of the urn, though, the level remained the same: near the bottom. I finally discovered – perhaps through having wet feet – that the problem consisted of an open tap at the bottom of the urn. All of the tea was on the floor! About this time, the younger woman saw that the kitchen was awash. "Get a mop!" she commanded. "This floor's like a skating rink!" As I now had to mop the floor, I presume that the drivers' morning tea was late after all.

I hung on to this job for the few required weeks, then transferred to the Wiri depot. By contrast, this place had a more relaxed atmosphere. Whereas the previous depot had been run by a mother and daughter, the Wiri one was run by two sisters, with the elder of the two being the manager. The two sisters were of Niue Island heritage, and there was also a cook (a white New Zealander like myself.) These three were all very friendly to me. Some of my duties were different here, and, to my relieved amazement, the cook usually washed her own equipment. My designation was still Dishwasher, though I again found this misleading, as, between washing dishes, I was expected to make toast, serve tea and coffee, wipe tables, collect plates, boil eggs, tidy the storeroom, among many other duties.

My first task of the morning was to place the cakes, which were delivered overnight, in the food cabinet. Next, I had to make the filled rolls and sandwiches for the day. Fillings had to be organised the day before, so that I would have boiled eggs, grated carrot, and so on, available. The cut rolls and the bottom slices of the sandwiches would be spread out on a bench, from there to receive a dollop of each filling in turn. I found this quite fiddly, but I would have enjoyed the task all right if the Manager had not continually tried to hurry me up. She thought that the job could be done more quickly than I was doing it. Accordingly, I did try to do it more quickly, but I was never as quick as the manager would like. She regularly baked scones in the morning, giving me a warm one for my morning tea (scones are one of my big pleasures in life).

Washing the dishes and making the toast at the same time was not the best combination for me. Having wet hands from the dishes, I would have to dry them before handling the bread. There was a big industrial toaster, which initiated me with a long, painful burn on my inner arm. There was also a deep frying vat for making chips, on which we all liked to nibble when there were any leftovers.

The most mystifying task I was called upon to do was "tidying the cabbages." On the storeroom shelves sat rows of cabbages, next to a pile of carrots and the occasional pumpkin. A cabbage is a living thing, like a cat, a palm tree, or an ostrich. One does not talk of – at least, not in my circle – of tidying cats, trees or ostriches – or cabbages. Living things just *are* – their appearance is an *is*-ness, a fact of existence. To put it another way: they are not untidy to begin with, so how can I tidy them? The concept of tidying them (or of tidying anything else, for that matter) is alien to me. Therefore, the requirement to do so struck anxiety into me. How would a tidy cabbage look? I had been sent into the storeroom to do it, so I knew that I had to somehow do something. I pulled the outermost leaf off each one, in case this would help. It did not improve the situation as far as I was concerned. Almost panicking, I fetched a cloth and wiped the shelf underneath each cabbage. I then changed their positions ever so slightly, but without seeing any rhyme or reason to this. I had now done all that was conceivably possible, but did not know whether the manager would agree. She came in to inspect. To my relief (but also my incomprehension), she now pronounced the cabbages beautifully tidy – "Well done!" – As I said earlier, aren't people funny?

The bus drivers, our customers – or, if not them, my work-mates – were near-continually calling out for plates, cups, saucers, knives, forks, tea-spoons, sugar, salt, and I was the one having to keep up with all requests, including, as described, the dishwashing, plate-collecting, toast-making and a number of other tasks. The fact that people were calling out for things meant that I was allowing the supply to run out, even though I was doing my best to fulfil my job requirements. I simply could not cope with a job which was multi-tasking in the extreme. I persevered because I thought that I would learn to master, if I stuck at it, handling a number of things at once. I had no way of knowing otherwise, at that time. What I found out, instead, was that trying my hardest, for twelve months, did not result in my learning how to multi-task – it merely resulted in high stress levels. It was not the fault of my Wiri depot colleagues, as they were all friendly and kind towards me. When a year was up, I accepted that this type of work was not suitable for me, and did not use any of my skill areas – in fact, it only high-lighted my areas of deficit. Wherever my place of achievement in life would be, it would not be here, in a cafeteria – and I left after my one year.

My next employment was at the Royal New Zealand Foundation for the Blind, in Parnell, Auckland. My position was that of Mailroom Assistant; or, one could equally well call it "Library Assistant," as I was working in the mailroom of the Talking Book and Braille Library. I happily answer to either designation, as the workings of the postal system are an area in which I am always very concerned. At first, I could scarcely make head nor tail of the work routine I was expected to carry out; however, the others, including the senior staff, did not seem to notice anything untoward. There was another new recruit learning the job, and, apparently, she found it even more difficult to comprehend than I did, leaving after a few weeks. That sort of made me the more "successful" of the two, which perhaps boosted my confidence. Another work-mate asked me whether I liked the job, but I was unable to decide this until I knew the work better. After two or three months, I understood the work sufficiently to settle into the position. It was physically demanding work, though: walking up and down the talking book (cassette) aisles most of the day, and, when I was not walking, I was running. This was in order to pick out talking books for our visually impaired mail-order clients, all over New Zealand. Another part of the day was devoted to shelving the returned talking books, so that was, again, walking or running up and down the aisles. The last part of the day was when we were packing the talking books into their specially padded posting containers. This was a companionable time, as we – four or five staff members – would all be standing close enough together to be able to converse. Sometimes, we would democratically select a talking book, put it into a player, and play ourselves a story whilst we did the packing.

There was an extended glitch when our manual system gave way to a new computerised system – and I had to learn parts of my job all over again. As this was my first encounter with computers, it took me quite a few sessions with the trainer even to begin to understand the basics of the system. Before grasping it, I felt very disoriented in my work, and, unable to foresee that it would all come right in the end, I thought more than once of leaving. Even the Deputy Manager of the RNZFB Library Services must have sometimes felt this way, as she played a big part in designing the computer programmes. Because our work was a one-off specialised service in New Zealand, there were no other examples for her to follow, so the programmes had to be tested on the factory floor – which is the time when they would decide whether or not they would work properly.

On finally mastering the computer system – and when the number of "hiccups" in the system reduced to a workable level – our work became much more streamlined than before. I gradually became one of the more experienced staff members, and was given extra "screens" on the computer which I was allowed to access. This allowed me to do troubleshooting for the few clients who were experiencing less than adequate service. In turn, this meant that I felt, and became, increasingly competent at my work. In fact, one night, at home, I wrote a report on "Progress So Far" regarding a particular computer behaviour, and put it in the Deputy Manager's in-tray. Next day, Kerrin was delighted, and made arrangements for me to be promoted to the office staff; I duly became a sort of secretary for her. With this change, I was told that a change of attire would be in order, and it would be nice if I would wear a skirt sometimes. Looking in clothes shops is one of my biggest botherations, so I picked out one green skirt, almost with my eyes shut, and wore that three times a week. Sometimes I would feel muddled and confused in this new job; and there was definitely much more multi-tasking than in the mailroom – in the mailroom, tasks were done one after the other, not all at once. Gradually, I went downhill in this new situation. One day, I could no longer think at all, and put all my papers, which I no longer knew what to do with, in Kerrin's in-tray. On seeing this, she looked at me as if to figure out what was going on – and guessed correctly. "Do you want to go back to the mailroom?" she asked. I nodded, as I was almost in tears. Again, I was lucky, as someone was leaving the mailroom staff, and in two weeks I was re-instated there.

Back to doing one thing at a time, I felt at home in my work environment. I was helping to provide a much-needed service; I had the satisfaction of belonging to a small, dedicated team; my work was routine and repetitive enough to provide calmness instead of anxiety; and, I could keep up with the play as regards the latest books, because the recording of these was done on the premises. Many of the staff were keen readers, and we had our own lending library. My working life chugged along relatively well in this milieu – although, during my eight years there, I was going through a lot of dramas and stresses in my social, home, and romantic spheres. This was an extended period of address changes, life changes, and even sexual orientation changes, as I struggled to find my place in the world. Looking back on it, I think this job must have helped me to keep functioning on at least one level, and was therefore very beneficial.

I was very sad when Kerrin, the Deputy Manager, told us all that she was leaving, in order to pursue training in a new career. She had been a dynamic, enthusiastic, and wonderfully people-friendly person to work for. I wrote my own speech of thanks and appreciation for her, and asked the manager for permission to read it out at the farewell party. Our manager, Maddison, gave her approval, although I kept the contents of my speech a well-guarded secret. When the time came, all the staff of the other RNZFB departments were also present, as Kerrin had been a well-loved person as well as a high-ranking staff member. During the eating, drinking and merriment, Maddison announced that I would now give my speech. Leaning on one of the columns for support, as I was very nervous – and, at this stage, very unaccustomed to public speaking – I began.

I had taken all of my phrases and sentences from our Talking Book titles, which were well-known titles to most assembled here. As is one of my quirkier talents, I linked the book titles up in such a way as to construct a true account of Kerrin's life amongst us, from beginning to end. People's faces changed from seriousness to cheerfulness, and, soon, some were bent double, laughing hysterically. I had not been able to anticipate how my speech would be received, but, by the end, there was no doubt. Kerrin's colleagues – and Kerrin herself – thought that my contribution had been marvellous. Maddison told me that I had "done well," Kerrin came and gave me a hug and a kiss, and, for days afterwards, various colleagues were asking me for copies of this "brilliant" creation.

As I write in Chapter 19 "Going to University and Three Important Friends," at the end of eight years in this job, I made the huge step, for me, of resigning in order to pursue full-time study. There was another factor involved in my decision to leave, however: the insidious beginning of Repetitive Strain Injury (Occupational Overuse Syndrome.) My love of repetition had finally been my undoing. When I found out what the problem was, I knew that I would not be able to stay in the mailroom, because certain repetitive tasks were a fact of life there. I felt sure that one particular task had caused the condition, because I could feel the arm muscles straining whenever I performed a certain movement; and I did not play sports, or engage in any other risk activities. I tried having two weeks off on sick leave, but this was insufficient to treat the problem. I was afraid of losing the use of my arm if I kept doing the same duties. An idea occurred to me: if I were to receive ACC (Accident Compensation Corporation) payments, then I could leave my job, which would stop my arm being further damaged, and would stop me being a liability to my employers; from there, I could plan a new future. I remembered our Manager, Maddison, once speaking to us about workplace injuries – saying that if this happened to one of us, not only would this be terrible, but she would also be in trouble with ACC. This was spoken about long before my own problem occurred, and, at the time (before Occupational Overuse Syndrome became commonplace), I thought that she was referring to sudden, violent injury only, such as a slipped vertebra. Therefore, years later, when my own case came up, I did not make that connection with "injury." I daresay that it was naive of me to think that the gradual loss of strength in my arm was not in the same category for ACC purposes, and that, therefore, no one would be "in trouble with ACC" if I applied for compensation. In fact, I thought that I was doing my workplace a favour, by finding an alternative income and thereby removing my employers' responsibilities towards me. I now understand that this was erroneous, muddled thinking, but, unfortunately, it was what I actually thought at the time.

I was soon catapulted into a space in which I did not want to be. As soon as I had applied to ACC about my arm, this meant that I was locked into a process. Work and Income New Zealand officers told me, as far as I could understand, that I was not eligible for a benefit unless ACC declined my application. Therefore, I then had to follow through with the ACC application. This took months, and, to my horror, turned into a battle between ACC and my employers, with me stuck somewhere in the middle. This was the last thing I wanted: I had always been a good, responsible, hard-working, loyal employee for the RNZFB – I had felt like "the golden-haired girl" – and now, because of my mistake in contacting ACC, I had made myself into a villain. This pained me very much, and still does. I had always respected, and been fond of, the managerial staff there (and still feel the same way), so causing trouble for them was the last thing I wanted or intended.

The ACC weekly payments eventually began, but I was far from happy about what it had taken to achieve this. I did not want to remain on compensation any longer than I had to, in any case. So I checked out what I had to know about going to university: whether I would be eligible for a student allowance and a note-taker. With the answers to both questions being "Yes," I was able to move into my new life when the first term started, three months later.

Chapter 18

Feathers with Everything! Part III

After we left the farm, I had to use ingenuity to get my "Feather Fix." Against her natural inclinations, Mum allowed me to install my wire pen on her lawn, containing a few bantams. And Lindsay didn't mind me having a large pet duck, until its behaviour became too difficult. After that, when I started living in other people's houses, I had to do without having poultry – even though these houses were surrounded by huge yards, perfectly suitable for a few hens or geese. Every time I see a spare piece of ground or an alley-way between buildings, I automatically size it up for the number of hens it would house. I fantasised about having a hen-house on the lawn of my workplace, but never got the necessary permission.

Eventually living in my own place again, in a small Mt. Eden unit, right underneath the mountain, I got the craving again. In hindsight, it was probably due to the shock of failing at relationships again, being on my own again, and wanting the comfort of my special interest – which included the tenderness of looking after living creatures. My big wire pen – constructed by Mum many years ago, which she has perhaps lived to regret – was parked on the concrete outside my back door, taking up all of my "back yard." I began with my specialist breed of Indian Game Bantams, which I had encountered in books and in poultry shows: a rare breed in New Zealand, they are stocky and the females have beautiful speckled plumage. At this stage, I had only a hen, so my breeding plans were thwarted. One evening, my little hen stood on top of the kitchen stove (which was turned off at the time) and cackled and squawked as loudly as she could. I wondered if the people upstairs could hear her, but no one complained.

Having a hen without a rooster, what happened next was inevitable: one day, I decided to shift house to somewhere with a lawn. When this was finally achieved (thanks to Mum and Eric again), I had a sizeable front yard, with a high fence. The most important thing, a chook-house, had to come next, so I hired a handyman. I then installed the three hens, and one rooster, of the Indian Game Bantam breed.

Living in town with a pet rooster has its complications. The main one is that you have to catch him every night, and put him somewhere (relatively) sound-proof, for when he starts his early morning crowing. In town, the only place where his 5 a.m. dawn chorus doesn't bother anyone is in my dining room. Actually, the bathroom is satisfactory, as well, but I've now got used to the set-up in the dining room. Because people do ask this, I will add that the rooster is in a *box* in the dining room – this is one place where "free range" doesn't apply. And it can be plural. That means more than one box, as game-cocks will fight to the death. (No, I don't give them the chance.) All of this means that I cannot stay at a friend's place for the night – unless I have caught the rooster(s) first. Next day, as with all pets, I will have to return home to feed and look after them, and to let the rooster(s) out. I guess all of this for the last ten years would qualify as an obsession.

The Indian Game Bantams bred prolifically for the first three years, and I had to sell a lot of them, hoping that their new homes would be kind. Some people bought them for breeding, as the Indian Game genes are the best for breeding heavy meat birds. The usual colour for the female is dark brown with chestnut brown speckles; up close, the speckles are intricate double lacing. The male of this variety is black. I knew, however, that there was a reverse colour variety of white background with brown lacing; but this is even rarer in New Zealand, and my enquiry to the one breeder I knew of resulted in no reply. Then, by chance, a farming couple near Waiuku offered me a white rooster, which, I could see, was the white variety of Indian Game – properly called Jubilee Indian Game. From this rooster, mated to a dark hen, I bred a batch of chicks, some of which were white, and which established me as a breeder of both colours.

One morning, I had an electrician in the house, and I still had a young Jubilee Indian Game cockerel in its box in the dining room. I proudly announced that I had a very rare variety of game-cock which I was going to show him, and went to catch it. Probably because I was talking instead of concentrating on what I was doing, I botched the job and the cockerel escaped into the house. He led me a merry chase through all of the downstairs rooms, making a few deposits on the carpet on the way, until jumping into a large bucket of herbal tea which was brewing in one corner. (The tea and the brewing were of the cold variety, by the way.) I know I've called it "Feathers with Everything," but even I couldn't face feathers in my *tea*, so it had to be thrown out.

Chapter 19

Going to University, and Three Important Friends

In my thirties, seven years into my mailroom assistant position at the Royal New Zealand Foundation for the Blind, I got the idea of going to university. Many of my work-mates were already part-time students, and then another had his work hours shortened so that he, too, could begin a degree. Our supervisor at the time was an understanding sort who was happy to rearrange one's hours to suit. I asked him, "If Bert can do that, may I do it too?"

I had my work hours reduced accordingly, to 25 hours per week, which, on the good pay rate of $12-something per hour, I could still live on. Not knowing the university enrolment procedure, I had missed the date for pre-enrolment, so I had to pay a penalty fee. I arranged to have the day off work for the actual enrolment. Arriving on the prescribed day, I found myself sent to the "Unsatisfactory Progress" room – due to a paper I had started 20 years ago, and not finished! This was a nasty shock, as now I did not know whether I would be accepted at all. When an official came to see me about it, it turned out all right, as, at that stage, I wanted to enrol for part-time study only, and that was still allowed with an "Unsatisfactory Progress" stamp on my record. Then began the process of standing in hours-long queues for the signatures from each department and the Dean of the Faculty. Several individuals made the most of this by walking up and down the queues, selling cut lunches from their baskets! This was a very wearying and frustrating day; I could hardly believe that what seemed such a straightforward task could be made into something so time-consuming.

In my initial enthusiasm, I had enrolled for two Russian language papers (all language departments seem to require that two papers be taken concurrently) and an English Literature paper: 19th Century English Literature. I had already learnt the Russian alphabet and a few words and phrases out of interest, so I had reason to believe that the subject would suit me. At that time, there was no Students' Enquiries Office where I could find out what to do, and no one else in my family had been to university, so I had to muddle along as best I could. I had not understood the information given in the university calendar regarding class and tutorial times, so it turned out that I had got this wrong, and that some of the class times did not, in fact, work in with my rearranged work hours. I had managed to find my way to at least some of the Russian language classes, and found that I did, as anticipated, love the subject. However, I was now faced with the heartbreaking fact that I would not be able to attend all of the classes and tutorials, which would jeopardise my progress too severely; I would have to withdraw from Russian. On top of that, I faced the horror of having to go through all the bureaucratic processes again, in order to *un*-enrol from Russian. I could foresee that this would take just as long as to enrol, and I did not like to ask my supervisor for another day off so soon. Just the thought of those queues and that stress of the first time around – with no one to whom I could turn for guidance – set off another anxiety state. So it was that I ended up in the waiting area of the psychiatric clinic at Auckland Hospital, feeling stressed, confused, overwhelmed, and unable to think what to do. A staff member came along and asked me what I was doing there, but he was unable to understand the nature of my difficulties.

After that nightmare was over, I could at least enjoy my remaining English Literature paper; in fact, I was enthralled with it. After hearing the first lecture on our first set book, *Emma*, I almost burst into applause – then noticed that nobody else was doing so, therefore it must not be the standard practice. I had not entered the realm of literary analysis before, and found it fascinating. This helped me to appreciate fiction more than I had previously, although certain types of fiction, e.g. 19th century literature, are (to this day) easier for me to understand than certain other types.

During the Easter break, I struggled with the coursework essay for the English Literature paper; as it was my first tertiary-level essay, I did not really understand what was required. I handed in my attempt anyway, and received a pass mark, though not a high grade. Just passing was a good feeling, at this early stage. I continued to love the lectures and tutorials. When the end-of-year exam time came around, though, my anxiety skyrocketed. As well as the actual exam, I had to work out where and when to go to read the exam-room allocation list, and then exactly where the correct exam room was, all at short notice before sitting down to write my answers. The university procedure was this way for the purpose of preventing students from stowing exam answers in the room beforehand; but it meant a lot of extra stress for me, because I could not find and familiarise myself with the room, and the route to it, beforehand. Throughout my life I have needed quietly to learn such things as new routes and new places well before the required time, in order to avoid high anxiety on the day; but this strategy was denied me by the university system. The fear had got to the point where even the suicidal thoughts were coming back. The Student Health Service was free, and I ended up there, getting a prescription for tranquillisers. I very nearly did not make it into the exam room at all – except for the fact that I took a tranquilliser at the right time, which meant that I could walk into the room. On being given the signal to start reading the exam paper, my mind was still so numb with fear that I could not work out how to answer the questions until late in the allocated time. This brain-freeze was not caused mainly by the pills but by fear – I know this because, in years to come, when I was no longer taking tranquillisers for exams, my brain was still too paralysed to think until at least half-way through the exam – which meant, of course, that I could not produce the result of which my intelligence was capable. For this, my first university exam, I received a low pass mark of C+ ; but I was pleased with any pass mark, the first time around.

A situation which was the bane of my university experience also illustrates something which happens in all aspects of my life, so I will now explain this further. Once I grasped what was required for university coursework essays, I excelled at them, earning A and A+ grades for all of my German Literature essays, and only A+ grades for those in Comparative Literature, right throughout my degree. As most other students know,

A and A+ grades are not handed out lightly at university level; some students never get to see an A grade. The magic ingredient, for me, was that coursework essays allowed me months in which to write them. This meant that I could think about the essay topic, research it, and write it over a long period, perfecting it as I went. The total opposite was, and is, the case for the exam essays! One has, for example, two hours in which to write two separate essays, or three hours for three essays. This puts a completely different time-frame, and a large dollop of urgency, on to the task. As well as that, as I have explained, was the stress I experienced in finding the exam-room allocation list, then the right room, immediately before the exam started. This could, and sometimes did, mean that I was already very nervous by the time I had found the room. And added to all that was the difficulty of having to switch my brain, suddenly and completely, from writing essay number one to writing essay number two (and, maybe, essay number three) – all within a short time . In other words, I was not allowed to keep concentrating on the topic in hand, but, just when I was getting deeply into the topic, I would be forced to switch to a new one – otherwise, of course, one would have completed only a proportion of the exam questions, and would fail the exam as a result. The factors which are noteworthy in the exam context – familiarisation with the environment beforehand, performance anxiety, difficulty with sudden new requirements, transition, and switching one's concentration to a new stimulus – are amongst the factors which have been significant for me in all areas throughout my life, and still are. This situation caused such a wide split in my coursework performance versus my exam performance that at least one teacher had difficulty understanding what was going on. This was particularly true for the higher stages of my university work. This also caused great frustration and anguish for me, when I had a coursework grade of A+ and was top of the class, only to then fall several grades in my final assessment because of my inability to cope with the exam requirements. The same can be said for any environment, including the workplace, in which my work on a continuous project might well be excellent, but when I am quickly changed from one task to another in an atmosphere of urgency, I may not be able to function at all. I have tried to improve in this area, but have been unable to overcome this difficulty. To add yet more to this issue: people who know that I am highly intelligent in some areas can have great difficulty in understanding that I am deficient in other areas. The split between my areas of high ability and low ability is so marked that some people assume that I am not trying; this then adds a layer of emotional upset to the situation, which, of course, makes it even more difficult for me to succeed at the task in hand. (For my guidelines on how to write university coursework essays, see my chapter near the end of the book: "Helpful Hints.")

Because of the above factors – and the ever-increasing feeling that I needed assistance with basic life issues – I was looking around for someone who could act as a guide and support person. That is, I was merely trying to think, at this stage, how such a miracle could come about. Although I loved learning, I had hoped to also meet like-minded people; but I had discovered that students rushed in and out of class, without forming any sort of friendly relationships. Of course, most of them probably had their own friends, with whom they had come to university; and I, now in my late thirties, was in a different age bracket to most. Perceiving that I was still on the outer of the world of people – and that I was having problems which other people did not seem to be having, such as near-constant anxiety over everyday incidents (especially changes) – I knew that there was something which was "not right" in the way I was functioning. I also suspected that I was capable of far better academic achievement than that which I was experiencing, because "something" was interfering with my mental processes. I thought that there must be someone who could help me, through a supportive role, to keep my equilibrium better than I was currently doing. It was a tricky question, because I realised that the vast majority of people already have full lives, and I did not want to be merely a nuisance; any person who became my "guide" would have to choose this role willingly, and there seemed little chance of this happening. So, how was I even to begin to ask for such a person? There was no such service available, that I knew of, and the now familiar word, "mentor," had not yet become a well-known concept in New Zealand society; this would only happen years later. Therefore, I was (to continue a theme which has run through my life) a forerunner in a new field when I advertised in the *Trade & Exchange* paper for a mentor. As this term was not yet in common currency, I could allow myself only low hopes for any positive result.

I did receive several responses, to which I replied. One man, who defined the word mentor as "friend," spent several hours talking to me, mainly on the subject of how he did not like living in Huntly. He did not seem to have any skills in the areas of life guidance or academic study, however, which were the kind of attributes I wanted; this acquaintanceship quickly faded away. Of the other two responses, one shone out above the rest: a man in his fifties, single, with a science degree, who had spiritual leanings, and who would like to give something back to the universe in the form of a couple of hours a fortnight with a person who needed guidance. This seemed ideal, and, after meeting each other, we both felt willing to embark on a "mentor–protégée" relationship.

This felt like the answer to all my prayers. On my first visit to Timothy's house, we had a lunch of tuna salad, then strolled along the pretty Carrington Walkway, along the path through the trees to the stream. Timothy knew the names of some of the spiders which I did not, and I knew a few plant names which he did not, and this formed another mutual interest. In his house was a corner with stones and decorations intended to inspire one's spiritual thoughts. Hugs and friendly touches were a welcome part of the relationship for me. Timothy seemed to be as charmed by me as I was by him.

On my second visit to Timothy's, we talked about our shared love of nature, and Timothy gradually introduced me to the New Age teachings, with leanings towards Buddhism more than towards Christianity. Sitting close and sharing friendly touches seemed normal and natural for the situation. After some time, Timothy posed a question which I did not expect: "Do you realise that if I moved my hand slightly, it would change the relationship to a sexual one?"

Oh – I had not thought of this. It was also an unwelcome turn of events for me. When I found the words to speak, I told him that I did not want to lose the mentor–protégée relationship, which, as far as I could understand, would happen if we became lovers. He said that he would think about the pros and cons of this question before our next meeting.

At our next meeting, Timothy said that he had deliberated over this, as well as consulting one of his own friends and advisors on the matter, and their collective conclusion was that "high sex," that is, a spiritually endowed sexual relationship, would be in keeping with the mentor–protégée roles which we already had, and which we would keep intact. By now, I loved and needed Timothy, and he was, after all, "older and wiser," a mentor, so he must have known what he was talking about, I believed.

Thus began a routine of my staying overnight at his house, and far oftener than once a fortnight. I enjoyed this new level of intimacy, for we were still continuing in our original roles as well: going for walks, playing scrabble, talking, and Timothy imparting the rudiments of his spiritual side to me. Now that I was a welcome visitor into his bedroom, I could see the special shrine he had permanently set up there for his meditations. He was also a regular t'ai chi practitioner, and showed me some of the moves. I discovered a book of Yeats's poems in his house, which I began to read avidly, though admitting to Timothy that I had very little idea, if any, of what they meant.

Two weeks into this new schedule, Timothy told me that he would have house guests for a while, so we would have to fit our relationship around that. I did not meet the house guests, nor did I expect to. It was now time to pre-enrol and enrol for my next university paper, if I was going to continue studying. Having been caught up, the previous year, by the euphoria of university life, I chose a paper in Linguistics. Again I had to wait in long queues in the hot sun, but this time around I had more idea of what to expect.

The next time Timothy and I met, there was a change: our sexual relationship was henceforth ended, he told me. He had found someone else: one of his house guests. I had grown to love and need this expression of love, so I was emotionally torn up. In shock, I wondered if the mentor–protégée relationship was also ended – but Timothy assured me that that part would still go on. How I could go on with it, however, what with the drastic change which had happened between us, I could not yet imagine. Timothy and the house guest – her name was Anna – were already engaged, he continued, showing me the photos of her and of the beautiful landscape in which he had proposed. As she was from overseas – Germany – she had had to go back there, and was there now. Timothy had an air ticket to go and stay with her in Germany, and would be leaving soon – for five weeks.

Horror upon horror! This was a triad of unexpected, and unwanted, major changes to my life: my love-life was ended (and not by my choice); Timothy had a new lover, and was marrying her; and, he was about to leave me for five weeks, which felt like a plunge back into icy aloneness. I felt devastated, frightened, and… in a day or so, when the news had had more time to sink in, angry. The anger was over the feeling that Timothy had just "used" me sexually, in order to get a temporary bit of fun for himself, without considering how I would feel when he chose to end it. It had been his idea to bring sex into our relationship in the first place, assuring me that it would be all right to do so.

I wrote down how I felt about this, as I was too upset emotionally to be able to speak my thoughts coherently. I then showed Timothy what I had written, adding that I would like him to know my feelings now, after which I would mention this no more. After discussing the issue and apologising to me, Timothy thought that a good way to end this would be to burn the piece of paper, so we did this over the top of the Carrington waterfall. It might have ended the incident for him, but some of the pain continued inside me.

It was now time for me to start my Linguistics paper at university. I already had a basic grasp of grammar, due to my earlier study of German. Other components of the course were not so easy for me, however: even though I consulted several people for extra help, I never felt that I fully understood the "tree diagrams" that represented the structure of sentences. One morning, on my way to class, I knew it was Timothy's hour for departure to Germany, and I felt deep sadness and anxiety. I had been given an assignment to do, and I wished that Timothy could at least look at it with me, as a supportive gesture. "How could I now survive five weeks without him?" I wondered. My body and mind went into a state which I call "low-grade survival" – something not much above hibernation.

Although anxious about whether I would be able to understand all the material, the rest of it was easy. In one section of the course, we were told to bring a small mirror to class: for gazing into our own mouths and throats! It still seems incredible to me that the vast majority of humans make all these noises, in complicated combinations – what we call "talking" – yet we do not know how we make them. What the tongue, the hard and soft palates, the teeth and lips get up to during this process is largely a mystery, without the use of a mirror. The section called "Morphology" was possibly my favourite: the study of word structure, for example how the word "look" can be extended to "looking," "looks" and "looked" through the addition of meaningful components.

Timothy's return finally took place, and, soon after, a visitor arrived from Germany! I was invited to come and meet Anna. This was another anxious moment, for how would we get on? If she did not like me, I could be banned from seeing Timothy ever again, I feared. Tall, blonde, and Nordic-looking was my first impression. Anna immediately revealed herself as a person of great friendliness and warmth. About ten minutes after first meeting her, I was totally won over. Now the situation had redeemed itself, for I had two friends instead of just one! The weekly outings were resumed, but now we were three. We shared idyllic trips to the beach, the bush, cafés…and I tentatively began trying out a little German language again.

In the middle of all this, I was invited to a group lunch by my old mates in the Access Radio team, and their friends. As I still had my job at this stage, I could afford to eat out sometimes. This was the third lunch that I had had with this group, at a frequency of once a year, at the restaurant on One Tree Hill. It was always a sumptuous affair, and we lingered as long as possible, through several courses and then on to coffee and nibbles. When I finally returned home that day – 8 August 1993 – Mum rang me up, to tell me that Eric, her second husband, my stepfather – had died.

Eric had been perfectly well that morning. Mum and he often went for walks together, but, on this occasion, Eric went for a walk by himself while Mum cooked dinner. Ordinarily, I would also have been at this dinner, but I had already excused myself because I was going to the group lunch, which I knew would extend well into the afternoon. When the other dinner guests – my brother and Aunty – arrived for dinner but there was still no Eric, there was cause for alarm. Fortunately, it was known that he was heading for Red Hill, a steep but picturesque climb which was a favourite walk of Mum and Eric's. By the time my brother and Mum arrived there, it was a matter for the police. Several police cars were there, and white lines had been painted to mark the position of Eric's body on the road. His identity had not been known until family members arrived. It seems that he had collapsed while walking down from the top of Red Hill.

Of Eric's own four adult children, one daughter had to fly back from Australia. The funeral was, therefore, set for 12 August – my birthday. It was a beautiful, non-religious service, with many old friends contributing interesting and funny reminiscences. My eyes and nose streaming, I also had a problem further down: a big scream, a huge animal howl, was fighting a life-and-death struggle to get itself out of my mouth. I know that this scream was not for Eric alone: much more, it was for my own real father, when, again, it had been kept inside me. It took me all of my strength, right throughout the ceremony, to keep this inside. It is a pity that such things have to kept in, "for appearances' sake," when I know only too well that they are better to be *out*. (This would be proven rather startlingly in the not too distant future.) Finally in the open air again, I could not stop crying (though this was not the same thing as the socially unacceptable howl). Relatives and friends of the family exchanged words with one another, and I made brief contact with a man named John. It was the kind of birthday which I hope I never have to repeat.

I was doing quite well at Linguistics, and had written out all of the material into study notes, a condensed version of the lecture notes, which I was learning in preparation for the exam. One Saturday, I had the morphology section of my study notes in my bag (all the better to revise one's material at all times), and left my bag on my car seat whilst I visited Timothy and Anna. The car was locked, but, on my return, a back window was smashed, and my bag was taken. There had not been much money in it, but my cheque book, money-machine card, driver's licence, bus concession ticket, and so on, were gone. This was traumatic enough, but it was not until a day or two later that I realised my study notes had also been in my bag – instant panic! With only two weeks left before the exam, I was now thrown back into the high anxiety which my study-notes strategy had attempted to avoid. At first paralysed by fear, I realised in time that I would simply have to rewrite my notes, that is, condense them from the lecture material, all over again. Only then could I feel satisfied that I had prepared myself as best I could. Although still needing a tranquilliser to get myself into the exam room, my extra rewriting must have paid off: I ended up with the final grade of an A.

The exam safely out of the way, I now did something much more daring than usual: I phoned a man I scarcely knew – John – leaving messages on his answer-phone until I got a response. When we did make contact, I invited him to my place for dinner. I made bacon and egg pie, a favourite dish of Lindsay's, which meant it was one of the few meals I knew how to cook. Later, I asked if we could go for a walk together, taking the opportunity to hold his hand. Finally locating my own source of power, I had also concluded that nothing happens unless one *makes* it happen, so I was determined at least to *try* to make something happen! I could hardly believe my own ears when I heard myself suggesting much more than holding hands. I was afraid that, unless I said what I wanted, the chance would be gone forever. I still think that this is true, at least a lot of the time. For most of my life I had hung back and waited for the right thing to happen – because I did not know how to make anything happen, and could not locate my own power. Now that (I thought) I knew what to do, I was going to make up for lost time!

My audacious suggestion of spending the night together probably took John by surprise; at any rate, he did not indulge my whim there and then. Nor did he end the acquaintance, so that was a good start. We were, and are, poles apart in many of our personality traits, so it felt amazing, to me, that we lasted for more than one date.

John was a self-employed house-trucker, doing the rounds of the gypsy fairs with his wooden crafts. His wooden bowls, vases, decorative boxes, and kauri coffee tables (from recycled kauri) were stunningly beautiful and creative, but my favourite pieces for everyday use were the little weed vases, every one unique. He also manufactured a range of wood waxes and massage waxes.

Our first excursion in the truck together was to Piha Beach, where we stayed for the weekend. Before university started again for the following year, we had another trip, this time to the Colville Music Festival and Craft Fair. Dozens of craftspeople were displaying their wares on tables and shelves. In order to go away for the weekend, I had to make arrangements for my pets: the hens, chicks, and rooster. I could shut up the hens and chicks in their sheds, with a supply of food and water, for two days. The rooster, however, either would have to be shut inside my house for the whole time, (because of the early morning crowing he would otherwise do outside) or, at that time, I could farm him out at a friend's farm. Seemingly unable to leave all traces of my poultry behind, I had brought two dozen Indian Game Bantam eggs, in case I could sell them as fertile eggs for hatching.

At the Colville Festival, in January 1994, it was very hot and the countryside was brown. One afternoon, wanting a change, I said to John that I would go for a walk; he had to stay behind and look after his sales stand. After walking along the road for a short distance, I found a little track which stayed within the shade of a stand of native trees. It was pleasantly peaceful to be alone, away from the crowds, the music, and the heat. As is my habit when I have the chance, I closely observed the different kinds of plants and insects on my way. One kind of plant which I hadn't seen very often was a prickly pear tree – a cactus bearing round fruits. I had read that some Native American peoples used these for food, so I sampled one. At that moment, I learned that the fruits – like every other part of the prickly pear tree – are covered with exceedingly fine hairs, but these hairs serve as sharp prickles, which get stuck in one's skin. I could not get them all out, so I continued my meander, discovering a beach and a rare bird sanctuary during my travels.

On my return to the festival and the craft stalls, I asked John whether he could see any prickly pear prickles stuck in my face. In order to get a good look, he instructed me to lie on the bed. It was quite a long job, as he kept finding more of the very fine prickles – even in my tongue! Having this operation lovingly done on oneself felt very caring and special. John apparently thought so too, for, at the end, he said "I love you!" This was the first time either of us had uttered these words to each other.

It was customary, on the last night of a craft fair, for everyone to have a shared dinner. That is, if one could find anything left in one's pantry which was fit to share. As half-eaten boxes of muesli would not do, the only suitable thing left in our truck was a dozen Indian Game Bantam eggs. Reluctantly, I boiled the water. When it had been boiling a while, and I seemed to be doing everything else but cooking the eggs, John said, "Well, put them in!" It could not be put off any longer, so in they went.

"There's another dozen Indian Game babies who will never be born!" I wailed.

"Oh, so that's the problem!" John replied. "You could have told me that before."

I was still working part-time at the Royal NZ Foundation for the Blind, which I mostly enjoyed. The combination of working and studying – and now, dating – was, for me, the best of all worlds. For my third year at university, I made a welcome discovery: one could get, if one was lucky, permission from a language department to take only one paper at a time, even though the university calendar stated that two papers were required. At any rate, the Germanic Languages Department allowed me to take one Stage I paper that year: that meant that I could fit this in with my part-time job, whereas two papers would not have fitted into my work schedule. I therefore enrolled for Stage I German Language, leaving the German literature paper aside for the moment. Now I had a big catch-up job to do: Stage I was not the lowest stage; Beginners' German was the entry stage, and Stage I assumed that the student already had a certain command of German. Yes, I had been good at German at school, but that was 25 years before! – and I had hardly practised it since then, except in my recent friendship with Anna. I knew that I would have to catch up in a hurry, but I preferred that to the "humiliation" of doing Beginners' German, when I felt that I should be beyond that point!

Accordingly, before classes started, I began brushing up my German from a book called *German Made Simple*. German may be, and is, many things, but none of them is "simple." It was just as well that I made these preparations, because Stage I German – and all of the following stages – were based very strongly on correct grammar. It was a comfort that I now had Anna to refer to, though her study background was in science rather than in the finer points of grammar (and I was to learn that university departments are stricter on these points than are the native speakers themselves!) In contrast to my school classes, speaking the language seemed to take a lower priority. To be fair to the department, I think the assumption was that students had spent time in Germany and were therefore fluent speakers. That was even more the case by the time one entered Stage II.

I enjoyed the fact that I was learning German again, although I was nervous in the classroom, feeling daunted by the apparently greater speaking ability of my classmates. On the occasions when the teacher asked me a question, my brain would often "freeze." Near the beginning of the course, the teacher handed out a long list of verbs – all of which, conjugated in their present and past tenses, had to be learned for a test less than a week away. This seemed more than I could manage at this juncture, and, voice a-quiver, I told the teacher so, after class. If I remember rightly, I was advised to just do my best. I did not fully master all of the verbs in time, but, at least my progress was better than nothing. Although, at this point in time, I was probably nearer the bottom of the class than the top, I had already decided to major in German! (You've got to admire my doggedness – maybe it was stubbornness – which made me stick to German through thick and thin, even though I actually found my other university subjects easier.) Another factor in its favour was that I now had Anna as a German-speaking helper. The Germanic Languages Department (who also taught Swedish and Dutch) did not give out marks leniently – so it was a proud achievement that I ended up with a final grade of B+.

During this year – 1994 – I was doing some German homework when I was startled by my hand suddenly skidding across the page, making a trail of ink where I didn't want it. This was the first sign of hand and arm weakness, which was to reach up to my right shoulder, creating problems for both work and study. I was gradually losing the use of my dominant arm and hand, which caused me increasing anxiety. After several trips to doctors, it was confirmed as Repetitive Strain Injury, nowadays called Occupational Overuse Syndrome. I felt sure that it was caused by my repetitive work, and by one task in particular, at my job. In this task, I could feel the muscles and tendons in my arm pulling each time I repeated the movement, i.e. every few seconds. I have never played any sports, and nor was there any other reason I could see for the problem. I now had to decide what to do: if I stayed in the job, the injury would probably worsen, and then I would lose all use of my arm, perhaps forever. This did not seem like a sensible decision; in fact, it scared me. I had already been toying with the idea of taking on full-time study at university the following year, and leaving my job, as I would be eligible for an adult student allowance. However, now there was another issue: how would I be able to write? – for the arm weakness was adversely affecting my ability to hold and use a pen.

Somebody must have told me that there were staff members called "Disability Co-ordinators" at the University of Auckland, and that they could help with this problem, because I somehow found this out and contacted them. Yes, not only could they help, but, luckily for me, their "note-taking service" was going to be fully launched for the first time in the coming year. This service consisted of paid persons who would accompany me at lectures and take the notes for me (and for every other student who had any type of disability whereby he or she needed this assistance). With this guarantee, I was able to make the decision to leave my job and enrol full-time at university.

It was a leap of faith, but I did it, enrolling for German papers, Maori papers and one in Anthropology. One of these was German Language Stage II, one was the German Literature paper which I had put off from the previous year, and one was German Linguistics, a Stage II paper. As soon as I heard my first poem in the German Literature paper, I was hooked for life: the sound effects and the rhythm of German rhyming poetry enthralled me. I made the required signature for the text book with my left hand: not being able to endure the thought of never writing again, I had taught myself to write with my left. My left hand was not, however, quick enough at high-speed writing to take lecture notes, so I still needed other assistance. I was allocated note-takers for some of my papers, and I was allowed to take a tape recorder to class for the others. As I am primarily a visually oriented person, I then needed to transcribe the taped lectures on to paper. I went to the Language Laboratory to try doing this, but all the booths were full on my first few visits. I asked the desk assistant if there was any time less busy than the others, and she gave me a helpful hint: come in at ten minutes before the hour, because then a lot of the students will start rushing off to their next lecture, and that's when you can grab a seat! This worked, and so I set up my tape, transcribing it slowly on to paper with my left hand. After every line or two of writing, I went through a series of arm exercises, as shown to me by my physiotherapist. All of this meant that transcribing one tape took hours, and I had three tapes a week for one subject. I also wrote a number of coursework essays with my left hand, sometimes having to rewrite large sections of them, when I wanted to change what I had written.

I was delighted to be steeped in academia, but stress levels were a problem: there were always tests looming, homework deadlines, essay deadlines, and, at the end of the year, the dreaded exams, to bring on anxiety. Also, now that I knew I could achieve excellent coursework grades, I became a perfectionist, which put more pressure on myself. The very thought of having six papers to complete (in the old system before semesterisation) seemed worrisome – six felt like a lot to juggle. I found out, the hard way, that the German Linguistics paper was very difficult for me, and that I should have saved it for later on, when I would be, hopefully, more advanced; but I had no way of knowing that beforehand. Besides, in my first full-time year, I succumbed to health problems from early on: a flu with a persistent cough, an infected toenail, and the irritable bowel syndrome which had developed. Struggling with poor health made the stress levels escalate; I became a frequent visitor to the Student Health Service.

A few days before my birthday in August 1995, there was the worst health shock of all: it seemed the herpes virus, which I had caught from the unpleasant character of ten years ago, was back again. Of course, I could not engage in lovemaking if there was any chance of this. Wanting to know for sure, I made arrangements to visit the Sexual Health Clinic at Auckland Hospital. I knew from last time that the time of the test is crucial, as the virus is diagnosable at only one stage of the outbreak. This meant that I might have to ask for time off work, as I had to get the test done on time. I told John that there was a problem – a problem whereby we could not make love for the time being. I still could not bear to utter that "H" word – until I knew for sure, at least. The test came back positive. Now I had to be brave and tell John – whilst knowing that this could end our relationship, which meant so much to me.

If I had managed to be stoic about it, perhaps it would have been easier for both of us. As it was, I was terribly upset and crying – having to tell my boyfriend I had herpes – and on my birthday! (It wasn't a happy birthday – last year's one had not been, either, with Eric's funeral.) John, too, must have gone into shock. Physically and psychologically, he seemed to pull away from me. This was an extra ghastly feeling to cope with – I was now untouchable. He said he needed time to think. Our relationship was "on hold" for the time being.

Around now, with such stress happening in my love-life, I was again seeing a counsellor at the Student Health Service regarding anxiety, which was making it difficult for me to function. I was pleasantly surprised to be given, this time, a very practical solution: there was such a thing as a "Limited Full-Time Course." If the Dean of the faculty approves it, a student may take fewer papers than the normally required number, and still be considered as "Full-Time" for the purposes of allowances, and so on. I desperately did not want to give up my studies, but reducing the number of papers would be a life-saver. As a former patient known to the psychiatric services, I was grateful that a day clinic staff member agreed to write me a letter stating that I had an anxiety disorder. The Dean of Arts was extremely friendly, and signed my application without question: I was now no longer taking Maori Language. I had agonised over which papers to keep and to drop. It did not seem to be sensible to drop papers in my major subject; and I loved Anthropology. I had also been very much enjoying Maori Language, but I reasoned that I could resume it the following year. I knew, also, that I could continue studying it from my books at home, as I had already done previously. It was not that I had experienced the slightest problem with studying Maori: so far, I have found it much easier than German! It was, however, simply the knowledge that I was taking six papers – and therefore having to deal with six batches of tests, coursework, exams, and so on – that had freaked me out.

Meanwhile, a doctor at the Sexual Health Clinic willingly agreed to talk with John about the dreaded disease. I don't know what she said, but I am grateful to her, and to John, for discussing it. As a result, after a week or so of being held at arm's length (for which I do not blame John), I was welcomed back to the relationship – though things could never be exactly the same again. After a series of outbreaks, I was prescribed medication – Zovirax in pill form – to keep the virus inactive and to protect my partner. I have had no more attacks whilst taking the medication, but, during trial periods of going off it, the virus has returned. I am, therefore, taking the pills permanently now, for as long as I am allowed to. One welcome side-effect is that I do not get cold sores, either, whilst I am taking the anti-herpes pills – because cold sores are also the herpes virus. I might as well add that there is a myth which says that getting cold sores early in life will immunise one against getting genital herpes later. It didn't work for me, anyway – I have been susceptible to cold sores since earliest child-hood, but that didn't prevent me from getting the other version of it.

I felt lucky that, when I told Timothy and Anna about this health issue, they were very supportive. Without their nurturing, it would have been even harder for me to deal with it. Our continuing outings included: a visit to the zoo (number one treat for me), a trip to South Kaipara beach, and Karekare beach, and sitting in a pub drinking Guinness; and home plea-sures such as Anna's good cooking and Timothy's photos of Africa. It was very interesting to hear Anna's account of how she gained her doctoral degree in Germany, and to see how, as a left-hander, she could do "mirror writing." Each time with them was so special for me.

As time went on, however, relations became strained between Timothy and me. His spiritual beliefs were getting on my nerves. I do not mind what beliefs people have, if they keep them basically to themselves; but I did not want to become a New Age follower, and I felt that this was what he wanted for me. Some of his beliefs – very close, as they were, to Eastern religions – became all the more unpalatable, the more I heard about them. For instance, there is the belief that if a person commits a wrongdoing in a past life, he or she will be forced to suffer in this life; though nobody can prove what anybody has done in "past lives," the belief seems to justify and condone cruelty carried out to supposed "past-life sinners" in *this* life. I have even read appalling statements in books, such as: "Don't be too sorry for the Jews (of the Holocaust), because they must have deserved it, due to their wrongdoing in previous lives." My response is that, as we do not have access to information from people's supposed past lives, we cannot use that as justification for what is done to them in this life. The belief seems, to me, to be an excuse for anyone to do anything they like to the Jews, or any other persecuted group of people. Similarly, I find the concept of "untouchability," as practised in India, obscene: how can a person be treated worse than vermin, due purely to an accident of birth? Such a situation is, to me, the ultimate in unfairness and injustice – with unfairness, as I have written earlier, to be one of the things I find hard to stand. I cannot even see the "logic" behind these beliefs. Timothy's ideas seemed, as far as I could understand, to be heading too far in this direction for my liking. As I say, I wouldn't have cared about that, as long as he kept it to himself; but I felt that his belief system was coming up too often, in one form or another. I also had the feeling that he thought he was spiritually "higher" than others. I had wanted guidance in the realms of life skills and academia, not in spirituality. Had I wanted the latter, I could have gone back to attending church, as I had done formerly. It seems (I now wonder) that perhaps I did not spell out clearly enough what I wanted in a mentor in the first place. To be fair to both of us, however, it had been a totally new exploration into unknown territory, and, as such, I had been unable to spell it out even for myself at the time when we first met. Besides,

I had not been able to foresee what would, or what could, happen. And by now, tempers had become rather frayed; sometimes, Timothy reprimanded me for no good reason. During our last meeting together, he came out with an angry outburst. Due to that, and the process leading up to it, I later wrote him a letter, in which I said, amongst other things, that I thought there was a problem with the power balance in our relationship. (Thanks are due again to my Sixth Form history lessons, in which I learnt about the Balance of Power concept!) Timothy's response was to post back all of the letters and cards I had written to him during our relationship: what bigger symbol of finality could there be, I asked myself.

Even worse than losing Timothy was having to lose Anna as well, as she was, of course, part of the package. All of this hurt me enormously; perhaps this is what I deserved. An off-shoot of this loss was that I no longer had a "support person" for my German studies; even if Anna could not always answer my queries, at least I had felt I had someone to ask. I grieved for a long time over losing my two special friends; in fact, it is still there, if I allow myself to think about it. Sometimes I dream about them, and, whenever I do, it is always a happy dream, bringing back the joyful times I had with them.

Of course, I still had John, who has been caring, supportive, and interested in my university study and my life ever since we met. In fact, he has been incredibly nurturing, which has very much assisted in my development. After we had known each other for a year, I gradually began to let John know things about my past. For many years, he had made a study of the phenomenon of psychological pain blocks, and he felt that these were holding me back. Because of our close relationship, I could now trust him enough to talk about matters which I had never told anyone before. One of these times resulted in the following incident.

Yellow Raisins
After one of his visits to Auckland, John drove me back to Waikino with him. He was keen to continue releasing my pain blocks, which were trapped inside and inhibiting my life. A confident driver, he said that he could do this during the journey (which was mostly rural). By now I knew that, at the very least, it would be a relief to let some of the worst ones out, along with the comfort of being with a trusted and loving person. John invited me to go ahead.

Seizing my chance, I started on the topic of my Dad (who died when I was ten) and the cows' tails. Shortly before he died, Dad took up the new idea, advertised in farming magazines at the time, of removing the bottom part of the cows' tails. This was because the cows had a tendency to swat the milking personnel (Dad, Mum, Aunty Freda, and Grandad) in the face during milking, with tails that were often thick and heavy with layers of cow dung. The new, advertised method of keeping the cows and the milking procedure more hygienic was to place a special kind of rubber ring around the upper part of the cows' tails, which, over the course of some weeks, cut off the blood circulation and caused the lower part of the tail to drop off.

I realise that this sounds gruesome. I had no part in Dad's decision, but, as a loving and impressionable child, I thought that my Dad could do no wrong. My father had no history of cruelty to animals that I knew of, after all. He loved our cats, which were allowed to sit on his lap at the meal table, much against Mum's wishes. One of them, Gussy, had once been a puny and bedraggled-looking kitten whom Dad had made two trips to obtain. Dad had brought home baby wild rabbits as pets for my brother and me, and they were lovingly cared for. His method of carrying kittens or baby rabbits was to put them inside the jersey he was wearing at the time, with their heads poking out through one of the sizeable holes. Dad's hens grew to a ripe old age, because he could not bring himself to kill them for dinner.

Observing the recipients of the rubber ring treatment, it was true that the cows seemed to suffer no discomfort from this procedure. However, after the loss of the main part of their tails, they could not effectively swat away the flies that landed on their bodies. This was where their problem – and my problem – came in.

Our farming neighbours reacted with horror to Dad's latest innovation, on the grounds that the cows could no longer protect themselves from flies, and told me loud and long what a horrible, cruel person he was. In the middle of this, Dad died, but the comments continued. I was already in unbearable pain from the loss of my beloved father, and, on top of that, I had to keep hearing that my father was some kind of monster who had deserved to die. One little neighbourhood girl – whilst playing on the slide which my Dad had built for my brother and me – came out with "B – and I are glad your father died, because he cut off the cows' tails." My inner pain was excruciating, and I ran away from her into our house; but I could not tell my mother what was wrong, because I knew that then she would start crying too; so, like all of the other times, I bottled it in. Being a child, I had only my family to confide in (as there were, in that time and place, no such things as school counsellors, or any other help which I could access), and as my family members had their own grief to deal with, they were unable to help me with mine.

A family member added to the horror I felt: whenever we saw a field of cows, there would be pointed comments as to whether the cows had tails or not. Then the comparison with my father's "cruelly treated" cows would be painfully drawn. It got to the stage where, if travelling anywhere with others, I would be terrified to see a paddock of cows, because I knew that the comments would be due to start. Our school bus driver, until then a man I had always thought of as warm and jovial, joined in the persecution – of a small, timid, grief-stricken child. In our dairy farming community, it was impossible to go anywhere without a paddock of cows being in sight and becoming the topic of conversation. Each time, I could feel my stomach and entrails shrivelling up into something the size and shape of a raisin. Although I felt unquenchable loyalty to my father, over the years I had reason to wish that he had thought about the consequences before taking the action he did. At the very least, it was lousy timing: doing something this controversial, then going and dying on me. It had not been my decision to remove the cows' tails, but, in his absence, it was I who paid the price.

By now, travelling along the country roads with John, I was screaming my pain out: this episode had never been told before, and it was raw. Eventually, John said to me, in a kindly voice, "Jen, we are coming up to some road works and I have to stop for the signal man – so would you try to keep quiet for a bit?"

During this trip I scarcely noticed the landscape, but finally we reached John's home in Waikino. Sooner or later, I paid a visit to the toilet. To my amazement, out of my body poured a yellow substance like partly-chewed whole kernel sweetcorn – though I knew I hadn't eaten any sweetcorn for a long time. Alternatively, it was like yellow shrivelled raisins – the raisins which, I felt, had taken the place of my insides so many times. Whatever it was, it took over a day to clear out, and I have never experienced anything like it before or since. Also, whatever it was, was it something that should have been inside me? – I wondered. And if it should not have been inside me, it is just as well that it came out. What would it have done to me if it had stayed inside me? – I hated to think. And why did it suddenly decide to come out? – I could see no triggering factor except for the screaming attack, the clearing of a chunk of mental suffering, right before the yellow flux; and this seemed to me, on a psychological and a gut level, to be the correct answer. Perhaps my life was saved by the removal of this pain, which had been stored inside me as "yellow raisins."

Postscript: Some years later, the idea of shortening the cows' tails, for reasons of hygiene, caught on amongst dairy farmers. Even some of our neighbours adopted the practice.

1996 marked the introduction of a new system, that of semesters, to the University of Auckland. Instead of taking six papers for a full year, a student would take three papers for half a year (a semester), and then another three for the next half of the year. I heard that most students disliked the new system – but I preferred it! As my previous reasoning explains, I was now *not* taking six papers at once – I was taking only three at once, and this felt psychologically better for me. The semester system also meant, of course, that what once took a whole year to learn now had to be packed into half a year – with the appropriate intensification of the subject. This is a point that many students complained about. I did not mind this, though, because it still suited my own way of working: to do *fewer* things at a time, but to do them more intensely, is what I prefer! So, at least *one* person was happy with the new system!

I discovered a new subject which I had not heard of previously: Comparative Literature. Now I had something else to be hooked on, as this seemed to be a subject invented especially for me. It was cross-cultural studies, languages, literature, translation studies, history, politics, religion, and any other relevant topic, mixed together into a meaningful whole. I took three papers in this subject during what was left of my degree. I also continued with my other subjects of German, Anthropology, Linguistics, and one more from English Literature. One of my very favourite papers was the Linguistics one called "Languages of the Pacific:" it fitted exactly what I wanted to know.

The German Literature papers (a necessary part of majoring in German) were one of my biggest delights. However, it broke my heart that, no matter how high my coursework marks were and no matter how hard I tried, I was unable to win the German Literature prize for any of the three years in which I studied it. Admittedly, during my first year I did not even know that there was a German Literature prize; but my fervour to be top of the class in Stages II and III made up for that lack. Unfortunately, as I described earlier in this chapter, I was unable to cope with the different conditions, and the anxiety, of the exams, thus bringing my year's points down too much to win the prize. At least, I deserved a prize for the best attendance, consistently excellent coursework, and the greatest effort and enthusiasm for the subject! (Or even a certificate would do!) Alas, no such prize exists.

As I was choosing subjects I loved, my Bachelor of Arts was a wonderfully fulfilling experience that I am so grateful to have had. The anxiety was a problem, but anything else I would have done at that time would probably also have caused anxiety, because that is part of my life. That is, it looks as though I will have anxiety no matter what I do, but I would rather spend the anxiety on doing something as positive as a university degree!

I was to finish my Bachelor of Arts, and to graduate in 1999. But just before that happened, a life-changing event took place...

Part Two

Part Two

Chapter 20

Revelations

In the second semester of 1998 (with only one more semester to do after that in order to complete my Bachelor of Arts), I was taking German Literature Stage III, Introduction to Maori Society Stage I, and a Stage II English paper, all of which I was very much enjoying.

Every week since I began my degree, I had been picking up a copy of *Next Week*, the university newsletter, which stated which seminars would be held in the near future. These seminars had nothing to do with students' own lectures and tutorials: they were extra presentations given by lecturers or guest speakers, and were open to the public. I usually found at least one that would be of great interest to me, and was, therefore, regularly attending extra lectures, because I loved being in the midst of learning and research. One day, in the latter half of the second semester of 1998, I attended a seminar given by Angela Arnold, of the Psychology Department of the university. She was in the process of becoming a doctor of psychology, but would have to wait a few more months to add PhD to her name.

Angela Arnold described, on this day, a little-known developmental disorder. Developmental disorders are conditions, present from birth onwards, which affect a person's development – making it slower in some areas, and uneven. Developmental disorder is not the same thing as intellectual impairment, nor is it the same thing as mental illness. The person with a developmental disorder is likely, however, to have some areas in their lives which look like intellectual problems or mental problems. In other areas, though, the person with a developmental disorder may be of normal or of above-average ability. Autism is one example of a developmental disorder. Autism is now known to exist on a wide spectrum: that is, there are severe forms of it, moderate forms, and mild forms. To cover all of this range, the term Autistic Spectrum Disorder (ASD) has been created. The condition which Angela Arnold was speaking about on this day – Asperger Syndrome (or Asperger's Disorder) – is at the mild end of the Autistic Spectrum.

Angela gave a checklist, i.e. a list of diagnostic criteria, for this condition. There are at least four different checklists available, which differ from one another on a few points, but which are all "near enough" for my purposes. All of the checklists emphasise differences such as social impairment, narrow interest, repetitive routines, speech peculiarities, non-verbal communication impairment (e.g. facial expressions), and the likely – but not essential – trait of motor skills and co-ordination difficulties. (In my opinion – speaking with hindsight, now – some checklists are, however, more accurate than others.)

As Angela (now Dr Arnold) has left New Zealand, I cannot say exactly which checklist she used in her seminar, but this is not of crucial importance. Whichever one she gave was elaborated on by her own explanations and examples, gleaned from her own experience in the field of developmental disorders. I will here show the checklist which was written by Gillberg and Gillberg (1989):

Diagnostic criteria for Asperger Syndrome:

1. Social impairment – extreme egocentricity (at least in two of the following):

    (a) inability to interact with peers

    (b) lack of desire to interact with peers

    (c) lack of appreciation of social cues

    (d) socially and emotionally inappropriate behaviour.

2. Narrow interest (at least one of the following):

    (a) exclusion of other activities

(b) repetitive adherence

(c) more rote than meaning.

3. Repetitive routines (at least one of the following):

(a) on self, in aspects of life

(b) on others.

4. Speech and language peculiarities (at least three of the following):

(a) delayed development

(b) superficially perfect expressive language

(c) formal pedantic language

(d) odd prosody, peculiar voice characteristics

(e) impairment of comprehension, including misinterpretations of literal/implied meanings.

5. Non-verbal communication problems (at least one of the following):

(a) limited use of gestures

(b) clumsy body language

(c) limited facial expression

(d) inappropriate expression

(e) peculiar stiff gaze.

6. Motor clumsiness

(a) poor performance on neuro-developmental examination.

Whether or not this was the checklist used in this seminar, Gillberg and Gillberg's diagnostic criteria are "close enough" to what was given. By now, I had changed from having a purely academic interest to a peculiar feeling inside.

Angela added some of the implications of these criteria: because of lack of understanding in the social sphere – and because of the individual's oddities in speech, interests, movements, etc. – the individual is often teased, tricked, or targeted by bullies. In point (e) of the "Speech and language peculiarities" section – also influenced by the person's social impairment and non-verbal communication problems – the person is likely to have trouble understanding humour; Angela went on to say that the type of humour most likely to be understood and enjoyed by such persons is word-play, or puns. At this, shock waves reverberated right throughout my body and mind – because everything Angela was saying applied to me.

As the seminar was of only an hour's duration, it must have ended soon after this point. I had an urgent need to make contact with this psychologist, Angela Arnold, before she disappeared out of the door, never to be seen again. I noted where the door was, in relation to her and to myself; I would have to stop her, somehow! For the moment, there were three other attendees surrounding her, asking her questions, so I waited for an opportunity. When my chance finally came, I went up to her and asked "What if this is me?" As soon as I had grabbed her attention in this way, I added, "I'll have to sit down!" – as I was feeling weak and shaky from shock.

Luckily, Angela Arnold was, and is, a very friendly and approachable person. She sat down with me and arranged to see me for a private chat. During the chat, Angela thought, from her own observations, and because I had identified the symptoms in myself, that there was a significant chance of my having this developmental disorder. I learnt that I could make an appointment with her for a formal assessment if I wished, in order to find out whether this really did apply to me. Angela added that, even if I gained a formal diagnosis, this would not do me any practical good: for there was no assistance available for adults with the condition. As I did not want this question to go unanswered for the rest of my life, and, aware of the possible dangers of self-diagnosis (e.g. going around believing that I had "something" if I actually did not), I decided to have the formal assessment.

For the rest of that seminar day I was wandering around in a daze. When should I tell John? – because, after all, I didn't have any official diagnosis, as yet. First of all, I thought the news could wait until the next day – until, spending a sleepless night, I phoned him at 3 a.m. He did not mind the inappropriate hour, as he agreed that this was a significant discovery. Angela had told me that I could contact the Autistic Association of New Zealand for more information. By doing so, I was able to buy a copy of Dr Tony Attwood's book *Asperger's Syndrome: A Guide for Parents and Professionals*. This book is, to this day, the definitive guide on Asperger

Syndrome, and I wholeheartedly recommend it to anyone who would like to find out more about this condition. In fact, as Dr Attwood's book covers the subject so comprehensively (though I may not agree with every last detail,) I will not attempt to write my own textbook on Asperger Syndrome within this volume. I am here using my own life experiences to supplement the "known facts" about Asperger Syndrome, and sometimes to challenge the "known facts." My aim is also to bring this scarcely-known condition to the awareness of the New Zealand public and professionals. As I said earlier, lived experience outweighs academic theory – therefore, I do not need to replicate the experts' text-books in order to produce something of worth; my own life story can now become something which will help others.

I had the formal assessment with Angela Arnold, resulting in the official diagnosis of the Syndrome. Not that that was any surprise by then – but I wanted it to be "official" or not at all. For one thing, my difficulties had not been understood by professionals in the past, or, even if they believed what I was telling them, they were unable to put it together into the correct category of either Developmental Disorder or Autistic Spectrum Disorder (of which Asperger Syndrome is one). Therefore, I could just imagine what would happen if I were to tell people that I had Asperger Syndrome: without an official diagnosis – that crucial "piece of paper" – I would still not be believed. Having lived with non-acknowledgement of my differences and difficulties for 43 years so far, I did not wish to carry on for the rest of my life in the same manner. At least, my close associates and I would now know the truth.

To say that this discovery was a bombshell would not be an exaggeration: it was a life-changing event. It reinterpreted most of my life in a new, understandable, and logical way. As with everything else in life, I would rather know the truth about things, the reason *why* something is happening in a certain way: and now, for the first time, I could understand why things had happened in certain ways. Even though I still have some of the difficulties associated with Asperger Syndrome, it helps 100 per cent to know *why* I am different – instead of having to think, as I did before meeting Angela Arnold, that I was "crazy," "stupid," "not able to get it all together."

By this time, I had only one semester left of my studies – then my degree would be completed. In the summer holidays before classes resumed, I returned to my holiday job of casual print finishing work in a printing centre. That is, I usually did little else besides punching and spiral-binding books, which is something I enjoyed. I had had some difficulties in this job previously, however – difficulties which were now recognisable as due to Asperger Syndrome – such as being terrified every time the electric stapler crashed, being unable to understand instructions at times, and being so terrified over a mistake that my brain had shut down. Therefore, in one sense, it might have helped me if I had told my supervisors that I have Asperger Syndrome. However, in this particular case – as I had already worked in the same place two or three times – I could not face the issue of telling the supervisors that I *now* had Asperger Syndrome, which would raise the questions of "Is this a new illness? If you had it last time, why didn't you tell me before?" etc., so I decided against it. The job was casual work, of only a few weeks' duration, so I hoped for the best.

Back in the classroom, I was finishing off my degree with Linguistics, English Literature and Comparative Literature. In the last-named subject, at Stage II level, I was, again, producing excellent coursework, but, in the mid-semester test, I performed at a much lower level. This was what had happened throughout my degree, as explained in Chapter 19: pressured situations make it very difficult for me to function, even when I am trying my hardest. When exam time came along again, I was desperate to end up with a final "A" in this subject, because my interest and my application were certainly of an "A" standard. Our lecturer, who also served as our tutor, had known me for three years, and knew of my devotion towards, and effort in, the subject. The day before the Comparative Literature exam – which, because I had finished my other exams, was also the second-to-last day of my entire degree – I suddenly decided to tell my teacher of the diagnosis and its implications. As he certainly would have had no idea of what he was about to hear, I was, and still am, highly impressed with his response: "It must be difficult having an invisible disability." That showed a very deep understanding of the situation, and I was very grateful to receive such acknowledgement (especially as this had been my first "experiment" in telling anyone besides John). I gave my teacher a pamphlet about Asperger

Syndrome, in case he ever acquired another student with this condition. He thanked me warmly for telling him this news, as he said he had been unable, until now, to understand the wide discrepancy between my coursework and my test and exam performance.

Remembering the kinds of problem that I had had at university – and those I had had in previous workplaces – I asked Angela Arnold if she would be able to write a letter briefly describing these, which I could show to employers (and teachers, if any) in the future. I was very happy with the document she produced, which outlined the main points I needed, and implied others:

> To whom it may concern:
>
> Jennifer has been recently diagnosed with Asperger's Disorder. This is a pervasive (lifelong) developmental disorder that is often described as a mild form of autism. Persons with Asperger's Disorder frequently have difficulty in examination situations and require extra time and separate examination areas. People with Asperger's Disorder typically have slower processing speeds, difficulty in multi-tasking, problems with distractibility and increased levels of anxiety in pressured situations. Consequently people with Asperger's frequently produce excellent course work but attain poor examination results.
>
> In work environments people with Asperger's require consideration of the above. Individuals also have difficulties in changes of routines and structures. In starting a new job, or acquiring new skills in a current job, specific coaching is required as to the specific job requirements. Tasks need to be broken down into smaller units and taught individually and in a specific structure. People with Asperger's are often very skilled in specific areas and can offer many unique abilities to employers.
>
> Should you require any further information please do not hesitate to contact me,
>
> Regards,
>
> Angela Arnold
> Registered Psychologist.

(*Author's note*: Angela Arnold has been awarded her Doctorate since then.)

When my exam results became available, I found that I had received an A–
for Comparative Literature. It had happened again: my coursework grade
of A+ had come down two grades to an A –, due to my poor exam performance. It just didn't seem fair, when I had put my heart and soul into my
university work, especially German Literature and Comparative Literature.
This time, though, I had the diagnosis. I went to the doctor at the Student
Health Service who was the one to see for aegrotat and grade review appli-
cations. Now she will understand why I went there with so many anxiety
attacks, I thought. Sitting in front of her, I made my request, stating that I
had just been diagnosed with Asperger Syndrome. "What the heck's that?"
she exclaimed. She had never heard of it, and did not seem to want to hear
about it. I did not feel like pursuing the subject with her.

I contacted Angela Arnold, who was willing to write out a form
requesting a reconsideration of my grade on the basis that Asperger
Syndrome had affected my exam performance. This request also had to be
approved by my Comparative Literature teacher, who, now that he knew of
my diagnosis, was all in favour of my grade being reviewed. The third
person who had to approve it, in one of the university offices, declined my
request, so I had to keep the A – grade. If he was anything like 99.99 per
cent of the population, he had never heard of Asperger Syndrome either.

I would now like to clear up a misconception about Asperger Syndrome:
that it is a brand new condition, and that there is suddenly an epidemic of
it. This illusion has been created by an accident of history: Dr Hans
Asperger's nationality.

In 1943, Dr Leo Kanner, an American, researched and named what we
now know as Autism. He used this term because the Greek word *autos*
means "self" – the autistic person appears to live in their own, self-
contained world. The individuals whom he studied were at the severely
affected end of the scale; therefore, to make this clear, such individuals are,
these days, often said to suffer from "Kanner's autism" or "classic autism."

In the same year, Dr Hans Asperger, an Austrian, researched another
group of individuals, also deciding to call them "autistic," from the Greek
derivation. (The two doctors who discovered autism, at practically the
same time, had not even heard of each other.) The children in Dr Asperger's
research group were at the milder end of the spectrum. Dr Asperger's
native language was German; therefore, he wrote up his discoveries in

German. At the time, the Second World War was in progress – making German-speakers, such as Hans Asperger, the enemies of Britain and the USA. Dr Asperger's house was bombed, and some of his papers were lost. Because he was on the enemy side, Dr Asperger's written work was not translated into English until the late 1980s! The next stage, of getting his discovered condition into the Diagnostic Manual, did not happen until 1994. Then, to distinguish it from Kanner's autism, the condition was named after him: Asperger Syndrome, (or, sometimes), Asperger's Disorder.

Therefore, an accident of history had caused this important information to remain unknown to the English-speaking world for fifty years. This resulted in all persons with Asperger Syndrome, up until 1994 at the very earliest, being unable to receive the correct diagnosis. Some individuals, of course, did have Asperger Syndrome during this information gap of fifty years – for I am one of them. Others would have been born decades and centuries too early, thus never having a chance of being diagnosed. This account shows the reason for Asperger Syndrome appearing to be a new disorder – yet it was identified in 1943. This also explains why there now seems to be an "epidemic" of new cases – because we, the individuals who have Asperger Syndrome, had to wait until now to be diagnosed, and so there is a large backlog of cases.

The delays and differences of my motor milestones (no crawling, walking at 22 months, unusual gait, awkwardness climbing stairs, etc.) can now be seen as an early sign of a developmental disorder, applying particularly to Asperger Syndrome. Judith Sheridan and Dr Tony Attwood have written a paper called "Abnormal Movements Among People with Pervasive Developmental Disorders," in which they state that "an experienced clinician can identify Autism by the way the child moves…and that this aspect of Autism requires further investigation."

Other hints of an Autistic Spectrum Disorder were: difficulty in knowing which way around my clothes were meant to go; my extreme "shyness" with anybody I did not know; my difficulty in participating in a conversation; not knowing how to play with the little girls, therefore mixing with an "inappropriate" group, the little boys; my unusual and obsessional interests which persisted long after the "appropriate" age for them was past (e.g. marble alleys, collecting bottle tops, catching water beetles, harvesting acorns, chestnuts and turnip seeds); my repetitive activities of, for instance, digging with a stick in the ground and walking repeatedly around the perimeter of the school; wanting, as a child, to spend a lot of time alone; preferring my solitary fantasy games to playing with other children; being a "walking dictionary" compared with other children; experiencing difficulty with decision-making; having a low threshold for frustration; and being excessively fearful, especially about changes, e.g. going up into the next class, which was a drama every new year. None of these things, on their own, mean that a person has Asperger Syndrome; but, when combined together, with other characteristics as well, the clinical picture shows itself. The characteristics which I have just listed are some which are observable by others; but there are just as many which are more hidden inside the person, and which are harder to notice unless one knows exactly what one is looking for, for example mental rigidity, major and ongoing identity problems, slower mental processing speed (except in one's special skill area), getting confused easily, difficulty with multi-tasking, difficulty with following a series of instructions, difficulties with spatial orientation (e.g. getting lost easily), difficulty in knowing what is going on in a social situation (not understanding social cues), sometimes not understanding jokes, becoming easily upset and taking a longer time (than "normal" people) to get over it, feeling increasing anxiety in a pressured situation…these and many other "invisible" traits are also part of the way in which Asperger Syndrome manifests itself in my case. Many other persons with Asperger Syndrome have these same traits, but they may not have every single one, and they may have some different ones – because persons with Asperger Syndrome are still individuals as well, not all peas in the same pod. I repeat: having one, two, or a few of these characteristics does not mean that a person has Asperger Syndrome – because everyone in the world has a few of them. With Asperger Syndrome (and other autistic conditions), it is also the intensity of the characteristic which is a factor. Persons with Asperger Syndrome have at least one "obsessional" interest, which would be indulged in for very long periods of time, if not stopped by an outside authority; and when someone else, for example a parent, does try to stop the activity, they may face fierce opposition.

It is when someone fits the requirements of one of the diagnostic checklists that there is a reason for diagnosis. And the reason for diagnosis is so that the person with Asperger Syndrome can begin to get assistance to learn life skills and to achieve. And the sooner this happens, the better. There are nowadays many ways in which children with this condition can be helped, for example by having a teacher aide who understands Asperger Syndrome, and by communications being conveyed visually as much as possible. Asperger adults in New Zealand, however, have few helpful services available to them. It also depends on which locality one lives in: cities are more likely to have services than small towns are.

My difficulties with relationships – tending to worsen as I progressed through adult life – had a lot to do with Asperger Syndrome, especially undiagnosed Asperger Syndrome. I had problems with recognising people's faces, if I had met them only once or a few times; let alone working out their facial expressions as well, which was a further obstacle. As I did not even *know* that I had difficulty reading facial expressions and body language (except for the most blatant ones: smiles and frowns); as I did not *know* that I often could not detect sarcasm, double meanings, hidden agendas and deception; and as I did not *know* that I could not pick up social cues (understand what was going on with other people) most of the time, I could not do anything to assist myself. If you *know* that you have a cut finger, you can put a band-aid on; but if you are unaware of the cut, you can't do anything about it. I knew that something was wrong, but I had no way of figuring out the mechanism of exactly what was going wrong, and why, and (therefore) what I could do about it. I could not improve my performance without knowing the answers to these questions – although I had *tried* to improve. Trying to achieve something when you don't know what the situation is in the first place is like trying to shoot a bullseye by firing crazily in all directions: the hit-and-miss method. It was certainly not lack of effort which had hampered me until now – in fact, I had often worn myself out with effort. The fact that I did not *know* what was lacking in my understanding meant that, the older I became, the more at risk I became of dangerous situations. I would not be able to tell, for instance, that a friendly, smiling man (or woman) had bad intentions. Yes, I was naive and trusting – and this is a trait of Asperger Syndrome. If we lack the essential brain wiring that deals with indirect communication and deception (the lack of which is a part of having Asperger Syndrome), then we are going to get into a lot of undesirable situations – by accident.

If I had received the diagnosis earlier in life, and had been told what this entailed, at least I would have been forewarned about possible dangers. I would then, at least, have known that dating, flatting and other social situations would be risk areas for me, and I could have chosen to do things differently. Also, I would have had access to support persons who understood my differences and who would have kept an eye on me to some extent. I could have asked such support persons for advice and guidance. I would have had the necessary data on which to base important life decisions. For instance, I now understand why I had less interest (than my peers) in dolls, and, later, babies; my brain was wired up differently. (I do not wish to imply that all females with Asperger Syndrome are exactly like me, however, as this is not so; some do marry and have babies.) For me, though, realising why I was different would have meant that I could at least make an educated decision about what to do with my life. I might then have chosen not to get married. Also, the information would have helped in choosing suitable jobs, and avoiding unsuitable ones: jobs which involve multi-tasking, frequent sudden changes in routine, a lot of pressure and anxiety, or having to think quickly on the spot, are not (as a general rule) suitable for persons with Asperger Syndrome. For example, my job in a cafeteria meant multi-tasking on a grand scale, which caused too much stress, and was therefore unsuitable. A person deserves, at least, to have the data with which to make a decision. As things worked out, I did not have this essential information (the diagnosis of Asperger Syndrome) at the time of getting married; therefore, I do not blame myself for making the wrong decision. Having made the wrong one, I think that our mutual decision to split up was the right one. It gave both of us a fresh start, and Lindsay is now remarried, with children.

There is still one major area in which I differ (perhaps) from the majority of others who have Asperger Syndrome. (Of course, in order to be sure of that, a very large survey would have to be done, ensuring that sufficient respondents with the relevant life experiences were included.) It seems to me that the "known fact" of people with Asperger Syndrome lacking empathy leads even some autism professionals into erroneous thinking. This "fact" then lets them believe that people with Asperger

Syndrome do not grieve, or not as much as "normal" people. In other words, this "known fact" is untrue and even dangerous, because then people with Asperger Syndrome cannot get the help they need, if major grief hits them. I am leading into the area of childhood trauma, caused by the death of my father when I was ten. This double phenomenon (Autistic Spectrum plus major bereavement in childhood) falls outside even most Autistic Spectrum experts' knowledge, and, as such, it seems I am on my own in writing my own theory about this.

I will meander into a byway for a moment. It is by no means uncommon for a person with Asperger Syndrome or autism to have another disability, or significant medical condition, or developmental issue, along with the Autistic Spectrum Disorder. For example, I have heard of individuals who have ASD combined with dyslexia, Down Syndrome, Tourette Syndrome, hearing impairment, or blindness. Of course, any other combinations are possible as well. In such cases, the individual may find that they are not being adequately and equally treated for both conditions. Also, most specialists are experts at one thing or the other, not both. And specialists in the fields of deafness, blindness, intellectual impairment, and so on, are not usually familiar with Autistic Spectrum Disorders – therefore, they are unlikely to take the implications fully into account when treating their specialty condition. My own situation was also "double trouble," that of two developmental conditions, both causing delays: Asperger Syndrome combined with major childhood bereavement (death of a parent). Professionals who fail to acknowledge this cause a continuation of the lack of understanding of childhood development such as I have already experienced in the past. The intensity of this loss at the age of ten was a far greater trauma to me than having Asperger Syndrome. I needed help for both, but received recognition of neither.

It is excruciatingly painful for any child to lose a parent (that is, the adult who loves them and looks after them in a parental role). This is true for any "normal" child. I now suspect, however, that it is, in some cases, even harder for an Autistic Spectrum (including Asperger Syndrome) child to get through this loss – because I know, from experience, how long it takes me to work my way through any issue (let alone an extremely emotional one). Once a feeling (e.g. pain or fear) is in the mind, it is an extremely long and difficult process to get it out again. It gets stuck in there, replaying over and over, sometimes for life. As I wrote earlier in this book, major frights take decades to seep out of my brain; and losing my father was the biggest terror of my life. Some parents and professionals realise that we Autistic Spectrum folks have trouble with feelings getting stuck inside us for a very long time – yet it seems that it is often too difficult for them to combine the two concepts: i.e. that childhood loss of a parent, the ultimate horror, could stay very much stuck inside, causing lifelong problems. Talking of being "stuck," I think that some theoreticians get stuck on their theories, for example, the theory that Autistic Spectrum individuals do not have feelings like other people do, and therefore do not grieve like other people do. (I argue that at least some Autistic Spectrum individuals grieve *more* than other people do.) No doubt, there will be some individuals who react one way, and some the other way (as I have learnt that there are exceptions to every rule in life). If there are exceptions to everything in life, then I would expect professionals to also recognise this fact, and therefore not to assume that one theory applies to all individuals. I have heard of several other persons with Asperger Syndrome whose life experiences add to my alternative theory, but I am not at liberty to talk about other people's private lives in this book. Once again, then, I am a pioneer in this field; so be it.

My wish is for individuals who are diagnosed with Asperger Syndrome, and their families, to feel happy and proud about this. Perhaps this is a tall order at the moment of first hearing the news. Later on, though, there is time for reflection about the good side of the situation. Some persons may need to do a mental shift as to what they call "positive" and "negative!" At least some of this is in the attitude of the beholder. To help get you started, here is a list; you may be able to add to it. (Thank you to Cathie, who began this list, with eight points.)

Positive aspects of having an Autistic Spectrum Disorder:

1.   Picture thinking: Creative and inventive, it enabled Temple Grandin to design cattle equipment and earn herself a Doctorate.

2.   Pleasure in repetitive activities: This can be a plus in many jobs.

3. Delight in details not noticed by "normal" people: for example the ants in the crack on the footpath; the moss in our front yard which I saw as a "miniature forest."

4. A different creative slant, i.e. uniqueness, for those ASD persons who have a creative talent.

5. Passion for one's special interests: We derive great pleasure and satisfaction from them.

6. Honesty: ASD people tend to be much more honest than "normal" people; we tend to have trouble understanding, and engaging in, trickery or deception.

7. Fashion labels: Regarding (so-called) "normal" people's need to wear the right labels on their clothing, I can only respond "That does not compute." For me, it's the same with any other material item which has status value for "normals:" I pity these people for what I see as their mental delusions.

8. Taking people at face value: As we are not impressed by the status markers, we give everyone an equal chance (this can be a risk factor for us, also).

9. For "very late starters," such as myself – every day brings new learning experiences and pleasures; we are not yet bored by what the world has to offer.

10. Intelligence: Persons with Asperger Syndrome are of average intelligence or higher; some ASD individuals can reach up into the brilliant range.

11. Memory: Long-term, and for particular subjects, can be exceptional; a plus for some jobs.

12. Focus: Can single-mindedly apply ourselves to a task, for example great scientists who persevered until they succeeded.

13. Loyalty: Unquestioning and total once given.

14. Precision in carrying out tasks: Repeating a routine exactly as taught, when this is required.

15. Commitment to work: Diligent, conscientious, reliable.

16. Forthrightness: With a strong moral code and sense of justice.

17. Non-squeamishness (for some ASD individuals): Ability to watch and participate willingly in unpleasant activities, such as operations on animals. (Not me, though!)

Dr Tony Attwood, author of *Asperger Syndrome: A Guide for Parents and Professionals*, also has a very positive attitude towards people with this condition. If you have Internet access, you can read one such article on his website. So, along with Dr Attwood, I invite you to feel the happiness of "Congratulations! It's Asperger Syndrome!"

Chapter 21

How I Chose a Cat Instead of a Kookaburra!

(Or: More Cognitive Issues)

I feel lucky to have established such a friendly relationship with the staff members at Newton's Seeds, Onehunga, where I buy poultry food in bulk. This saves me from the constant task of buying it in small quantities from grocery shops, which are also unreliable at stocking it. The only drawback of going to Newton's was that, until recently, I drove there – which was scary for me at the best of times, and, as Newton's is situated in an industrial area, I had to share the road with many big, articulated trucks.

Once there, I am greeted warmly by Doug, Marion and the other workers, which is very pleasant for me. A cat from the mouse-catching team is likely to install itself on the counter for petting. It seems to me that the cats have too many cat-biscuits available in their food dispenser, overflowing on to the floor; would this dampen down their interest in their work, I wonder? I have often been in rather a dither whilst on the premises, due to anxiety about the drive there and back, and trying to remember all of the things I intended to look at or buy there. I need to write my shopping list beforehand, otherwise the array of goods distracts me so much that I forget what I went there for. Newton's has always been a very interesting place for me, because I am fascinated by the variety of seeds, some of which I have grown in order to see what the plants look like, for example, sorghum and pigeon peas. On sale also are gardening tools, canary vitamins, and fresh honey.

On my last visit (in December 2001), whilst meandering through the aisles I overheard another customer being offered a free calendar for the year 2002. Oh, goody, I thought, remembering that in the previous year I had been given a free calendar. That year, there had been a choice of two calendars: the only difference was the large colour picture – one could choose between a parakeet and a dog. The slight difficulty was that the cal- endars were hidden out the back; I presume this was because they were intended only for regular customers and not for everybody, and I could understand this rationale. This circumstance made it more difficult to choose, however, as one would have to say, sight unseen, whether one wanted the parakeet or the dog, and then that particular calendar would be brought out. As I am not a "dog person" (although there are exceptions to this rule), I opted for the parakeet. The latter turned out to be a pretty, green bird climbing in a eucalyptus tree, with which I was very pleased.

This year, the choice was, according to a male staff member, between a cockatoo and a cat. At least, this is what I thought I heard him say; in my somewhat dithery state, perhaps I got this wrong. At any rate, my mind conjured up the picture of a white, sulphur-crested cockatoo, such as I had seen at the zoo. I like these birds well enough at the zoo, but I do not care for them in other settings; for example, not as a pet. I have always been fond of cats, however, so this fact made up my mind for me. Another couple were already at the counter, and going through their own deci- sion-making process: staff member Marion had returned from the back room with the calendar of their choice, and, as she held it up, I could see very well that it was a *kookaburra* – not a cockatoo. I had, however, already asked for "the cat, please," and she had now gone to fetch that. But now that the other choice was a kookaburra and not a cockatoo, I began to wish that I had chosen the kookaburra. When Marion returned with the cat calendar for me, the couple then declared that they liked this better than the kookaburra, so Marion rushed the kookaburra calendar back to the back-room and returned with a cat calendar for them.

All of this happened so fast – plus, there was the disconcerting change of option between (as I thought) a cockatoo and a kookaburra – that I was not able to keep up with the goings-on and state that I now wanted the kookaburra instead of the cat; also, I was too embarrassed to say that I had changed my mind, and did not want to send poor Marion rushing to the back-room yet again. It seems, in retrospect, that it would have been all too easy – had I been a "normal" person with correspondingly faster reaction times – to have piped up, right at the moment when the couple rejected the kookaburra, stating that I would have their calendar and they could have mine, thus exchanging the two picture choices. However, I have never been "normal" in this respect, needing more time than the average person in order to weigh up my options, come to a decision, cope with the sudden change of options (in this case, changing my decision at rapid-fire pace – which can be a very difficult thing for me to do), and mentally process data in general; therefore, as usual, I missed the crucial moment. Though I was left reeling from the quick-fire chain of events, in which I had ended up making an unintended decision, I am still very happy with my pretty, useful and free "cat" calendar. Now that this lovely calendar is up on my wall, I couldn't care less about the kookaburra. It is the moment of decision-making which is (often) the difficulty for me. Although this is an insignificant and amusing incident, it is also an excellent example of what happens to me all of the time, which is why I have included it here.

This had been a relatively "easy" choice, of only two items; imagine, if you can, what I am like when presented with an array of options! I have sometimes come out of cafés with nothing, because the dazzling display of dozens of items was too much for me. On other occasions, I have had to be helped, by understanding companions, to choose something. Pressure from other people to "hurry up" adds anxiety to the situation, thus making it all the more difficult; though I am aware of the need to be considerate of other people waiting in a queue. If anxiety builds up too much (usually in a more important matter than the lunch menu), at some stage on the scale my brain can go into "shut-down," at which point no further thinking is possible. Sometimes, when this happens, I am able to operate on "auto-pilot," that is, without thinking, as long as it is an activity with which I am thoroughly familiar. For anything less familiar, however, the shut-down will mean that further thinking and acting will have to wait until I have calmed down, had a rest, had "time out."

Any kind of thinking and doing require that I am near top form, i.e. not overtired, overwhelmed, too anxious, unduly pressured, or too hungry. These requirements are increased about 100 per cent when I am learning a new task (of the sort which is not in my special skill category). For any activity which is outside my special skill area, I am likely to be slow on the uptake, to need the task broken down into its smallest components, and to need frequent repetition and practice until I have mastered each component, then the full sequence. This way of teaching people with an Autistic Spectrum Disorder is now common practice amongst ASD professionals, but is not necessarily followed by the person's teachers and employers, which can result in frustration for the teacher, and escalating anxiety for the Autistic Spectrum person, sometimes to the point of mental shut-down. When that point has been reached, any further teaching is impossible, yet the teacher may still be trying to do so. The teacher unfamiliar with ASD is then likely to misinterpret the person's inability as "non-compliance," "not listening," "being unco-operative," "being lazy," etc.

As suggested by the incident of the cat and the kookaburra, it is difficult and stressful for me to cross a busy road, due to the very quick assessments of speed and distance which have to be made, and then instantly acted upon. By the time I have judged the speed and distance of oncoming vehicles, it is often too late for me to make my move. Not all stretches of road have pedestrian crossings or islands in the middle of the road, for example the Great South Road in Penrose, at the place where I have to cross to enter my workplace every morning. This road, like many others in Auckland, has four lanes and is very busy at rush hour (the time at which I have to cross it). I would rather do without the extra daily stress which this causes me. So far I have written about crossing on foot; it is even worse for me by car, as my slower processing speeds make me feel very nervous as a driver, and I am well aware of the extra damage which a car can cause.

I began driving at the age of fifteen, when I lived with my family in a rural area of South Auckland. In such a location, it was necessary for every possible family member to be able to drive, in case of any emergency. Certainly, the roads of our district were, at that time, almost devoid of vehicles, so it was not too anxiety-provoking for me to learn under these conditions. The roads of Auckland and surrounding districts have become increasingly busy, hazardous, and fast-moving since then. Though I have never had a car accident of any significance (nothing more than the occasional scrape and minor bump), I have phased driving out of my life. I now live in a suburb of Auckland City, and have found that, without a car, I can still continue with about 99 per cent of my usual lifestyle. My choice of dwelling was deliberately made according to major public transport routes, and I looked for – and found – a job within fifteen minutes' walk of my home. Journeys to other centres can be made by bus or train, and, in fact, I love being able to sit back and enjoy the trip, without the worry of negotiating the traffic, losing one's way, or finding parking when I get there (all major issues for me). For the rare occasion on which I may attend a party late at night, there are taxis – which also means that I can enjoy a beer or two, which would not be possible if driving afterwards. And even Newton's Seeds will deliver goods for a small fee. Owning a car uses up a lot of money in fees, insurance, and maintenance; even if, like me, one does not drive it very often. Giving it up has been a plus!

Please note: I do not wish to imply that everybody with Asperger Syndrome should refrain from driving. I do not think that this is true, and it would not be up to me, in any case, to make that judgement of their abilities. If there is any question mark over a person's ability in this area, this should be assessed and decided by a medical professional. It may be that, in this sphere of life, I am more impaired than the average person with Asperger Syndrome.

Chapter 22

Feathers with Everything! Part IV

Due to my restricted poultry-breeding facilities in town, I set up a "run-off" at my brother and sister-in-law's farm at Karaka, South Auckland. My first attempt, using an abandoned calf-rearing shed, met with dismal failure: no matter how many holes and apertures I closed up, the shed was always overrun with huge rats, which ate the eggs, the fowls' food, and I was afraid the fowls would be next. I spent at least $100 on bags of cement, which I would mix in small amounts in a bucket, then constructing edges around the already concreted shed floor. I knew how to use lengths of wood to hold the wet cement in place, and, although I spent many dusty, sweaty hours in this activity, it was very satisfying work. However, my efforts were unsuccessful: come nightfall, the rat population would be the same as before, and I could not understand how they were still getting in.

At the end of one such day, I was still messing around in this shed when I heard a cow approaching, swishing through the grass with snuffling breaths. There was nothing unusual about that, and I thought nothing of it, until – with a loud snick, I heard the door latch fasten on the outside. The cow had locked me in! I rushed to check the door, and it was true. My stomach did a flip-flop: with darkness falling, a stinking chook-house full of rats was the last place I wanted to spend the night. There was not even anywhere clean to lie down. There was another door at the end of the chook-yard, but I had long ago tied this shut with thick twine, otherwise the cows and donkey could open the door. Now, my only hope was to cut the fastenings somehow. The chook-house was a long way from any houses, and, anyway, I felt too embarrassed to scream my head off, with the prospect of then having to explain that a cow had locked me in. The villain of the piece was calmly cropping the grass outside. I frantically looked around for any sharp objects. Fortunately, my somewhat untidy habits meant that there were a few items of junk to be found, such as an empty tin, plus the trowel with which I had been doing the concreting. My insides throbbing with fear, I had to get on with it quickly, or it would be dark as well. I rubbed the edge of the trowel against the twine, and just kept going. Although it was a high-strength type of twine, it had been exposed to the weather for a long time, and I could tell that I was gradually cutting through each tiny strand. With the darkness uncomfortably close, I finally cut it right through, escaping with huge relief and trembling limbs.

I next moved my operations to a disused cow-shed, which was still in excellent repair. Its construction totally of concrete, the rats were unable to get in, unless through the open door when someone was visiting the shed; for these occasional ones, a dose of rat-bait in strategic places did the trick. (In case you were wondering why I didn't use rat bait in the first shed – one has to place the poison somewhere where the fowls can definitely not eat it, and there was no safe place in the calf-shed, whereas there were parts of the cow-shed which were fenced off from the fowls.) The cow-shed could be partitioned off into two breeding pens, which, of course, resulted in my enthusiasm getting the better of me – hatching and rearing dozens of chicks. I was still using only clucky hens for hatching, as the one electric incubator I tried using was a disaster.

John – my man friend – had moved on to the farm and was living there in his house-truck. He was using the other end of the cow-shed – the part without my poultry pens – as a workshop. In order to walk easily from the back of his truck to the cow-shed, he installed a plank connecting one to the other. The only trouble was, he never had the use of the plank to himself. Whenever he tried to "walk the plank," my nephew's pet Red Shaver hen would be in front of him – in fact, underfoot. Care would have to be taken so as not to trip over her and fall off the gangway. Nor was she satisfied when she had reached the other side: she would then have to reposition herself in front of John's feet and repeat the performance on the way back across the plank. This would go on all day!

One afternoon, when I was visiting John at the farm, we were having a cup of tea in his house-truck, my back against the large window. Suddenly there was a loud bump right behind my head, against the glass, and I slopped my tea with fright. It was the Red Shaver again – not content to be left out of the proceedings, she had attempted to join us by flying through the window, not realising it was shut. She was unharmed by this, and in future preferred, if the gangplank was not in place, to hop up the steps. John could never have a door or window open without her coming in for a visit. Once, we found her on top of the phone, "dialling" a number with her feet – so, making expensive toll calls was another of her naughty behaviours that John had to beware of.

My hatching and rearing activities in the cow-shed were partly in continuation of my specialty breed of Indian Game Bantams, and partly my experiments in colour, size, and shape – using different breeds of fowls. Also, for some years I had a pen of Old English Game Fowls; these were very special to me, but, unfortunately, the rooster of the breed was of a hysterical temperament, to say the least. His extremely loud and continuous screaming sessions could be provoked by my mere appearance some distance away. The noise was ear-splitting and distressing for me, nor could I calm him down by extended periods of handling him at night (most fowls will become used to their handler in time, but this one was possibly mentally ill, or autistic, I thought). I also thought it questionable to breed youngsters from a bird with such an unsuitable temperament. Therefore, although this rooster was strikingly beautiful, with his white and gold plumage (the colour pattern known as "pile"), I eventually gave him up and found a new home for him.

Before this happened, though, my rooster Rafael performed a few useful functions: he accompanied me in my University of Auckland graduation photos, and he played his part in providing fertile eggs for Michelle, my sister-in-law. Michelle decided, around this time, that she wanted some fowls of her own, and, as she did not want bantams, Rafael was the only stud-rooster available right then. My nephew's Red Shaver hen had gone clucky, so she was given the fertile eggs to hatch.

The first batch of chicks grew up and bred with the original Shaver hen, producing a pretty line of fowls, with the highly-strung Old English Game temperament diluted out of sight by the docile Shaver personality. They perched at night in a large clump of Chinese Lantern bushes, beneath the kitchen window. When a few more generations of these birds had reproduced, the fowl population around Michelle and Keith's house became a concern. As any poultry breeder knows, one ends up with a preponderance of roosters – with only one rooster being necessary for breeding, whilst the others eat tons of valuable chicken feed. Something would have to be done!

Over the ensuing months, Keith used various combinations of trickery, trapping, and even shooting to reduce the numbers of roosters. His efforts were not keeping pace, however, with the fowls' success rate in "going forth and multiplying." When a man phoned me requesting "a brown rooster" for his farm, I saw that as a chance for at least one of the excess males to go to a good home. On telling Keith and Michelle about this, together we decided to catch as many roosters as possible on the following Saturday night. With my poultry contacts in town, I could dispose of the unwanted extras – although most would not be going to "good homes," but to people's cooking pots, I knew. There is simply no way to find kind homes for dozens of spare roosters.

During one such episode, an acquaintance, Ali, had arrived with his cardboard boxes and his little preschool daughter. I had my carrying cages full of roosters in the laundry, so that, if there were to be an escape artist amongst them, we could, hopefully, contain the mishap to that one small room. We began the process of transferring the roosters from my cages to the boxes. The neighbour's cat, curious as always, had come in to investigate. Seeing the front door open, I thought it better to shut it, just in case of a major escape. As often happens, one of the roosters turned out to be a raucous screamer (although all we were doing was catching it). This frightened Ali's little daughter, who began crying loudly. At this, the cat also set up a terrified wailing, and tried to get out of the house – but, alas, the door was now shut, and I was wedged between the washing machine, a pile of cages, assorted boxes, and two other people, so I could not, at this moment, go to let the cat out. With the rooster, the child, and the cat all screaming, it sounded like some sort of madhouse – though not exactly something unfamiliar to me, in my lifestyle of "Feathers with Everything."

When the day arrived for rooster-catching at my brother's, I took a good look at the Chinese Lantern bushes. This is one of my favourite species of plant, but, for our present purposes, they were certainly a dense thicket. Keith and Michelle expressed doubts as to whether any roosters could be caught at all, as they were, by now, so wary and paranoid about humans. Come nightfall, Keith volunteered to venture into the jungle. Once inside it, I could see no trace of him, nor of the roosters. Michelle and I had been given banana boxes to throw over any escapees from the thicket. Michelle, my niece Lizzie, and I were lined up along the edge of the greenery, awaiting developments. A series of clucks (in rising tones of consternation), squawks, crashings through the undergrowth, mutterings and curses ensued. The thicket pulsated in and out in time to the sound effects, so that I was soon doubled up with uncontrollable laughter. Michelle succumbed to the same condition, so that I was aware that, if a rooster were to burst suddenly out of the bushes, we would have no chance of doing anything sensible with our banana boxes. Then an arm stretched upwards, holding aloft a brown rooster. That one went into a cage, and Keith dove down again for the next. A loud scream heralded the capture of the second, who was put into another cage. When Keith got to the white one, last on our agenda, he was said to be "impossible to catch."

"He's coming out, he's heading your way!" Keith called out, so Michelle and I tried to pull ourselves together. Then, "Sh—, I've stepped on him!" Keith yelled. Well, that's the end of it, I thought – the rooster won't be still sitting there after that. I thought I saw a white streak disappear into the darkness. Just when the white rooster seemed an impossible dream, Keith's upraised hand held the prize triumphant. That one was a throwback to his Old English Game ancestry – his rich gold trimmings glowing against his white plumage – so I kept him as a replacement breeding rooster. Now that he was caught, he sat quietly in my arms. (Well, I was holding on to his legs rather securely.) Considering the temperament of his grandfather, this one was much easier to tame. He went into the Old English Game breeding pen for the time being, while the captives came back with me to the city.

Next day, the man who wanted "a brown rooster only – no other colour will do" liked all of them so much that he took all of them to his farm! I was thrilled with the happy ending for all the roosters. Keith and Michelle were also glad to get rid of them, and, I'm happy to say, Keith emerged unscathed from his jungle adventure.

Chapter 23

My Life Now

Armed with my new, life-changing knowledge, I registered with two supported employment agencies – Workbridge and Workforce – and set about doing something useful while I was waiting. The end of 1999 was approaching. My first idea of where to do voluntary work was World Vision – because I knew their office was near my previous workplace in Newmarket, and another volunteer there told me that there were plenty of mail-outs to do. As mail-outs are one of my favourite activities – as well as World Vision being one of my favourite charitable organisations – I kept this in mind as a good choice. Before finally deciding, however, I contacted the Autistic Association, then situated in the grounds of Greenlane Hospital, Auckland – in case they had any useful work I could do. As the main office person and I were playing "phone tag" on the answerphones for a week or two, I very nearly gave up; but then, we made contact, and it turned out that the Association had a big pile of newsletters waiting to go out, but with no one to process them. In that case, I was the right person for them.

The office of the Autistic Association was one of many in the Parent and Family Resource Centre building. This old building was one of the historic types, quaint and picturesque; our office was upstairs, with a lovely view. Inside the room was a computer, a desk under the window, a bookshelf against the wall, and – no room for anything else. Not much bigger than a telephone box, two was a crowd. For the purposes of doing the mail-out, there was a spare desk outside in the corridor, at which I worked.

From there, one could see out of a different window on to a building which was used for experimental work on pigs: the squealing would alert one to the fact that a new truck-load had arrived.

The staff members then were the Co-ordinator, a part-time fundraiser, a volunteer, and Gretchen, the Programme Developer. At that stage, I only glimpsed Gretchen in passing, as her work was carried out away from the office. I had more contact with the other three, who were very friendly and welcoming to me. After a mail-out was completed, there seemed to be little work suitable for me to do, which I began to find frustrating. A short time before the Christmas of 1999, the Co-ordinator left and a new staff member started work there. We first met on the doorstep of the historic Greenlane Hospital building. Her name was Priya, and she was fresh from London, with a wealth of knowledge on autism, and a delightful cockney accent. One of the first things she did was to organise my work so that I would go there for three days only, with the other days off, so that I would still have a life outside of my voluntary job.

The Autistic Association was about to move to new premises, as our old building was deemed unsafe and was marked for demolition. Several committee members came in to sort and pack the contents of the office. I came along too, but, as I have very little idea of how to sort and tidy things in any case (let alone other people's things), I was of no use on this occasion.

The office reopened in an old house in the grounds of Mt. Richmond Special School, Otahuhu, Auckland. Now, we were spoiled for choice as to where to put our desks: the house was (and is) quite large. Gretchen and I took one room as our shared office; Priya took another, which she would soon be sharing with a new staff member; and there was a spacious lounge for meetings. My first request was for the key for our new post office box, which was granted; now, my first errand of the day was to collect the mail before coming in to the office. Priya asked me whether I wanted supervision. Though unsure as to what this meant, I replied "Yes," which meant that Priya officially became my supervisor, and we had regular supervision meetings – for the furtherance of my career and personal goals.

A few weeks later, the new person started: Christina, who was appointed as the new Co-ordinator, whilst Priya's role was now that of Information Field Officer. I soon discovered that Christina, and her young daughter, Abi, shared my love of newly ripened chestnuts, honey-locust seed pods, wood and grasses and feathers. We would get the "warm fuzzies" together over finding new items for our nature collections. Christina and I were also library-lovers of the first order, so we could share our enthusiasm for that subject. Gretchen, Christina, Priya, and I found that we all worked very well together. I was now allowed to answer the phones, directing calls to the other three as required. Or, if the enquiry was for literature, or just to speak to someone about Asperger Syndrome, I could deal with the call myself. I began my career of fielding hundreds of calls on Asperger Syndrome; and many times, the caller – usually a parent of a newly diagnosed child – seemed to find my inside knowledge reassuring. I have a university degree, after all – so the situation is far from being the end of the world. I tried to be sensitive to the rawness of the caller's feelings, though.

To add variety to my day and to my repertoire, Priya taught me how to make "proper" coffee in the percolator, which was served regularly to my colleagues. I would go out to buy milk and lunches; Lorraine taught me to do the banking; and I would keep the photocopied literature stocked up, which was used for mailing to callers who wanted information. My three days per week at the office were now full of activity, fun, and agreeable company. My three colleagues greatly appreciated and valued my insider knowledge of Asperger Syndrome, sometimes asking me my opinions. Priya and Gretchen started to take me out with them to do presentations to schools, where my contribution was always praised as being wonderfully authentic – more real than any textbook could ever be. I had the idea, which was allowed and encouraged, of holding a "Grandparents' Workshop" on Asperger Syndrome – because I suspected that, sometimes, extended family members wanted to ask questions, but did not always want to share their concerns with their own family. I gave this presentation, with Priya and Christina present, and it seemed to go down very well.

My life was now so fulfilling and happy that I often told people I was "dying of happiness." I was still on a benefit, because I was waiting for the supported employment agencies to find me a suitable job – though I was to find out that this would be a very lengthy process. There was also the chance that I would be offered a paid position where I was – several persons told me that that is how things tend to work. In the meantime, though, I was building my confidence, extending my skills, and enjoying myself as never before. Sometimes we even cooked meals in the office: Priya cooked an Indian speciality called dhal, and Gretchen made Greek salad. By telling Priya of my aspirations during our supervision meetings, some of these wishes could come true, for example the Grandparents' Workshop (as mentioned), contributions to the monthly newsletter, extending my presentations still further, going on the occasional home visit, and…things even more unimaginable were yet to come my way.

One day, Priya and I took the ferry to Waiheke Island – all expenses paid for – to do a presentation on Asperger Syndrome to a group of professionals. The day was sunny, the scenery was beautiful, and…Priya had recently given up smoking, which was very difficult for her. I felt sorry for her, but there was not much I could do about it, except tell her how brave she was and how well she was doing. By now, I was giving a much bigger portion of the shared presentations, and we were able to switch back and forth amongst our topics like magic.

A documentary-maker, Sue Younger, approached the Autistic Association (Auckland Branch) and asked for volunteers to take part in a TV programme on autism and Asperger Syndrome. The committee thought that I would be a suitable candidate, along with Harold (another Asperger adult), and various children and families. I was thrilled to be chosen, although my feelings on the subject would go full circle before the project was finished. The documentary, *Life Among Strangers*, would finally be screened in October 2000; (copies are available at the Association – since then renamed "Autism NZ" – for members to hire). The following are some of my experiences during the making of the programme.

What it was like being a TV Star

The filming of the television documentary on autism, *Life Among Strangers*, was certainly a new experience for me. I thought it might be fun, as well as promoting much-needed awareness of Asperger Syndrome in New Zealand.

Sue Younger (the Documentary Maker), and her team of Peter the Cameraman and Terry and Eugene the Lighting Men, were a pleasure to spend time with. Sometimes they bought me lunch. My bantam rooster was not so thrilled about being picked up and put down five times for the camera, however.

It was not easy getting used to having a camera "in my face," though. During the piece about the Asperger Social Group party, the voice-over commented that "Jen is very nervous." The presence of a film camera a few feet away, pointing at me, had something to do with that! Also at that party, someone let off an extremely loud firecracker, causing me to dive for cover into the furthest corner, only to be persuaded out when the film crew assured me that "It's safe now, Jen!" I considered the "unexpected loud noise" and its response to be an appropriate episode for the documentary, but later found out that it had not been included.

Finally, the evening of the participants' preview screening arrived. I was allowed to take John for moral support. It was interesting to meet the other "film stars," but I was a bit too nervous to make the most of this opportunity. The programme met with my approval until the segment with the bus came on, and I watched, with growing horror, as the person they called Jen appeared on the screen. Yes, I had been filmed boarding the bus, visiting the library, catching the rooster, so I knew that it had to be me. Without these clues, however, this person was difficult for me to recognise. I began gripping John's hand with enough ferocity to risk stopping the blood supply. For months afterwards, I spent an unprecedented amount of time in front of the mirror, trying to reconcile the person I saw there with the person on the programme. I would try to catch out this impostor by surprising it with a mirror confrontation.

The documentary preview having sent me into shock, I was then unable to tell anyone that the TV programme was coming up. I knew that I urgently had to do so, as most of my relatives had yet to be told that I have Asperger Syndrome, let alone that I would soon be talking about it on TV! I am a person of late diagnosis, having been (accidentally) diagnosed at 43 years old, and I am now 46. Getting used to the idea that I have Asperger Syndrome has been a process in itself, so I had not yet told more than a few close family and friends. When the TV screening was due in ten days, I knew that I really, really had to do it – though the letter I would write to them was already well underway in my brain. To soften the blow, I emphasised the point about Asperger Syndrome often being connected to high intelligence! I was not to find out my family members' reactions, however, until after the documentary appeared on TV, and I was concerned about this.

In the meantime, my request to Sue Younger for a second preview (in the attempt to settle my nerves) was granted. Sue showed, as ever, great sensitivity and kindness towards me, even inviting me to watch it again in the comfort of her living room. The second time around, I could take in much more, and even enjoyed it.

Priya and Gretchen (my colleagues) and I watched the real documentary at the office, all the better to answer the 0800 calls. As soon as the programme ended, the phones started (and would not ease off until 31 October). Would I be stared at as soon as I stepped out of my door next morning, I wondered? No, I found out with relief.

At the end of the month, we Auckland Branch staff were on the plane for the Autism Conference in Wellington, so it was a breathtaking time for me. At the conference, I suddenly found out what superstardom is like! Everyone recognised me and praised my efforts, which was extremely heart-warming. To add to the sense of luxury, we stayed in hotel rooms, went out for coffee, had breakfast in cafés, saw fantastic scenery, flew in planes... (but that is another story). Both at the conference and when answering phones back in Auckland, people never stopped telling me how wonderful the documentary had been, and how helpful my part in it. As I had predicted, a large proportion of these callers were adults who identified themselves with Harold and me, and who felt that they had Asperger Syndrome, as yet undiagnosed.

Therefore, my aim in participating in the programme had been achieved, and I am so glad that I had the opportunity to do so. And, oh yes, I received phone calls from some of my down-country relatives, telling me how proud they were of me, so the story has a perfect ending. After all my terror about the prospect of being seen by three million people, I am now enjoying my new-found fame. I would be happy to give presentations on my insights into Asperger Syndrome anywhere I am invited to go.

As I said, superstardom was heady stuff – too much of that, and I could become a Hollywood super-brat! However, more was to come!

The Christmas holiday was coming up again, and, with it, closure of the office, and a long holiday for Priya back to England, her home country – all of this was too much change for my liking (for someone who does not like all the hype and stress of Christmas in any case). Before all of this happened, Priya gave me a pile of interesting magazines for me to read over the break, and asked me the question: would I like to be the Keynote Speaker for the Autism One-Day Conference (Auckland Branch) in the following March? This was a very great honour, and I was both thrilled and stunned. I accepted the offer, knowing that I had a big task ahead of me: to write a speech that would pass my own high standards. I soon started to see the form that it would take, however. Christina helped me very much by staying in touch with me over the holiday break, and Priya was not beyond communication after all, as we exchanged e-mails to and from England. In one of my e-mails, I asked Priya what she thought I should include in my speech; she replied that she trusted me totally, as anything I wrote would be brilliant. I was, and still am, very touched by her confidence in me. If the Keynote Speech were to be a flop, a lot of the disgrace would have been on Priya's head, for giving the job to the wrong person. Therefore, it was obvious that she believed that this would not happen!

When the big day arrived, I was very nervous. No one who was present had even heard, or read, the Keynote Speech! I had to hope that it would touch the right note. Highly conscious of the strict one-hour time frame into which it had to fit, I felt that my mouth was on a treadmill – I could barely stop for breath. Nor could I tell from the audience whether they were enjoying it or not: this type of evaluation is likely to be too much for someone with Asperger Syndrome!

At the end of the speech, everyone clapped, and some people came up to meet me. Some looked radiant, a few people were wiping tears from their eyes, and one or two hugged me – cautiously asking me if this was all right. I realised that the speech had been very well received. My man friend, John, took me by the arm to lead me off to morning tea. I had to be led, as I felt like a stunned mullet – all of my energy and effort had gone into the speech, and now I could not think any more. John got me a cup of coffee and biscuits, for even this was beyond my abilities for the time being. Although my energy levels and thinking ability had gone into a sudden slump – due to having a very important project, and then completing it – I was in a very happy state, in fact, euphoric, because I had completed the project successfully. I find that this phenomenon happens when I have a project (of whatever sort) which requires a lot of thought and effort over a long time – the sudden completion, if successful, causes a slump in energy and thinking ability, although I am perfectly happy. I have also found that this can be a part of Asperger Syndrome, as I have compared notes with others. During the "slump," we should not have too much expected of us! In fact, John's response of leading me around by the arm for the rest of the day was very helpful – exactly what I needed.

Again, I was a hero for the day, afterwards settling back into my voluntary work at the Autistic Association for my three days per week. By now, though, things had started to change: Christina left to pursue her MA and doctorate in psychology; and, a few months later, Priya also resigned. Gretchen and I were still there, teaming up as co-presenters in a series of workshops about Asperger Syndrome, which are still ongoing, and which enjoy very positive feedback. A new co-ordinator, Kay, joined us. Kay and I soon found that we had a very good working relationship; with her area of expertise being "classical" autism, and mine being Asperger's, we complemented each other.

I was now feeling, however, that a change would have to take place regarding my career. It had become obvious that no funding was available for my role there, and never would be. The thought of leaving my work with autism broke my heart, but there was no paid job there for me. I did not want to remain on a social security benefit forever, and every so often social security officers would ask me about my job intentions. I asked the supported employment agencies to actively look for a paid position for me, but that process went too slowly for me. Therefore, I finally wrote myself a letter of introduction – including a list of the pros and cons of Asperger employees – and walked up and down my road.

Around the time when I saw the need to leave my voluntary job in favour of paid work, a new staff member started at the Autistic Association: Julie. We hardly had the chance to work together, but I could feel the warmth of her personality and her caring nature straightaway.

Living, as I do, on the edge of an industrial area, I thought that the best place to start looking for a job would be in my own back yard, so to speak. The vast majority of receptionists smiled and treated me warmly, promising to hand my letter to their manager. In one building, I had the feeling that I had accidentally burst into a board meeting, and hastily withdrew. In the reception area of another building, a man came up to me and told me, rather abruptly, that I was trespassing: "Didn't you see the No Trespassing sign?" On my way out, I looked for the sign, but saw none; and, in any case,

I cannot see how approaching a reception desk can be labelled as "trespassing" – why have a receptionist at all, then, if no one is allowed in?

Over three sessions, I covered 64 local businesses. This made me feel better than if I had done nothing. Soon afterwards, during an afternoon at my Autistic Association desk, a phone call came from an employer: he was interested in offering me a job. I was suddenly very excited and very scared! The Managing Director was too busy to interview me that day, but we arranged a time for the following Monday. Christina kindly offered to come with me as a support person. We met the Managing Director (John), and the Centre Manager (Lee) – suddenly I had a job as a print finisher at Copy Solutions, Penrose, Auckland.

In the meantime, Priya, Christina, and Kay (employees and ex-employees of the Autistic Association, Auckland Branch) had been writing letters without my knowledge, with the result that I was chosen to receive a Volunteer Award from Auckland City Council. The presentation ceremony, which Mum, my brother, my sister-in-law, and I attended, was held at the Mt. Wellington council rooms, and included refreshments and short speeches by local councillors. It was a lovely evening, in which a dozen or so volunteers were shown the utmost appreciation and were presented with flowers, a video and a large commemorative plaque. This took place the night before I was to start my new job: quite a rite of passage, marking the change between my voluntary work and my new paid job. Now that I would be working for five days a week, I would no longer be able to spend my three days – or any days – in the office of the Autistic Association. This was a wrench for me, but it could not be helped. Although no longer in the office, I have continued voluntarily organising a social gathering and a pen-pal club for Asperger adults and teens, as well as regularly contributing to the monthly newsletter. Also, as I have mentioned, Gretchen and I have continued running our workshops on Asperger Syndrome, for which I am now paid a fee. In these ways, I can still be a part of the Asperger and autistic wider community.

Next morning, I was rather nervous; on arrival at work, I was taken to meet the other staff members of the copy centre. With a relatively small number of employees – ten in all – the workplace had the friendly atmosphere which is seldom found in a large establishment. My colleagues included sales reps, printing operators, a courier driver, a graphic designer and a clerical person. Everyone was helpful towards me, and Managing Director John said "Welcome aboard!"

Thanks to my previous, short holiday stints at the university copy centre, I had one relevant skill already: punching pages on the electric paper punch, and spiral binding (using plastic coils to bind the pages into books). Indeed, this previous experience was why I had approached printing firms for work during my latest job search. Now, though, there were many new things to learn, and I hoped that I would not be learning them all at once. Fortunately for me, for my first two days, there was a huge stack of papers which had to be folded-and-stapled into booklets, using the folding-and-stapling machine – and this was the same thing over and over again, thus removing the need for much brain-work on my part, whilst I acclimatised myself to my new environment. The rhythmic sounds of the machine, and my repetitive movements of feeding the papers in, lulled me into a pleasurable state similar to that brought about by my marble alleys when I was a youngster. I did get aches and pains in a variety of places, due to the unaccustomed type of work; though, I found out, this was temporary. I had no way of knowing whether my first two days' work had been satisfactory, which was of such concern to me that I had to ask the managing director; he assured me that I was doing well and was a valuable staff member.

My supervisor, Lee, wrote up a list for me of tasks to do when I first came in each morning. This was helpful, and I supplemented it with my own written notes, every time I was given instructions. For instance, I was to check and replenish the paper in three printing machines along the front window. At first, even this was complicated, as each machine stocked different sizes and grades of paper, necessitating that I always doublecheck which paper I was putting into which tray. Also, I was shown how to read the meters on all the machines: as every type of machine had a radically different method for getting to the meter reading, this was another skill which took some time to master. Having written all the instructions down, of course, meant that I had no worries about this: I could refer to my notes each time. Last on my list was the task of cleaning the machines' screens with cleaning fluid and a cloth.

These morning duties were usually finished by 9 a.m., after which time Lee or one of my senior colleagues would find me the next job to do. As other individuals with Asperger Syndrome will identify with, I would have preferred always to have known which jobs I would be given, throughout the day; but, in a business such as a copy centre, even the managers could never predict which jobs would come up next, so I was nearly always on the edge of uncertainty. Even after being given a set job to do, the arrival of another customer would often rearrange the job priorities, meaning that I would have to leave one job partly done and switch to another. This was not always easy for me, as (along with many others who have Asperger Syndrome) I much prefer to stick to one task until it is finished, only then turning to the new task: that is, doing one thing at a time. I tried to be a diligent worker, but had no idea of how to judge my performance. Most of the time, the jobs seemed to chug along the production line and out of the door with little or no trouble, so I had to assume that all was going well. I had the satisfaction of belonging to a small, dedicated team – as their one and only "Print Finisher." I was oh so proud of this title!

As I was still writing articles – on "Adult Issues" – for the Autistic Association (Auckland Branch) newsletter, my new job naturally came up as something to write about. The September 2001 newsletter contained the following column from me.

Adult Autistic and Asperger Issues

1. Our "Relaxed" Asperger Social Group (adults & teens) met again in July; this time we had twelve people. All seemed to enjoy it. The venue is our Auckland Branch office, 32 Albion Road, Otahuhu. The next gathering will be Saturday 22 September. Please tell any eligible persons about this social group. If you wish to join the other, more active, Asperger Social Group, please enquire at the office for the contact people for this.

2. Autistic Spectrum Pen-Pal and E-Mail Pal Club: As I am no longer a volunteer in the office, I thought I could streamline this, to make it easier for me to do from home... [I have omitted the rest of the details here].

3. I have a job (as mentioned in my last column.) Now I have been a print finisher in a copy centre for one month, and I have

settled in more. I completed a month's work there on 12 August, which coincided with my 46th birthday! A print finisher does the final processes on the products (books, booklets, documents, posters) that the printers have printed. This can be folding, stapling, punching with an electric puncher, and binding with plastic coils or wire. I have been enjoying this. My colleagues have all been very friendly and helpful. I would like to say a big THANK YOU to my employers, John and Lee, for giving me this chance, and a new start, at a time when the 63 other work-places I visited did not. Thank you also to Auckland Branch staff members Kay, Gretchen, and Julie, for listening to my work adventures and thereby helping me settle in. (They will also lend you a listening ear, if you contact the office.) Some issues that have come up for me regarding full-time work:

(a) The big transition from my voluntary job to full-time paid work.

(b) Coping when learning a new task does not go right first time (though most tasks have gone well).

(c) Trying to perform a new task when the radio was playing loudly (multi-tasking); as I had already written down all the steps of my new task, I concentrated as hard as I could on my written notes and managed to override the sound enough to do the task (plus, as I am now 46, I have progressed in some areas of life).

(d) Coping with sudden changes in the task I am doing; if a new "rush job" comes in, someone will interrupt the task I am doing and instruct me to do the new task; though I do not like this, so far I have managed.

(e) The stomach and gut problems which are a daily reality for many Autistic Spectrum people can make full-time work difficult.

Straightaway after writing this column, I knew (which I had suspected from the start) that full-time work was proving too much for me, physically and psychologically. I asked John, the Managing Director, if I could move down to part-time hours: thirty hours per week. Fortunately, he is an understanding sort of person, and he agreed to my request. My six hours per day were still spread over five days per week.

In the course of my job, I was given quite a few lots of wire binding to do, which I enjoyed (after the initial confusion, experienced each time, as to which way around the bindings were supposed to go). Doing a big batch of them was fun for me, and they usually turned out well (though some other workers seemed to have occasional difficulty with wire binding). The paper-folding machine was more problematic for me – it seemed to depend "which way you held your mouth," at least at first. Not going right meant screwing the paper up, folding it in the wrong place, and jamming the machine. Even this temperamental beast gradually improved over time. I found out that laminating posters, and then trimming the edges on a special trimmer, was very enjoyable. Sometimes I was given collating to do: walking up and down a row of pages, putting them in order to form books. One day, as I described in Chapter 9 "Co-ordination Issues," the pages were very numerous and extremely slippery. I had tried my very hardest, all morning, to handle the collated books (as yet unbound) without dropping them. Suddenly, a colleague asked me a question – just as I was getting my grip on another pile of pages – which resulted in my dropping the whole thing on the floor – and they were un-numbered pages. Too anxious and confused to sort out the mess, I had to own up to my supervisor, who had to spend half an hour restoring the pages to order. Afterwards, I could easily recognise it as a case of being distracted at the wrong moment – at a time when I was already having to concentrate my hardest not to make a mistake. I am not blaming anybody; simply making an observation.

On 12 January I made it to my six month milestone, of which I was very proud. The premises were shut, at the time, for our annual Christmas holiday. The day before we were to return to work, my man friend, John, and I were together, and made a trip to the Museum of Transport and Technology. It was an interesting day; I very much enjoyed the in-house film about Jean Batten, the famous aviator. That was also the day on which I experienced the symptom of bleeding from the bowel. I felt anxious about this, but lucky that John was with me for moral support. On our return to work, our Managing Director came to tell me that I had earned a pay rise, to take effect next pay day! This was a thrill. At the same time, however, I had to visit the doctor, who ordered a colonoscopy. My friend John was back at his Waihi address by now, and my Mum came with me to the clinic. So it was that, two days after I got a pay rise, I received the diagnosis of bowel cancer.

Poor Mum was thrown into shock more quickly than I was. As I have medical insurance (which I had doggedly kept paying for in spite of my lean years on a benefit), I now had the option of a quicker admission via private hospital. Now that I had the diagnosis of cancer, I did not want to wait – I wanted it dealt with as quickly as possible. The colonoscopy clinic staff referred me to a surgeon and a hospital: I obtained the first possible admission date, for the following week.

It was probably fortunate that my first and foremost anxiety was for the care of my poultry – this kept me from thinking about the actual operation beforehand. My two breeding roosters were farmed out to my brother and sister-in-law's place in the country. Even though I actually wanted to part with one of these roosters (to a good breeding home) in any case, there was now not time to arrange this, so the farming-out was done as an emergency measure. I had three adolescent birds, at least one of which was a male, which I had to do something with before admission – as, in hospital, I would not be able to supervise the "roosters in, roosters out" procedure which I perform every night at home. Sadly, I had to let these three birds go, even though I had not yet satisfied myself that all were, in fact, males; I could not risk the consequences of male birds coming into their crowing capacity whilst I was away. As for the others, my Mum offered to care for them each day – unfortunately for her, there was not much choice but to do so. This meant a lot of travelling for Mum, from her house to mine once a day, except for a couple of times when my friend John came up from Waikino for a visit; on those occasions, John would feed my birds, visit me in hospital, and let Mum have the day off. I did not like having to leave others responsible for my pets, but the whole cancer episode had happened so suddenly; and, besides, I did not want to have to give up my pets completely, simply because I was going into hospital.

I could write another whole chapter on the terrors of being in hospital for major surgery for ten days – probably made worse by the anxieties inherent in Asperger Syndrome, for example never knowing what was going to happen to me next. However, such a chapter would be difficult for most readers to stomach, and my talents are probably better utilised elsewhere.

Suffice it to say that now, at the time of writing, I have been back home for 20 hours, and very relieved to be back in familiar territory. I am now in recuperation mode, off work for two months. I was discharged with the good news of an "A1" cancer outcome: the surgeon said that this is the best possible test grade, which only 15 per cent of rectal cancer patients end up with. It means that I have a 99 per cent chance of no further recurrence of the cancer; (no one can ever guarantee 100 per cent). This is the latest episode of my life to date.

Chapter 24

Some Implications
of very Late Diagnosis

1.   As you can see from my experiences, it can be difficult for an
     adult with Asperger Syndrome to obtain the correct diagnosis
     (which is the first step in obtaining any understanding or help).
     By now, you will have seen what the obstacles are: largely,
     professionals (doctors, psychologists, teachers, etc.) who are not
     aware of Autistic Spectrum Disorders. Unless *somebody* in the
     adult's life becomes aware of Asperger Syndrome (or mild
     autism), there is no possibility of the adult being assessed in the
     correct way.

     More often than not, at the present time, it is the adult who
     is the one who finally realises what the problem is. This can be
     from watching a TV programme, or seeing an article, on
     Autistic Spectrum Disorders. In my own case, I realised due to
     attending a university lecture on the subject. Once you have
     discovered it in such a way, there is more chance of being
     correctly diagnosed, especially if you can carry the book or
     article into the doctor's office and use it as evidence. Of course,
     even then, some professionals will not necessarily believe you;
     and some professionals do not like being told anything new,
     especially by their patients. I would strongly recommend that
     the patient take a support person with him or her to the

professional; the support person can do some, or most, of the talking.

But it is those adults who have no way of discovering what their problem is who are at the biggest disadvantage. This was the same for me, until the age of 43. By the time a person has reached their late thirties or beyond, he or she may well have become "brainwashed" into thinking that he/she is just "stupid," "inadequate" in some way. The undiagnosed Asperger adult does not have any reason to look for information on Asperger Syndrome (AS) – because how can you research something that you do not know exists? The same logic does not apply to the professionals, as it is their *job* to learn about as wide a range of disorders as possible, and their responsibility to up-skill themselves as new medical knowledge becomes available. The adult with AS also has a variety of difficulties which hamper his or her functioning, which make it harder for him or her to follow the problem through to its solution. After all, if you do not *know* that you are missing out on perceiving up to 90 per cent of what is going on in a conversation or social situation, how can you work out *why* you are feeling confused? You need to be given the answer (i.e. the correct diagnosis) before you can realise what is missing, in order to begin to address the problem.

2.   Logically following from point one, the undiagnosed adult with AS becomes more confused and anxious about life, more and more "on the outer" of the social world, and grows more and more to feel that he or she cannot understand other people, and that they cannot understand him or her. He or she is more than likely to have experienced bullying or to have been taken advantage of by others, as people with AS can easily be tricked and manipulated by others. (This is due to our difficulty with understanding social situations, e.g. we usually have trouble perceiving underlying agendas.) All of this, therefore, is likely to lead the undiagnosed adult with AS to retreat and withdraw from other people, at least in whatever spheres are possible, for example one's home life. Such adults, if unmarried, are likely to become loners (in one or more spheres of life). The type who

tends towards being a loner is then likely to become ever more eccentric, as he or she has no "reality check" with other people. This set of circumstances can go into a downwards spiral, with the eccentricity tending to keep other people away as well. The next thing that can follow is that the adult lives in more and more of his or her own fantasy world. This is more-or-less forced upon him or her, as he/she cannot mesh with the "real" world of other people. As a result of this, if the undiagnosed adult ever does come to the attention of mental health professionals, he or she is likely to be diagnosed with schizophrenia, psychosis, or similar. This is because the professional has seen only the end result of Asperger Syndrome, but without seeing the cause, and what led up to, the psychosis. Then, the patient can end up getting inappropriate and harmful treatment, for example antipsychotic drugs, which may not be suitable for someone with AS; and, as well as this, he or she will fail to get the appropriate understanding and help necessary for someone with AS. Also, the wrong diagnosis is something which can stick to a person for life, with subsequent medical professionals never questioning the original diagnosis.

Another mental health scenario which is possible (and which happened to me) is the following misdiagnosis – Persons with AS typically process and understand concepts in a concrete way, for example abstract concepts are typically put into a "visible, tactile" form so that we can think about them more easily. This is allied to picture thinking, and can be a very original, creative way of thinking. An undiagnosed AS adult can go ever further with this process, until the various parts of his or her own personality are partitioned into separate personalities, with separate names. Before my own diagnosis, I, too, saw myself as being inhabited by different entities, both good and bad. Now I understand how this happened. However, this phenomenon can also be misunderstood by mental health professionals, who, on hearing of an array of personalities, will immediately think Multiple Personality Disorder. Indeed, as in the last example, it may have come to a diagnosable stage, but the professional is not seeing and understanding the *how* and *why* of the condition: that it is a result of undiagnosed Asperger Syndrome (in our hypothetical patient). Again, the unaware professional will proceed to treat the patient for Multiple Personality Disorder, but without realising that the underlying cause is undiagnosed Asperger Syndrome.

The same goes for Anxiety Disorder, Depression, Social Phobia and probably other diagnoses: these conditions can all be caused by Asperger Syndrome, especially if undiagnosed. Mental health professionals need to be aware of this.

3. Living to one's late thirties or beyond without the correct diagnosis of AS causes a person to feel invalidated in their experience. As the undiagnosed AS adult is having different experiences from most "normal" people, he or she is not living the same reality, "not sharing the same planet." If he or she tried to share his or her experiences with others at a younger age, he or she would have become aware of their differences, and then probably stopped sharing his experiences as an adult. Not only does this cause a fracture in one's social relating, but it serves to make the adult go on feeling invalidated, unacknowledged, for a lifetime…at least, until one receives (if one ever does receive) the diagnosis. This is why I made sure that I obtained an official diagnosis, on paper, in black and white. Even after the diagnosis (which I have now had for three years), I still feel the fear that others may not believe me. For this reason, I am comforted by knowing that the diagnosis is official, (that is, not just in my own imagination). If I have to go to somewhere like the Social Security department or to a doctor, I can take the official piece of paper with me as proof. This need for validation may be something which will carry on for the rest of my life (as yet, I don't know).

4. The adult with undiagnosed AS, as I wrote earlier, tends to live in his or her own private world. Not feeling the same as other people – not feeling "normal," makes some of us try very hard to "get by" as normal, to pass the "unwritten tests." (One adult with late diagnosis of AS – Liane Holliday-Willey – has written her autobiography and called it *Pretending to be Normal*). Without

doing a survey, I cannot tell if this is typical of most AS individuals, but I suspect it is common enough. As we lack the inbuilt unwritten rules of social interaction, we have to observe very carefully, use trial and error, and try to work it all out via our powers of reason.

One positive outcome of all this can be that, by the time we have reached our forties or so, we may, through all our efforts, have worked out how society and the world works – *better* than "normal" people have. Because we have been forced to study society and the world consciously (whereas this knowledge is largely innate or acquired unconsciously with "normals,") we may be able, later in life, to understand these things *more* thoroughly than "normals" do. This is a similar phenomenon to the situation where a Chinese student, knowing no English, comes to live in New Zealand – and two or three years later is Dux of the school and is able to speak and write perfect English, whereas most New Zealanders cannot use their own language to such a high standard! The hypothetical Chinese student has achieved this superior ability from consciously studying English (very hard); whereas those of us who have grown up speaking English have not usually studied it so carefully! The conclusion of both of these examples is this: the people who are on the "outer" of the dominant culture are forced to observe it and study it very diligently, in order to learn the unwritten rules of the culture, thereby enabling themselves to obey the rules, thus fitting in to the culture; but the people who are members of the dominant culture do not even completely know what its rules *are*, not having had to struggle to fit in; they have always automatically been "in."

I am not the one who first wrote this rather enlightening explanation: I once read it in a book review, but, unfortunately, cannot now track down the author, although I have tried. (If any readers can tell me the name of the author, and his book, I would be grateful.)

In turn, all of what I have written in point four leads to a further link: the phenomenon of "passing." Passing was first used to refer to light-coloured Black people passing as Whites into White society. One can certainly not blame them for wanting to do so, as this was in the days of oppression against Blacks in the USA. If one could get away with it, passing as white meant an education, a good job, mixing with a new echelon of people, prospects...a whole new, and better, life. The downside was that those who managed to slip into White society lost their Black contacts, their friends, family (because they could not risk being seen in Black society; and, sometimes, Black society rejected them as a result of their passing) as well as their very sense of identity, their self. Also, the subterfuge which was involved in maintaining the pretence was very stressful, so that some, although "successful" at passing, nevertheless were "unsuccessful" at coping with the stress and inner loneliness of it all, and fell prey to mental illnesses.

Nowadays, "passing" has been extended to the phenomenon of any Outsider successfully getting into the dominant culture, through pretending to be one of them. This is a similar situation to how autistic and Asperger Syndrome adults cope in the dominant culture of "normals." Whether or not we totally succeed (and thereby fool other people), many of us are constantly trying to "pass" as normal. Some Asperger Syndrome adults do pass for normal, at least some of the time, but the conscious effort of trying to be someone other than what we are can be an enormous stress. Therefore, is all that stress worth it? Nowadays, the concept (if not always the reality) of "celebrating diversity" is known in modern society. Ethnic minorities are reclaiming (and with all good reason) their right to exist as different, but equal, persons. It is also fine, nowadays, to be Gay or Lesbian. People with disabilities are also coming in from the outer, to participate in mainstream society. So, why do people with an Autistic Spectrum condition have to keep on pretending to be "normal," instead of just being who we are?

Of course, we who have Asperger's or autism do have to learn a lot of things in order to fit in even minimally (not like in the bad old days of "handicapped" children being placed in institutions, there to be taught nothing, which then reinforced the stereotype that such children could learn nothing.) But we can also be proud of who we are, we can say "I have Asperger Syndrome" if we need to or want to, we should be allowed to be a bit different if that is really how we are – we do not *have* to be Mr or Mrs J Average in Normal-town. The need for parents, teachers, or other professionals to stamp out every trace of "difference" is what extinguishes our abilities, our creativity. The need of certain psychiatric personnel to eradicate my "differences" caused me to lose my valuable tool of picture thinking. If these same "professionals" got loose in NASA, there would be no brilliant, inventive scientists left.

5. Again, linked to the above, is the phenomenon of "coming out." My experience of coming out as a gay person allows me to draw this comparison. (I have some authenticity with which to do this, as I spent six or seven years identifying as gay – as you will know if you have read my earlier chapters.) Suddenly getting the Asperger or autistic diagnosis as an adult puts you in a similar position. You often want to tell your parents – but you fear the reaction this may cause. In my own case, I waited a year to tell my Mum! – because I was anxious lest the news upset her. As it happened, it did not upset her, but only confirmed her feeling – which had started as soon as I was born, she told me! – that something was different about me. Mum has been extremely supportive towards me; all the more since hearing my diagnosis.

For other individuals, however, it is not always so successful. Returning to the Gay theme, I knew of one woman whose parents permanently disowned her when she came out to them. Therefore, I would not categorically state that everybody should automatically go through the same process. I have also heard of an Asperger adult whose parents did not accept the news in a way which was supportive towards her. For the Asperger adult, having to tell one's parents is the opposite way around to most medical situations: for most congenital conditions (present at birth), it is the parents who have to tell the child about the condition, not the other way around. For an Asperger adult to get a late diagnosis, it follows that his or her parents are in an older age group – which can mean that they are too old, too conservative in their ideas, to accept the news. As they have grown old with their "Johnny" always having been this way, they are not always able to accept that Johnny is this way because of a developmental disorder, a neurological condition, and they may simply not want to know. Such a situation is, of course, a sad and a difficult one for the Asperger adult.

Whilst I cannot – and will not – tell every Asperger adult that he or she *must* tell the diagnosis to anyone, I myself have my own feelings about the importance of coming out. Yes, I was lucky with my Mum's reaction, but I have also told others, some of whom I did not (according to some people's opinions) strictly *have* to tell. For instance, as soon as I went out looking for a job again (my first job after the diagnosis), I told every prospective employer that I had AS – before they offered me anything! In this way, nobody could say that I had tricked them into employing me – they made that decision already knowing that I have AS. (And yes, I did get a job this way!) I know that some folks would say "Why on earth tell them that – because the employer will probably not take you on, with that knowledge!" Yes, I realise that I run that risk. But it is a risk which I choose, and want, to take – because I need to be accepted with the AS, or not at all.

I know that it has a lot to do with my late diagnosis – therefore, being forced to live with a "secret," though a secret not of my making, or of my choosing. I had to live 43 years with the secret that something was different about me – and sometimes, something was just plain wrong with me – even though I did not *want* to have this secret. Because this "thing" had no name, no official recognition, I was forced to live with an unnamed entity. As I am a person who much prefers to be open and honest, living with this unknown, unknowable secret was a constant source of anxiety. So, now that I have the diagnosis, I can get rid of the secret – and good riddance!!! *I no longer want to live that "secret life!"* I no longer want to creep around trying to follow someone else's norms – I have Asperger Syndrome, *and this is OK!*

As well as my "We're here – get used to it" announcement, above, I have other reasons for choosing to be "out" about my AS. In the matter of employment, I feel the need to tell my employer and supervisor (and sometimes my colleagues as well), because of my relatively high anxiety levels, which are "normal" for me. Apparently, other people can detect my high anxiety levels in any case, so it is better for them to know that this is part of my AS, than for them to keep on wondering what is wrong.

As well as this, there are other AS traits which can surface in the workplace (and which contribute to the anxiety): a keen startle response to sudden noises or movements; problems with multi-tasking (including working with distracting stimuli present); difficulties with learning new tasks; difficulty with sudden changes in routine; and sometimes misunderstanding what is said to me, especially when others are joking. Because these situations do occur in my workplace, I find it much easier all round if my supervisor (etc.) already knows that these are traits of AS. Otherwise, if I did not tell, I would again be living that unwanted secret life.

Some people fear that letting the diagnosis be known will invite teasing and taunting from unkind workmates (or fellow students, or whomever). OK – I cannot guarantee that it won't. But from what I've heard from some others with AS, they get teased and taunted even *without* their workmates knowing the correct diagnosis – they get called such names as Stupid, Crazy, Un-Co, (add on whatever names you can think of). Therefore, I still tend to think that things might be no worse if these tormentors knew the *correct* term – Asperger Syndrome – for the person's peculiarities. Could such insensitive people be any worse than they are already being in any case? Also, telling them that the AS adult has a legitimate condition puts the responsibility for decent behaviour on to them; they no longer have any excuse for tormenting the person, as he or she has a recognised disability. In fact, for the workmates to continue tormenting a disabled colleague would constitute breaking the law under the Equal Rights legislation. If this were to be proven, (and I admit that the operative word is "if"), they could land themselves in trouble.

For me, it is a case of that saying of Jesus: "The Truth will set you free." Getting rid of that one big secret certainly makes me feel liberated!

Chapter 25

The Stone Age Connection

This is my own foray into "Evolutionary Psychology." I have included it for a reason; it is relevant to the rest of my book. The first section is an introduction to the subject of prehistoric humans. The second section extends further, into the human brain and language, and looks at how these topics are relevant to people with an Autistic Spectrum Disorder.

The Cro-Magnon people were the first "fully modern" human beings, the ancestors of everyone who is alive today – so the scientists say. The Cro-Magnons lived in the Upper Paleolithic (Late Stone Age), which began 40,000 years ago.

The Neandertals, a type of "archaic" human, didn't quite make it to "fully modern" status, and the question remains as to why. Nowadays, most authorities believe that the Neandertals somehow died out, whilst the Cro-Magnon people took over the world. The Neandertals lived during the Middle Paleolithic (Middle Stone Age), and their culture is called the Mousterian. Their remains have been found mainly in France, Germany, Spain, Yugoslavia and the Middle East.

The Neandertals started out as victims of "bad press," as the first-discovered skeleton was described by a "scientist" who wanted to make them seem as inhuman as possible. In reality, the Neandertals were of a stocky build, but, "shaved, bathed and dressed in a suit, they would have passed as normal commuters on the New York subway." (Shreeve 1995) Their demise wasn't due to a shortage of grey matter, as they had at least as large a brain as modern humans, with some individuals possessing a bigger brain than us.

It has been discovered that, in some parts of the world, for example, Israel, the Cro-Magnons and Neandertals lived at the same time, virtually side by side, sharing the same culture, for thousands of years. "Two distinct kinds of human, sharing *one* culture, were apparently squeezed together in an area not much larger than the state of New Jersey. Rather than resolving the paradox, the new dating techniques only teased out its riddles: If two different kinds of human were behaving the same way in the same place at the same time, how can we call them different? ...If modern humans do not descend from Neandertals but replace them instead, why did it take them so long to get the job done? Can one call so long a process 'replacement?'" (Shreeve 1995, p.183)

In 1990, author James Shreeve was shown a Neandertal mandible from Zafarraya cave in southern Spain. At the time, it was said to be around 30,000 years old; more recently, the fossil has been re-dated as around 28,000 years old. "So their moment of extinction creeps ever closer to the present" (Shreeve 1995, p.342) This is further evidence that our fore-fathers and the Neandertals were co-existing... (and maybe more than co-existing?)

Some have disputed whether earlier hominids than us, and in particular the Neandertals, had fully acquired human language. The achievements of the Neandertals, which include what appears to be ceremonial burial of their dead, indicate the use of abstract thinking, which, in turn, suggests a complex form of language.

Language as we know it today may have developed its various facets at different points in time, however. "Linguist Derek Bickerton has suggested that the last major feature of fully modern language to emerge was the concept of time itself – a past and future tense." (Shreeve 1995, p.308)

Human language is no longer considered to be an all-or-nothing proposition. Recent research indicates that there is no discrete "Language Centre" in the human brain. Instead of this, the different facets that go to make up language are situated in different parts of the brain. Vocabulary, therefore, is stored separately from grammar; the other separate storage areas include comprehension, physical sound production, the communica-tion concept, indirect meaning, and so forth. These findings support what is currently known about language use in Autistic Spectrum Disorders and in some other neurological conditions. For example, a person with autism may be able to recite the contents of the telephone directory from A to F – with perfect recall and pronunciation. However, the person may not have any comprehension of the information which he is reciting; the feat does not require any knowledge of grammar; and the exercise is highly unlikely to be what "normal" folks call "communicating." Individuals who have an Autistic Spectrum Disorder are known for their tendency, even when able to physically produce speech, to be lacking in other components of language use. This state of affairs becomes possible when we understand that all of these different components are stored in separate parts of the brain – with some parts of the brain intact, and others impaired. (Paraphrased from a talk by Professor Michael Corballis, speaking on behalf of Stephen Pinker, "Varsity Hour," Planet FM, 104.6 FM, New Zealand Radio, 14 April 2001).

Further to Bickerton's comments (Shreeve 1995, p.308), if time was the last feature of language to evolve, this suggests another separate part of the brain, with its own possibility of being intact or impaired. Some individuals who have Asperger Syndrome, although very intelligent in other areas, have great difficulty with the concept of time and the skill of learning to tell the time.

> Archaics like the Neandertals may have rubbed their bodies with ocher, worn hawk feathers in their hair, or otherwise adorned their persons. But there is no evidence of such a wholesale, formalised effort to transform elements of the material world into social messages [as occurs in later, Cro-Magnon, humans]. The universal human habit of ornamenting the body to communicate gender, social status, group affiliation, and other information about the wearer appears to have sprung into being at the beginning of the Upper Paleolithic [Cro-Magnon times, fully modern human]. (Shreeve 1995, p.320)

As for the need to display one's gender, social status, and group affiliation, this is difficult for some of us who have Asperger Syndrome to understand. For myself – and, as I have recently discovered, for some other adults with Asperger Syndrome – the issues of gender, social status, group affiliation, race, colour, sexual preference, choice of clothing, and other "markers" are irrelevant. For those of us who are "wired up" this way, the real issues about a person are their character, ethics, inner qualities, achievements, interests, and intelligence level.

"To the extent that a Neandertal's social world was more homogeneous and straightforward than ours, so, I believe, was a Neandertal's sense of self." (Shreeve 1995, p.321) Some Asperger adults, (such as myself), portray our social selves more "straightforwardly" than do "normal" people in that we do not see the need for the trappings of status and so on. In fact, (speaking for myself), I not only dispense with such trappings, but see them, (when I see them at all), as a negative trait of "normal" people. To me, this trait seems not only illogical but also unpalatable – because it implies that people can be, and should be, pre-judged by outward appearances. This superficial evaluation is one of the very things of which some Asperger individuals disapprove intensely.

The Asperger individual may turn out to be a surprise package. This is because many of us do not feel the same need to outwardly display statements about ourselves. Underneath an ordinary or shabby exterior may well exist a complex private self. There is a partial comparison with some other situations in human society: when the Europeans first met the Australian Aboriginals, for instance. Because the material technology of the First Australians was relatively simple, the Europeans made incorrect assumptions based on superficial assessments. The Europeans considered the First Australians to be "primitive" and inferior, basing their dealings with them on this assumption. When European researchers bothered to investigate, however, they found the First Australian cultures to be immensely rich and detailed in such spheres as language, environmental knowledge, cosmology, the arts, social structure and spirituality. Aboriginal languages, far from being "primitive," are complex and elegant; the structure of some of them, for example Dyirbal, resembles that of Latin. This is just one more example of a minority group being misunderstood and dismissed by a majority group which was unwilling to question its own assumptions.

I have addressed the issue of "self-hood" in other chapters also, including "Identity and Boundary Issues" and "Some Implications of Very Late Diagnosis." It is poignant that the persons whose very definition – autistic – is taken from the Greek word for "self" – "autos" – are the same persons who often experience more-than-average problems with their identity, that is, the sense of self.

> If they had not gone extinct, I suspect their world today would not be greatly different from their world 50,000 years ago, not because Neandertals and other archaics lacked the power to innovate, but because, to them, innovation was anathema... Their conservatism was profound and immense, as voluminous as the great cranial vaults in which they stored the remembered minutiae of their days. Novelty, strangeness, surprise – strangeness in all its forms was assiduously avoided... (Shreeve 1995, p.339)

Most families of a person who has an Autistic Spectrum Disorder will have noticed that the person avoids change and attempts to stay within familiar territory and experiences. I have seen a pictorial check-list for ASD which states: "Variety is *not* the spice of life" [for a person with an Autistic Spectrum Disorder].

> Neandertal society would be new-averse, circumscribed by the known... I imagine Neandertals regarding strangers not as an anxious, imminent threat, but as a sort of superfluous blur on the very fringe of awareness. Strangers do not matter. (Shreeve 1995, p.339)

> Neandertal social circumstances would render Neandertals politically transparent, more gullible. But more honest too... What I see is a world that mandates directness. (Shreeve 1995, p.340)

Chimpanzees are known to be able to engage in deception, which is one of the many points in which they resemble modern humans. Individuals who have an Autistic Spectrum Disorder, on the other hand, tend to be much more honest than "normal" humans; it is very difficult for us to deceive, lie or cheat, and some never learn this "social skill."

> Neandertals did not paint their caves with the images of animals [in contrast to the later Cro-Magnon people]. But perhaps they had no need to distill life into representations, because its essences were already revealed to their senses... (Shreeve 1995, p.341)

Perhaps they already had the images of animals, and of everything else, inside their heads, and picture thinking was how they thought – like

Temple Grandin, and many others on the Autistic Spectrum (Grandin 1995).

> Compared to our own, the Neandertal world would be more com-
> fortable, but infinitely less spectacular…none of the vastly intricate
> economic and political systems we have devised to make it all hang
> together…none of the heated, sustained hatred and aggression of
> war, no oppression of one folk by another, no contamination of the
> one earth by all. (Shreeve 1995, p.341)

Autistic Spectrum individuals tend to feel strongly about issues of fairness and justice – which leads us to despise war, oppression, and despoliation of the earth.

Studies of the parts of the brain have revealed that the frontal lobe is responsible for the ability to adapt to sudden change. Though the Neandertals had the same size brain as modern humans – and some Neandertal individuals had a bigger brain than we do – their frontal lobes are thought to have been smaller and the back regions larger, compared to moderns. The back brain would give the Neandertals more memory storage space, something they probably needed for survival in their tough environment. Shreeve has commented that they were conservatives, avoiding change. As a general statement, persons with an Autistic Spectrum Disorder, who are also thought to have a difference or impairment in the frontal lobe region, share this avoidance of change. At the same time, many ASD individuals (like the Neandertals) have a very impressive memory capacity.

I, myself, would be delighted if anyone could prove that I am a throw-back to the Neandertals. These people had the brains and brawn to survive the Ice Age – which included catching woolly mammoths for dinner, using only stone tools. How many of we "moderns" could achieve that level of skill?

Chapter 26

Helpful Hints for others with Asperger Syndrome

(and Our Helpers, and the Community in general)

These suggestions are ones which have helped me. Of course, I cannot guarantee that they will help everyone who has Asperger Syndrome. If they do help others, I am happy about this.

Also, by the time you have read through to this chapter, you will have found many examples of things which *did* help me, and things which *didn't* help me. These instances will assist you to understand which sorts of things are good, and not so good, for someone like me. However, not all individuals with Asperger Syndrome are exactly the same either. I grew up as the passive, timid, anxious type of Asperger person; there is another type of Asperger person whose behaviour tends more towards hyperactivity or aggression. Therefore, I am unable to say whether what suits "Type A" will also suit "Type B." The underlying reasons for both types of outward behaviour are thought to be the same, however.

1. Being prepared!

Being prepared is probably my most useful strategy. For many things in life we can prepare in advance (I realise that for some other things, we cannot). Being as prepared as I *can* be makes me feel calmer in a situation. For those things which can be anticipated, I find it helps me a lot if I plan ahead of time.

For example, I try very hard to plan my life into manageable chunks, of a manageable day, week, and month. This means that sometimes I have to turn down offers of activities and outings, because I know (from experience) that I will become stressed, overwhelmed, and panicky if I try to do too much in one day, week, or month. Before my diagnosis of Asperger Syndrome, I would try to do as many things in a day and in a week as "normal" people do – but it would stress me out so much that I sometimes became physically ill. Now that I know that I am different, I know that I have to play by different rules – not the rules which suit "normal" people. The way in which I mean this is not simply making excuses; it is adapting one's life so that it is manageable, do-able and enjoyable. To give an analogy – a person with a missing arm or leg adapts their life to make activities possible and pleasurable for themselves; a person with AS has an invisible deficit (as well as positive attributes), but it is still a deficit which needs taking into consideration. We might as well make things easier for ourselves instead of harder – which is what "strategies" and "helpful hints" are.

If there is more than one significant thing to do in one day, then, at the very least, I need to allow adequate time and a rest in between activities. If one has a job, this is already the "one significant thing to do in one day," and adding anything else to the day may be too much. This is especially true if travelling to a different place is involved, because my navigation skills cannot always be relied upon, so finding new places can take me a long time – so that, if I have not allowed enough time, I could end up rushed and stressed. Rushing from one place to another is always anxiety-provoking for me, so this is all the more reason for me to plan a sensible and relaxed schedule in advance. This may include, as I mentioned, declining extra activities which will fill up my timetable, and so put too much pressure on me.

If I have to go to a new place for the first time, I find it helps if I do a trial run at an earlier date. Especially for events like a job interview or a meeting, it helps a lot when I know that I have already travelled there and found the right place. Part of the exercise is working out the bus route, (phoning the bus company, if necessary, to find out the route details), or studying the road map, if travelling by car. In the case of driving the car, studying the map (for me) is not usually enough: I must write out the names of the roads or streets. I write them in the order in which I will encounter them, along with "L" for left turn or "R" for right turn, or "Straight Ahead", or "Pass." The side streets which I will pass are also written in their correct order on the piece of paper, with "Pass" written beside them, so that I can mentally check them off as I go. Going past the named streets lets me know when I am getting close to the next turning that I have to take. That is, I have added to my piece of paper "After going past Brown Street on the left, take the next right turning into Apple Road."

Because I have already written down my instructions to myself, that makes it easier for me to remember them when driving. It is also easier to glance at my large handwriting, while driving, than to read a map! – No, I definitely do not recommend reading a map while driving! – I sometimes have to stop the car in order to re-read the next stage of my journey, and that is the safest way to do it: while stationary.

This method is also easier if, like me, you start to get so anxious about the route that you find it very difficult, or impossible, to understand the map any more! My comprehension of maps seems to disappear under stress. (Of course, you might be very different from me in this respect, and be skilled at reading maps; some Asperger individuals have maps as their special interest.)

It can sometimes take me two or more "dummy runs" before I successfully master the route and find the right place. Therefore, it is all the better for me to make my mistakes and learn from them *before* the actual appointment day! Yes, all these preparations take up extra time; for going a long way to an unknown area, I allow at least half a day (or, in summertime, you could try out the journey during one of the long evenings). Something I do when I get there is to walk all around the "target area," sometimes for hours, to get my bearings. This is one reason why "ordinary" things seem to take me longer to accomplish than for "normal" people – because I'm doing all these practice runs! And that's OK! This strategy avoids my feeling stressed on the day.

2. Rest and relaxing activities

In my opinion, people with Asperger Syndrome or autism need to have rest and relaxing activities built into their timetable (as does everyone), but AS persons may need it even more. This is because the increased anxiety levels with which we live can cause us to become tired, or burnt out, more quickly. As I wrote in point one, having one's timetable too full is a likely source of stress and overwhelm, and should be avoided.

The person with Asperger Syndrome may, at times, simply like "tuning out," staring into space. If this is relaxing, so be it. The brain is probably using this time to process the day's input.

Whether or not the person has "tune out" times, he or she will have one or several special interests – passions – which can go as far as being obsessions. This feature is one of the diagnostic criteria for Asperger Syndrome. The person finds these activities enjoyable and relaxing, may use up most of their time on them, and be difficult to drag away from them. I am, myself, far from being in control of my special interests – in fact, it seems that they control me. I am not really in a position, therefore, to say how the special interests can be dampened down! Because the person with AS usually knows a great deal about their special interest, this feels like an island of calm and reliability to him/her – it may be the one area in life in which he/she can excel, and in which he/she receives no unwelcome surprises. It is important, therefore, for the person with AS to keep their special interests, in order to keep this area of relaxation and mastery intact. I realise, however, that there is often a problem in finding a balance between the special interest and the rest of the person's life. (In the case of dangerous passions, such as lighting fires or using guns, the person does need to be controlled or stopped – but most special interests are not in this category.)

Parents or helpers may be able to assist the person with AS to find a balance in their timetable. It is probably easier if the person receives their diagnosis of AS in childhood – thus giving parents and helpers more chance to modify his or her behaviour. I can speak from my own perspective only – as an adult who obtained the diagnosis at 43 years old – and from this perspective, I can say that it is easier for me to accept "behaviour modification" now that I know *why* I need this! I am not having official therapy, but "unofficial" assistance from certain friends and family members…such as, how to organise my living space. I still feel great frustration and anxiety, at times, when other people want to change anything in my surroundings, or in my usual activities – but, now that I have the diagnosis, I can *reason* with myself as to why I do, at times, need to accept changes, and others' help and advice. If I did not have the diagnosis, I am sure that I would not tolerate such "interventions" in my life! My intelligence and reasoning ability are able to overcome this resistance only because I have the diagnosis, which explains to me what difficulties I have, and why, and (therefore) what assistance I might need. So, it *could* happen that a child who is told about their diagnosis of AS may have a similar positive reaction (of course, I cannot guarantee it, especially as every person is an individual). That is, it could happen that an AS child may find it easier to accept change and intervention if he or she understands the diagnosis, thereby understanding why he or she needs assistance in certain areas – because AS people like being able to reason things out, to understand them as a rational cause-and-effect proposition. (As well as understanding one's deficits, of course, the child should also be encouraged to be proud of the positive aspects of having AS – such as honesty, fairness, special skills, etc.) As for myself, I usually have much more trouble with things which I do not understand, or expect, than with things which are fully explained!

So – after all that preamble – because I now understand the reason *why,* I am able to, at least some of the time(!) – change my life a little bit, or allow someone else to do it for me. After all, if I did exactly what I wanted to all day (indulging in my special interests), I would only ever mess around with my poultry, and go to the library! Anything else which I do is an acknowledgement, by me, that I have to live in the "normal" world! (Oh, that's not quite true: I do have some special people in my life, too!)

The point I am getting around to is that parents or helpers, or the aware AS person themselves, may be able to use the person's special interests as an incentive to do other things in their day. For example, if I work in the morning (whatever it is that needs doing most urgently), then I can allow myself to go to the library in the afternoon – at least, on some days. I still think, however, that *some* time per week for the special interest needs to be non-negotiable – it is allowed no matter what, so that the person can gain their relaxation and enjoyment of life. For the person to earn *more* time than that, they might need to work for it – by doing their homework, or helping with chores, or whatever. The more aware the person is of their AS, the more he or she *may* be able to accept these rules of "normal" life – which, he/she will then understand, are there for his/her betterment.

As I wrote above, I am far from being an "advanced soul" in this subject! When I become one, I'll write a new book!

Liane Holliday Willey – another adult who has Asperger Syndrome – has given some helpful hints for people with AS in her book, *Pretending to be Normal.*

3. Essay writing at university

In 1999, I finished my Bachelor of Arts at the University of Auckland. The biggest challenge for me, each semester, was the exam time. The second-biggest challenge of the semester was the essay. An essay can be worth 30 per cent to 40 per cent of your paper's marks – check out what percentage it is worth – and therefore, if you get high marks for it, this will save you from depending totally on the exam for your passing grade. I could never understand why so many other students prided themselves (or so they said) on writing their essays at 3 a.m. on the day of the deadline! This will result in a mark which is less than the student is capable of. It would have also, had I tried it, resulted in a panic attack which would have prevented me from being able to write the essay. (I chose not to try it!) If you are doing a degree for the enjoyment, learning, and personal fulfilment which it provides, you will want to make a good effort for the essay. My own guidelines (which may or may not help others) are:

(a)   It helps a lot if you have chosen a course of study in which you are interested! If you find your studies too boring or too difficult, my comments may not apply to you.

(b)   Mark the deadline date for the essay on your calendar and in your appointment diary! The lecturer should have written the date on the sheet of essay topics; doublecheck that you have copied the date correctly.

(c)   Some departments hand out the sheet of essay topics straightaway during the first class! I liked this, as I could then get my brain started on one of the topics. One topic may immediately seem more interesting to you, or may be one for which you already have some thoughts. If two topics seem equally suitable at first, keep your brain open to both possibilities for a bit longer (maybe two weeks). If all of the topics seem mystifying at first, never mind: this is what the classes, and your reading, are for – to explain the subject to you.

(d) Keep up to date with the required reading for your paper(s), both textbooks and class hand-outs. This will not only ensure you a better grasp of the subject throughout the paper, but will also provide you with most, if not all, of the ideas you will need for the essay. This is, of course, obvious, but not all students do their reading. Yes, it can be difficult to keep up with all the required reading for three papers at once, if you are studying full time. This is why I recommend starting your required reading in the holidays, before the classes start. The departmental handbooks list which texts you need to read for each paper, so try your hardest to get at least some of these texts, second-hand or from the university library or public library, during the holidays. This will give you a head start before the pressure of classes is on. It may even mean that as soon as you see the list of essay topics, you already have some ideas!

(e) If you are unsure as to the meaning of an essay topic, do check it out with the tutor or lecturer. You must be certain of what is required, otherwise you will not be able to answer the question correctly, and you will receive a very low mark or a zero.
     By the way, if you have a tutor (who teaches at the tutorial classes), approach him or her first. The lecturer should be approached only if there is no tutor, or if the tutor cannot help you. Large departments generally provide tutors; small departments sometimes do not. In the latter case, the lecturer may also teach at the tutorial classes.

(f) If you are too nervous to talk to your tutor, in order to clarify matters, then this is an additional issue: you should have already registered yourself with the Disability Co-ordinators at the university (the University of Auckland has this service), telling them that you have Asperger Syndrome or autism. Then, the Disability Co-ordinators can contact the department in which you are studying, and discuss your needs with your tutor, if you are unable to do this yourself, or if you would like support to do this. By the way, you do not need to have a specific problem, such as not understanding the essay question, in order to register with the Disability Co-ordinators: it pays to contact them when you enrol, so that you will have understanding support throughout your university degree. (I think that the enrolment forms these days have a box you can tick, if you have any form of disability, so that you can automatically receive this assistance.)

(g)   When you have decided that one (or two) essay topics look more promising than the others, read and think with this topic constantly in mind. When you read, or hear on TV, something that is relevant to your essay topic, make a note of it before you forget. Your other university papers may well contribute to the topic: my subjects of German, Comparative Literature, Anthropology, English and Linguistics often gave insights to each other. Newspapers, magazines, and your recreational books may also, by chance, happen to deal with the topic. For university, you must be able to quote authors, book or article titles, and dates; or programme name and date, if a TV programme, – so add these details to your essay preparation notes. Put your notes on one sheet of paper per essay, or in a notebook, so they are not scattered around and lost. After gathering information and ideas for two weeks or so, you will need to narrow it down to one topic (if you had two possible choices at the start).

(h)   As soon as possible, start writing a "rough copy" on the topic, using whatever information and ideas you have so far. The first attempt may look silly, but this is one way, (I don't know if there are other ways), of getting your brain focused on the topic, and starting the thoughts flowing. I have read that the subconscious part of the brain even works on problem-solving while we are asleep! Therefore, use the writing method to tell your brain what the essay topic is, and it will start to "simmer away" in the background, working on its own. As you get more and better thoughts on the subject, add these to your rough draft. You still need to ferret out as much information as you can on the essay topic, by reading your required texts, skimming through any other material that seems relevant to the subject, and by keeping your eyes and ears open to opportunities when that subject unexpectedly appears, e.g. in the news. The more data you give your subconscious mind, the more it can work for you. This "slow simmering" method needs to be started early, but it results in a better, more thoughtful essay. If you are lucky, this mental processing will help you to connect pieces of information in ways which are new for you; these new connections can usually be used as creative ideas for your essay.

(i)   Most teachers will tell you to structure your essay with "a beginning, a middle, and an end." When writing down your first thoughts, don't think about a beginning or an end (unless these spring to mind by themselves). One needs to get enough information to write the *middle*, that is, the main points, "the meat and vegetables" part. Only after you have got the middle part sorted out, will you be able to see what the beginning and the end should be like (in my opinion!) The beginning is an introduction to the topic, and the end is the conclusion (soup and dessert, respectively). The middle, or main points, of your essay will be likely to suggest their own introduction and conclusion, which you can then write last of all.

(j)   If you quote from any books, articles, TV programmes, etc., you will need to reference these, both in the essay and in a bibliography at the end of your essay. Departmental handbooks often have a chapter on how to do this; or, the department may provide a separate guide-book with this information. Different departments can have different referencing rules, so follow the rules of the department for whom you are writing the essay.

(k)   Handing the essay in! Make sure, before the deadline, that you
know where and when to hand in your essay. Some
departments have Essay Deposit Boxes. If you have been told to
put it in such a box, make very sure that it is the correct box for
that paper. The paper number, e.g. 233.101, should be written
on the box; double check what your paper number is, before
parting with your essay! Also, if planning to deliver your essay
at 4 p.m. or later, ensure that the building will still be open. I
have heard of a student who tried to hand in her essay after 4,
but the building was locked, so that she could not hand it in; it
was the day of the deadline, so the essay was no longer
accepted, and was not marked, resulting in a zero for her
coursework, thereby jeopardising her entire paper. To avoid
such disasters, it is better to hand the essay in well before the
last minute.

(l)   Best of luck! If your essay mark is lower than you expected,
your tutor has probably written comments on it, about how it
could have been done better. It's a learning curve. If you need
more clarification or help, ask your tutor; if this is a problem for
you, refer back to point (f).

4. The academic setting: Things that helped me, and things that would have helped me

This section is written partly for the employees of tertiary education institutions, e.g. universities and technical institutes, describing those things
which help a student with Asperger Syndrome or autism.

For those readers who themselves have Asperger Syndrome or autism,
these hints may still help you, because you will find out what sorts of issues
you may need to address before starting academic study.

(a)   A course guidance office, with staff who do not mind frequent
repeat visits(!), would have helped me. The University of
Auckland now has such an office, but it did not exist at the time
when I was a student there. As soon as I discovered that there
was such a thing as a degree structure (which needs to be
followed in order to fulfil the degree requirements), I wanted to

check and re-check that my studies were on the right track. I often thought of a new question which I wanted to ask, as well as needing reassurance on my previously asked questions. Asking the same question repeatedly, in order to obtain reassurance, is an Autistic Spectrum trait which some of us have. After I have been reassured enough times, I do end up feeling satisfied and calm. Without having this readily available source of information, though, I experienced more anxiety than I needed to have had.

Also, as I was the first person in my immediate family to go to university, I had no understanding of the university "system," the way things worked (e.g. for enrolment); it would have helped me a lot if I had had someone to ask, right from the start.

(b)   The note-taking service (organised by the Disability Co-ordinators at the University of Auckland), helped me enormously. When I began full-time study, the note-taking service had just been fully launched. A note-taker is a paid employee of the university who accompanies the student to lectures (if he or she has a disability) and writes the lecture notes for the student. At this time, I had Occupational Overuse Syndrome (OOS) in my writing arm, which is why I needed this assistance. Although I taught myself to write with my left hand, this was still not fast enough for the high-speed requirements of taking down lecture notes. Any other disability which impairs the student's ability to take lecture notes will qualify him or her for this service, e.g. visual impairment, hearing impairment, cerebral palsy, dyslexia. For those individuals with an Autistic Spectrum Disorder who have fine motor skills problems – in this case, for writing – the Disability Co-ordinators will supply a note-taker. (Of course, supplying a note-taker to anyone also depends on whether there are enough note-takers to fill all of the available positions.)

(c)   In the noisy, crowded, bustling campus environment, many Asperger and autistic students would be likely to want a quiet room in which to withdraw. Ideally, this room would be restricted to students with a disability, there would be no expectation to socialise, and there would be somewhere to lie down if desired.

(d)   Some students with an Autistic Spectrum Disorder – as well as those with other learning disabilities, e.g. Dyslexia – need a Buddy to help them learn their way around the university library and its catalogue system.

(e)   Navigation around the campus was a problem for me for some time, and Buddy assistance over an extended period would have been helpful.

(The two types of Buddies mentioned in points (d) and(e) could be combined in the same person: perhaps a paid employee of the university, working as part of the Disability Services.)

(f)   Computer lessons: these were, and still are, an issue for me, as I am an older person who encountered computers only late in life. The university did provide free computer workshops, but these were not compatible with my way of learning. For me, the two hours of instruction was far too long: I was soon overwhelmed, and could learn nothing. In order for me to learn anything (in this subject or in any other unfamiliar subject), I need short, repetitive sessions – only gradually moving on to new material. For most other Autistic Spectrum students, computer lessons may not be a problem. However, the learning method which helps us best (when learning unfamiliar subjects) is the same as I wrote above: shorter sessions are better than long ones; unless the long ones repeat the material and introduce new material only at a rate at which the student can assimilate.

(g)   Visual problems affect some persons with an Autistic Spectrum Disorder. For example, some cannot cope with fluorescent lights, as they register every flicker of the lights. On some outdoor stairs (particularly the ones coated with lots of little pebbles), I had trouble seeing where each step began and ended, causing a potential risk of falling. This was solved when someone painted a yellow line on the edge of each step.

(h) The difference between my coursework performance and my exam performance was very noticeable, as described in chapter19 "Going to University, and Three Important Friends." This was because coursework allowed me weeks or months to do my work carefully, whereas exams required quick thinking, adaptability, and the ability to work well under pressure. Persons with an Autistic Spectrum Disorder often have problems when required to think quickly under pressure, so we are likely to find exams very difficult and stressful, and to be unable to display our knowledge of the subject. An alternative could, theoretically, be provided by the university, allowing students with ASD the option of completing additional coursework instead of sitting the exam. In fact, all students could be offered this choice.

(i) When sitting exams, I found the university system of having to find out the location of the exam room at the last minute very stressful, thus adding a lot more anxiety to the occasion. Also, some ASD students may have a problem with sitting the exam in a crowded room. Alternatives could be one's own private exam room, or having a help-desk set up with Buddies who will accompany students to their exam room (thus ensuring that they get to the correct room without additional stress).

(j) The Disability Co-ordinators, and the Student Health Service, at the university or technical institute need to have a basic understanding of autistic spectrum disorders, if they are to assist such students. I was not able to benefit from this myself, as I received the diagnosis of Asperger Syndrome in the last semester of my degree. As Asperger Syndrome is still a little-known condition, many people in professional positions need to upskill themselves in order to be able to assist their Asperger clients. Reading this book, or any others from the Suggestions for Further Reading at the end of this book, would be a good start.

(k) It was interesting for me to experience the changeover from "Six Papers Studied All Year" to semesterisation, which meant "Three Papers Studied Each Half-Year." As this change occurred part-way through my degree, I am in a position to say which situation suited me better. While most students seemed to be complaining about the new system, I *preferred* it. This is because it suits my way of working better to be doing *fewer* things, even if more thoroughly, rather than doing *more* things, even if more broadly! From what I now know of Asperger Syndrome, (e.g. difficulty in doing a lot of things at once), I suspect that I am not the only Asperger student who prefers taking fewer papers at a time.

(l) The Limited Full-Time Course regulations, to be permitted at the discretion of the Dean of the Faculty, enabled me, during difficult times, to continue my studies. If a student (due to medical issues, disability, etc.) finds a full-time study course too much, he or she may be able to be a "Limited Full-Time Course" student, that is, taking fewer papers, whilst being considered full-time for the purposes of student allowances. The student should be prepared to provide written evidence of why he or she needs this consideration. (Although I did not yet have the diagnosis of Asperger Syndrome, a Mental Health day clinic staff member wrote a letter stating that I had an anxiety disorder.) In my own case, the Dean was extremely friendly and helpful. If anticipating, before beginning one's degree, that one will need special consideration, it would probably be best to contact the Dean (or his representative) beforehand, so as to explain the situation. There may be other suggestions that the Dean knows about. Otherwise, the Disability Co-ordinators at the university may be able to offer sufficient support in other ways.

Glossary, and Notes on the Maori Language

The indigenous language of New Zealand is Maori, a Polynesian language which belongs to the Austronesian language family. Polynesian people sailed to New Zealand approximately one thousand years ago; their descendants, now called Maori, live in New Zealand. Other languages which belong to the Austronesian family include Malay, Hawaiian, Tagalog (national language, officially called "Pilipino", of the Phillippines), and a number of indigenous languages of Taiwan. The number of languages in the family is estimated at between 500 and 1,000. Languages of the Australian Aboriginals, and the majority of the languages of Papua New Guinea, do not belong to the Austronesian language family. One hundred and fifty years ago, Britain began the colonisation of New Zealand, bringing with it the English language, which belongs to the Indo-European language family.

Maori is a vowel-based language, with every word ending in a vowel; in this sense, it resembles Italian. By comparison, English and German are consonant-based languages. The length of the vowels is an important feature of Maori: meanings of words can be totally different depending on whether a vowel is long or short.

Maori is written phonetically, except for one feature: many books written in Maori (especially the older ones) do not indicate the all-important vowel lengths, thus causing difficulty for beginners learning the language. Nowadays, this distinction can be made by placing a macron (dash) over long vowels, or by writing the vowel twice for long vowels, thus: Maaori (which is the correct pronunciation of the word "Maori." However, in order to look up words in most dictionaries, one needs to use the usual spelling minus the repeated vowels, i.e. Maori, not Maaori.

I will, therefore, give the usual spelling of the Maori words used in my book, followed by their phonetic spelling. Where there is no change in spelling, this indicates that the vowels are short, as opposed to long.

Haka (haka); Fierce dance accompanied by chant; also called by some "posture dancing." New Zealand's All Blacks rugby team performs a haka before each game. (Mentioned in Chapter 10 of this book).

Kauri (kauri); Agathis australis, a forest tree native to NZ; also its resin, the collecting of which was the livelihood of some earlier New Zealanders. (The resin, or gum, is mentioned in Chapter 1 of this book; the timber is mentioned in Chapter 19).

Moko (moko); tattoo; lizard. (The markings on the bodies of some lizards has caused the double meaning). This word is mentioned in Chapter 10 of this book.

Pukeko (puukeko); Porphyrio melanotus, swamp hen, a common native bird of NZ. As well as inhabiting rural areas, it is often to be seen in groups on the side of Auckland motorways (where the road crosses a swamp or tidal inlet). This bird is mentioned in Chapter 11 of this book.

Punga: In my family (New Zealanders of European descent) this word is used to mean a variety of tree fern, native to NZ; however, on consulting my Maori dictionary, I can find no mention of it. Perhaps it is an item of NZ English which has strayed from its original source. (Mentioned in Chapter 4 of this book).

Taro (taro); Colocasia antiquorum, a plant cultivated for food. Taro is a very popular food plant with other Polynesian groups of people who have more recently settled in New Zealand, e.g. the Samoans. Some New Zealanders of other ethnic groups, e.g. myself, also enjoy it. (Mentioned in Chapter 14 of this book).

Flax: (an English word, used to denote the native NZ plant Phormium tenax). The Maori word for it is Harakeke. This plant was, and is, used in traditional Maori crafts and industries, e.g. the weaving of baskets and the bindings for sea-faring canoes (pre-European Maori did not have metal, and therefore no nails). Its very strong fibres allow it to be used for these purposes. However, its English common name is misleading, as, outside of NZ, the name "flax" denotes a plant of very different appearance. (Flax is mentioned in Chapter 16 of this book).

Jandals: (a word of New Zealand English). Rubber thongs which are a very popular item of footwear in New Zealand. (Mentioned in Chapter 11 of this book).